I Remember When

A Memoir of One Who Served

1944 - 1946

Kenneth Vander Molen

To:

Living Stones Academy

Remember and be thankful

Kenneth Vander Molen

Chapbook Press

Chapbook Press
Schuler Books
2660 28th Street SE
Grand Rapids, MI 49512
(616) 942-7330
www.schulerbooks.com

Printed at Schuler Books in Grand Rapids, MI on the Espresso Book Machine®

ISBN 13: 9781936243426
ISBN 10: 1936243423

In memory of my wife, Jeanne.

This book will also belong to our children, grandchildren and great grandchildren with the prayer that they will never have to experience a war of this magnitude.

Blessed is every one who fears the Lord,
Who walks in his ways.

When you eat the labor of your hands.
You shall be happy,
And it shall be well with you.

Your wife shall be like a fruitful vine
In the very heart of your house,
Your children like olive plants
All around your table.
Behold, thus shall the man be blessed
Who fears the Lord.

The Lord bless you out of Zion,
And may you see the good of
Jerusalem
All the days of your life.
Yes, may you see your children's
Children.

Peace be upon Israel!

Psalm 128:1-6

CONTENTS

Author's Notes

While reading the book, *A Soldier's Story* by General Omar Nelson Bradley, he wrote and I quote, *"The reader may find errors attributable in part to inaccurate sources and to faulty recollection. To those who may feel themselves wronged, I freely acknowledge that this is in part a book of opinion and that the opinion is my own."*

I agree 100% with General of the Army Omar Nelson Bradley.

Even though General Bradley served as the Commander of the 12th Army Group in the European Theater, he was the GI's General. He understood the rifleman's view.

Another quote from General Bradley, *"The rifleman fights without promise of either reward or relief. Behind every river there's another hill – and behind that hill, another river. After weeks or months in the line only a wound can offer him the comfort of safety, shelter and a bed. Those who are left to fight, fight on, evading death but knowing that with each day of evasion they have exhausted one more chance for survival. Sooner or later, unless victory comes this chase must end on the litter or in the grave."*

Sergeant Green, Unit Unknown, *"No man, however he may talk, has the remotest idea of what an ordinary infantry soldier endures."*

During my wartime service, I had come in contact with many people who have been an influence on this journey.

I owe a great debt to my Americal Division Comrades, who have made the supreme sacrifice and who remain nameless in the following story. They shall always be missed but not forgotten.

I thank my twin brother Gordon, who was with me while in basic training and all through the war starting from September 1944 until we were discharged together at Ft. Sheridan, Illinois in December

1946. He is a veteran of the Americal Division who was awarded the Purple Heart for wounds received in action. I relied on him for information regarding certain dates and events. I am grateful for his perspective.

To John Zeilstra, a Navy veteran who served aboard the LST-909 during kamikaze attacks off the coast of Mindoro and Okinawa, Philippine Islands. John was very helpful to me in explaining how the LSTs operated during the invasion of the Philippines. It was the Navy that got me to the Pacific and returned me home. He encouraged me to complete this journal.

Also, Thomas Zeilstra, who helped with technical computer support. His advice and knowledge of computers was greatly appreciated.

Dr. Robert Swierenga, from Hope College who took time from his busy schedule to read my manuscript. It was an honor to have him review my book and I appreciate his wise comments.

Staff Sergeant Jack Morton of Company "G" taught me how to survive the horrors of war. His leadership and understanding can never be wholly understood unless you had walked in his combat boots. Jack was the one man whom you would want at your side during the dark hours of night in enemy territory. Jack received a field commission to the rank of second lieutenant. Many years after the war, I made contact with Jack and have on file a few of his letters to me. Jack died in 2009.

Finally, I lovingly express my appreciation to my wife Jeanne for creative guidance as my editor and for her proof reading. She listened to me for many hours as I explained how the war was fought. We spent numerous hours together at the public library researching historical events. She also encouraged me to purchase books about the Second World War. I am completely awestruck with her command of the English language. Without Jeanne by my side, this book would never have been written.

In all these things we are more than conquerors
through him who loved us.
For I am sure that neither death, nor life, nor angels,
nor principalities, nor things present, nor things to come,
nor powers, nor height, nor depth,
nor anything else in all creation,
will be able to separate us from the love of God
in Christ Jesus our Lord.

Romans 8:37-39

Chapter I
YEARS OF INNOCENCE
September 1939 – August 1944

I was just 13 years old when the Germans invaded Poland, which was the start of World War II. The date was 1 September 1939, and this will be a good place to introduce how I got involved with World War II.

I am a twin and my brother's name is Gordon. So whatever happens to me, usually happened to him as well. We were living at 2662 Manistique, Detroit, Michigan. My older brother Clarence was married and living in Cincinnati, Ohio with his wife, Grace. I was attending Grosse Pointe Christian Day School and in the seventh grade. By the eighth grade, I was among twelve students that graduated, and then went on to Jackson Public School.

United States was neutral at that time so really the war didn't mean a whole lot to me at that moment. America didn't have a large standing Army and we didn't want to get into a European War. Living in Detroit at the time and being close to Canada (part of the British Empire) the tunnel and bridge between the United States and Canada was restricted. The Canadian Government placed military guards at these border crossings; however, with proper credentials you didn't have any trouble at these check points.

By 1941, food items like coffee and sugar were hard to get. We had to save all our tin cans and bring them to the collection depot. This reminds me of what we do today in our recycling. I started to work after school on Friday evening and all day Saturday at Holbrook's Super Market on Harper Avenue. My first paycheck was for $3.75 of which they took 4 cents out for Social Security. Our store manager told us that coffee was going to be rationed that next day and informed us that we could purchase as much coffee as we could carry in a grocery bag. Since Gordon was employed with me, we took home a goodly amount. We packed as many cans of coffee as possible into those bags. While going home on the bus, it was really crowded, the bag that I carried ripped open and a couple of cans of coffee rolled down the bus aisle. I quickly picked up the

13

coffee and got off that bus, but fast! You never wanted a person to know that you had something that was in short supply. People would think you were hoarding and this wasn't done during the war emergency.

That was not the end of that tale of coffee. Of course when we got home, Mother was really happy to have this coffee being a good Hollander, we needed our coffee. It seems like on Sunday after church some of the ladies of church came over for some coffee and cookies and remarked to my mother that she seemed to be the only person in church who had any coffee on hand. So right away my mother goes down to the basement and brings up three cans of coffee and gives it to the ladies of church! I had worked so hard to get that coffee home and now mother was just giving it away. At least, I had hoped she would have asked for a few dollars in return.

I attended Jackson Intermediate High School in 1941. Mrs. Hobbs was our homeroom teacher and there were forty-six students in her class. I am to the right of the teacher, second row, in the picture above.

14

More and more of the men were going into service, even though we were not at war many were called into active service. My older brother, Clarence went down to the Draft Board and took his physical and he had high blood pressure and so was placed in 4-F. If you were in good health then you were 1-A, so being in 4-F meant that women and children went first. At least that is what Clarence used to tell us. Even to this day I do not know why Clarence was 4-F.

Five minutes before eight o'clock on the morning of Sunday, 7 December 1941 Hawaii Time, 366 Japanese bombers and fighters attacked Pearl Harbor. My brother and I were members of the Junior Choir of the First Christian Reformed Church and on that Sunday we had a practice session getting ready for a Christmas service. Our choir director was Mr. Dewey Westra. During this practice the janitor came in and talked to Mr. Westra and told him that it was just announced on the radio that the Japanese had bombed Pearl Harbor. Dewey Westra said that we still had about one half hour of singing practice and after that we could go home.

Running home quickly, we turned the radio on and heard for ourselves about the Japanese bombing of the Hawaiian Islands. All we knew was that we had suffered some damage. Most Americans did not know how bad the damage was at Pearl Harbor. I got out a world map to locate where in the world was Pearl Harbor. The news was controlled so we would not give the enemy any information on how successful the bombing had been.

My dad was working for Merchants Fur Company, located in Detroit on 206 East Grand River Avenue. He was a furrier that is a person who makes fur coats. I was in the 10th grade at Southeastern High School. The year was 1942 and at Southeastern they had a ROTC program. I can remember when I first saw the ROTC program while visiting friends in Chicago. It was at that time that I decided on the military service. I recall taking a real interest in History. Being in Southeastern High School we had a more extensive program of education than in the 10th grade. I was studying American History, South American History and English History. I recall one teacher in English Literature, who came from

England, taught us about Macbeth, William Shakespeare and the Canterbury Tales. I really enjoyed her class; in fact I got an A.

One time during class we had heard that there was a lot of bombing occurring in London. This teacher was from London and she had a son in the Royal Air Force. I recollect her crying in class when the bombing was going on. Maybe this is why I think a lot of the British people and the war effort. Little did I realize that many years later I would be visiting that country and seeing all the places that I had learned while in high school.

I had lots of fun while in the 11th grade. I was now working down town at Merchant Fur Company, the same place that my father was employed. I signed up and was now a member of the Southeastern High School Reserved Officers Training Corps, complete with a really cool uniform. I made a big impression on the young ladies around school. I went to a lot of football games, not to see the games but because I was in ROTC and was able to guard the crowds of kids. By volunteering for guard duty, I was awarded a ribbon on my uniform. I "guarded", one time at the Masonic Temple downtown Detroit, the cast of Irving Berlin's show called, "This Is The Army". I met Irvin Berlin in person and it was a real thrill for me. Also had the opportunity to hear Lily Pons. I noted that she had the smallest feet I have ever seen. Her husband was Andre Kosstelanetz, a well-known opera conductor. I persuaded my mother that I needed a military overcoat to go with my uniform. Then I went out and purchased just what I wanted with my own money.

Our ROTC would compete with other Detroit High School ROTC units held at Briggs Stadium. At these Field Day exercises there were lots of marching, setting up tents and doing the manual of arms with rifles. Even though we had military training in high school, I never had fired a gun. To be able to fire a rifle, you had to be in the 12th grade. I held the rank of sergeant.

On 11 November, I marched down Woodward Avenue in the annual Armistice Day Parade as a member of Southeaster's ROTC unit. It was great to be a member of the military. There were

16

military personnel present requiring us to salute all officers. It was a great experience.

From now on there would be no weather reports on the radio. This was ordered to prevent the enemy from getting this information.

I was seeing a girl from Southeastern who meant a lot to me. Her name was Mary Margaret Liddane. She had a sister named Nancy and also a brother who I never met. Mary Margaret lived on Harper Ave and I would walk her home from school on the days that I did not work. We would go sometimes to Belle Isle in Detroit and she taught me how to play tennis. Some times we would go canoeing around the

island. We really had lots to talk about and she was a very loving person. Since neither of us had a car, we did all of traveling by bus or streetcars. Only one thing that was wrong with our relationship, she was Catholic. I remember once when I took her to my home to introduce her to my mother, the first thing my mother asked "was she Catholic or a Christian?" That's the way things were in those days. She did give me a picture with her sister next to her. This was taken in Chandler Park.

On 7 August 1943, I was 17 years old and in the hospital with an appendectomy. This operation was not in my plans for the future.

7 August 1944, I would become 18 and subject to the draft. I had one more year to finish high school. My plans were to register for the draft on August 1944, pass my physical and then enter the Army on September 1944. That way I wouldn't have to finish my last year of high school.

According to the Selective Service Act, on the day before our 18th birthday, we were required by law to register with our local draft board. On August 6, my brother and I registered for the draft. We went to Jefferson Avenue, our local draft board number 17 and registered with them. We were told that we were to report for our physicals sometime before 1 September. That was good timing because school didn't start until 3 September.

The Registration Certificate for the draft shows that I was white, blue eyes, 5 ft 10 ½, 173 pounds, blond hair and light completion.

The bottom line crossed out reads; *scar on back of left ear*. This was in reference to brother Gordon, as he had a scar behind his left ear. The next line reads, *appendix scar* referring to my appendectomy the year before.

Even the Army got us mixed up.

My brother and I made plans to fly to Cincinnati. We wanted to spend some time with Clarence and Grace. We left Detroit City Airport and flew to Dayton, Ohio. Dayton was a military base so we had to have the curtains drawn when we flew in! We landed in Cincinnati for our short vacation. On Thursday, 17 August while in Cincinnati, we received (via the mail) our questionnaire, which we had to fill out. This form was one of the first steps required before our physical examination could take place. There were questions about education, family background and whether we had any previous military service.

Returning to Detroit, we both went before the consistory of the church and professed our faith. This was not done because we were going into service as so many people were doing, but because we were ready to profess our faith in Christ and felt that this was the right time. We were asked all the questions in our catechism book. It was no wonder that so few young people wanted to make profession of their faith. We received a small serviceman's Bible from the church.

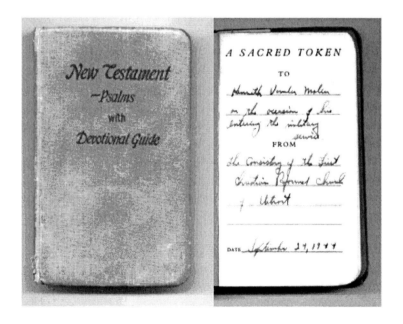

I carried that New Testament with me all the time I was in service and read it. I especially remembered being comforted, when in combat, reading Romans 8, *"Nothing can separate me from the love of God, which is in Christ Jesus my Lord."* I even underlined those verses and they are that way even today.

When I was elected an elder in our church, I carried that New Testament on hospital calls and home visits.

When my grandson, John Mark Vander Molen entered the Marine Corps service I gave him that Bible.

On Monday, 28 August 1944 I went downtown and had a complete physical examination. They looked at everything and even looked at places I didn't know I had! As soon as I was finished, the doctor said that I was 1-A. I asked, "When will I be called into service?" I didn't mention that I had one more year of school to complete.

He replied, "You will probably be called up in about five months." That was not what I wanted to hear because in just seven days I would be back in school. I had to think of something fast. I inquired, "Is there any way to get in the service faster than waiting five months?" Without looking up from his work the answer was what I wanted to hear. "Sign up now for immediate induction and you will leave for service on 25 September 1944." I signed up on the dotted line right then and there! Gordon also agreed with this plan so we would be leaving together.

I was going to be in service in twenty-eight days. Of course, I never told my parents that I had signed up for immediate induction. I just said that I passed the physical and would be waiting to hear from the President as to when I would be entering service. They never expected that I would be called on 25 September 1944. I know that they would have wanted me to finish my education first. I placed service to my country first and education second.

Chapter II
CHICAGO, ILLINOIS
September 1944

Mother had the idea that I would not be able to pass the physical because she thought I had a bad kidney or something like that. My appendix had been removed so surely that would keep me out and don't forget, I had another year of schooling. Mother was sure that I would get a deferment for any of those reasons. She wanted me to buy new school clothes.

It was Thursday, 7 September that I received the formal greetings from the Franklin D. Roosevelt, President of the United States. It was a form letter that stated when to report for service. I was, along with my brother Gordon, to appear on 25 September 1944 for induction into the United States Service at Chicago, Illinois. I was glad, Mother cried.

The last few days at home before we entered the service went by very slowly. We had orders to report in Chicago on Monday, 25 September we left Sunday afternoon from the Michigan Central Station. We didn't have a car so I believe that Herm Van Donselaar, a friend of my folks, brought us to the station. I carried just a small bag containing clothes.

I don't believe my mother was at the station, but I do remember that my father was there. I made up my mind that I would not look back but walk straight ahead and enter into the train car, which was assigned to inductees.

The first night would be spent at the Conrad Stevens Hotel and on Monday we would be inducted into the service of our country. We did not know which branch of service we would be entering into but I was hoping for the Army.

My brother and I sat next to each other and started to talk with some of the fellows around us. There were men much older than the rest of us, one being Mike Van Couwenberghe. I believe he was 25 years old and married. We traveled through the countryside as the landscape swept by. The train stopped to pick up more inductees in Kalamazoo. Some ladies from the local Red Cross came on board and gave us doughnuts and coffee. A paper napkin was printed with musical notes around the border, with the words of a song that was very popular at that time, "I've Got A Gal In Kalamazoo."

After arriving in Chicago, our supper was served in the hotel. We were assigned to a room and told to be up at 6 a.m. Most of us went to bed early and slept well. This was the last evening that I would be sleeping as a civilian for some time to come. Some fellows spent their last night drinking Chicago dry. The next morning left them with a severe hang over.

The following pages are copies of my physical examination and induction records. My Army serial number has been entered on this form. There is a lot of information on these pages. Page 26 shows my transfer to IRTC Camp Robinson, Arkansas.

DSS Form 221
(Revised 9-2-44)

REPORT OF
PHYSICAL EXAMINATION AND INDUCTION

Masterplate Imprint

VANDER BOLEN, KENNETH   L 36 918 144

(Local Board of Origin Date Stamp with Code)

Section I.—GENERAL (Local board will prepare from latest information available).

	Do Not Use
	LEGMENT

1. Name _____ VANDER BOLEN _____ KENNETH _____ WESLEY
   (Last—in capitals)   (First)   (Middle)

2. Present address ____ 2662 Manistique Ave. Detroit Wayne Michigan
   (Street or rural route)   (Town or city)   (County)   (State)

3. Registrant's order No. __ V-13299 __   4. Social Security No. _____

5. Marital status: Single ☒ Married ☐ Widower ☐ Divorced ☐ Separated ☐

6. Number of Group 4 children ____ --- ____   7. Birthdate of registrant __ 8 __ __ 7 __ __ 26 __
   (Month)   (Day)   (Year)

8. Birthplace of registrant ____ Detroit _____ Michigan _____ U.S.A.
   (Town or city)   (State)   (If country)

9. Race: White ☒ Negro ☐ Other (specify) _____

10. Citizenship: (a) United States citizen: Yes ☒ No ☐ (b) First papers ____ ☐ No ☐ (c) If not citizen of United States, citizen or subject of (specify country) _____

11. Court record: (a) Convicted of a crime other than minor traffic violation: Yes ☐ No ☒
    (b) If "yes," specify crime, date, location of court, and sentence _____
    (c) Now on parole, conditional release, probation, or suspended sentence: Yes ☐ No ☒
    (d) If answer to (c) is "yes," has necessary release or waiver been secured: Yes ☐ No ☐

12. United States military service: (a) Previous service: None ☒ Army ☐ National Guard ☐ Navy ☐ Marine Corps ☐ Coast Guard ☐
    (b) Date of discharge _____   (c) Type of discharge _____

13. Education: (Number of years completed) Elementary school __ 8 __ High school __ 3 __ Trade, night, or business school _____ College or university _____

14. Occupation and industry: (a) Title and duties of present job __ Fur Cleaner ____ (iii)
    _____ Clean Fur coats _____
    (b) Length of experience: Years __ 2? __ Months _____
    (c) Business of present employer _____

15. Employment class (present job): Employee ☒ Independent worker ☐ Employer ☐ Unpaid family worker ☐
    Student ☒ Unemployed ☐

16. (a) Number of times previously sent to Induction Station ____ none ____   E-120
    (b) Date last sent _____   (c) Was this a preinduction physical examination: Yes ☐ No ☐

17. If transferred for induction or referred for Class IV-E final-type physical examination, local board of transfer is Local Board No. _____, County or city of _____ State of _____

INSTRUCTIONS—ORIGINAL

1. To Local Board.—The Original DSS Form 221 will be prepared and distributed as set forth in Instruction No. 1 for Form 221.
2. To the Armed Forces.—The induction station will make the following disposition of this Original Copy of DSS Form 221:
   (a) For registrants inducted: (1) By the Army, this Original will be forwarded from the induction station to the reception center for extraction of data, then to the Service Command Headquarters for machine record ... then to The Adjutant General, War Department, Washington, D. C. (2) By the Navy or Coast Guard, this Original ... ded from the induction station through the Main Recruiting Station to the Bureau of Personnel, Washington ... Marine Corps, this original will be sent from the induction station direct to the Commandant, Headquarters, U. S ... ington, D. C.
   (b) For registrants rejected: This Original of DSS Form 221 will be marked ... "Rejected by the Armed Forces" and will be sent together with the Second Copy of DSS Form 221 to ... Director of Selective Service.
   (c) For registrants sent for preinduction physical examination: This Original of DSS Form 221 will be sent with the ... Copy of DSS Form 221 to State Director of Selective Service.
   ... For Class IV-E registrants sent for final-type physical examination: This Original along with First Copy and Second Copy of DSS Form 221 will be returned to the local board.

23

SECTION II.—LOCAL BOARD EXAMINATION AND CLASSIFICATION.

18. Medical History (c) Has registrant had spells of unconsciousness, convulsions, fits, epilepsy, tuberculosis, asthma, hay fever, diabetes, earache, stomach ulcer, rheumatic fever, heart trouble, chronic or frequent colds, syphilis or manifestations, or has been addicted to alcohol, narcotics, or habit-forming drugs...

(b) Specify other defects or diseases claimed by registrant ....

(c) I certify that the answers to Items 18 (a) and 18 (b) are correct. ....

(d) Signature of registrant .... (e) Date ....

19. (a) Does examining physician have documentary evidence confirming statements in Item 18: Yes ☐ No ☐ (b) If not, does examining physician have any evidence which would substantiate statements in Item 18: Yes ☐ No ☐ (c) If yes, specify ....

(d) Serological test (syphilis): First specimen: Date _9 - 1 - 44_ Result _neg._
    Second specimen: Date .... Result ....

(e) Does above-named registrant have any defects set forth in List of Defects (Form 220). (If in doubt answer "No" and give details): Yes ☐ No ☐ If answer is "Yes," describe the defects in the order of their significance ....

(f) REMARKS ....

(g) Signature of examining physician ....

(h) Place .... Date ....

20. (a) Was local board physical examination waived: Yes ☐ No ☐ (b) If yes, under what Section of Regulations ....

(c) This local board has classified the above-named registrant in Class ....
(d) Signature of member of local board ....
(e) Place _Detroit, Mich_ (f) Date _8-25-44_

SECTION III.—MISCELLANEOUS (To be filled out at induction station for only those registrants accepted for military service).

21. (a) Organization and serial number of previous U. S. military service (if known) _None_

(b) Reason for discharge _None_
(c) Religious preference (voluntary for Army) _Protestant_

22. (a) Nearest relative (other than wife or minor child) (Name first) _Martha Flierman Vander Molen_
(b) Relationship _mother_ (c) Address _2662 Manistique Ave., Detroit, Michigan_
(Number and street or rural route, if none, so state)   (City, town, or post office)   (State or country)

(d) Person to be notified in case of emergency (Name first) _Martha Flierman Vander Molen_
(e) Relationship _mother_ (f) Address _same as above_
(If friend, so state)   (Number and street or rural route, if none, so state)   (City, town or post office)   (State or country)

23. (a) The persons eligible to be my beneficiary are: _None_
(Full name of wife, if no wife, or if she is deceased or divorced, so state)   (Wife's full address)

none

(Full name and address of each minor child and each dependent child over 21 years of age)

(If there are none, so state. If the address is the same as the wife's, so state. Do not repeat address)

(b) In the event of my leaving no widow or child, I then designate as my beneficiary to receive the six months' death gratuity the dependent relative whose name, relationship and address are shown below:
Martha Flierman Vander Molen (mother) Same as above

(If designated beneficiary is declared, may remit then in own handwriting: "I decline to designate any person as my beneficiary")

(c) In the event of the death or disqualification of the last-named dependent relative, I then designate as my beneficiary to receive the six months' death gratuity, the dependent relative whose name, relationship, and address are shown below:
Cecil Vander Molen (father) Same as mother's

(If beneficiary is named is from the last named or alternate is declined, man must state in own handwriting, "I decline to designate as my beneficiary")

24. (a) Signature of registrant _Kenneth_ (First name) _Wesley_ (Middle name) _Vander Molen_ (Last name)

(b) Witness ___ APIS., CHICAGO, ILL. on _25 September_ 19_44_

M. J. Warner
(Signature of witness attesting)

M. J. WARNER, 1st Lt. WAC.
(Name of witness typed)   (Grade and organization)

(PAGE 2)   aca

24

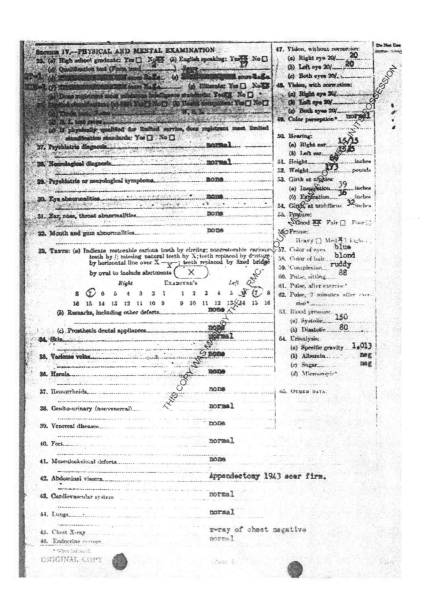

25. (a) High school graduate: Yes ☐ No ☒   (d) English speaking: Yes ☒ No ☐
(b) Qualification test (Form ___) raw score ___
(e) ___ score ___
(g) Illiterate: Yes ☐ No ☒
(h) ___ Yes ☐ No ☐
W. ___

(m) If physically qualified for limited service, does registrant meet limited examination standards: Yes ☐ No ☐

27. Psychiatric diagnosis ___ normal
28. Neurological diagnosis ___ normal
29. Psychiatric or neurological symptoms ___ none
30. Eye abnormalities ___ none
31. Ear, nose, throat abnormalities ___ none
32. Mouth and gum abnormalities ___ none
33. TEETH: (a) Indicate restorable carious teeth by circling; nonrestorable carious teeth by /; missing natural teeth by X; teeth replaced by denture by horizontal line over X —X—; teeth replaced by fixed bridge by oval to include abutments ◯

                Right   EXAMINEE'S   Left
        8 ⑦ 6 5 4 3 2 1   1 2 3 4 5 ⑦ 8
        16 15 14 13 12 11 10 9   9 10 11 12 13 14 15 16

(b) Remarks, including other defects ___ none
(c) Prosthetic dental appliances ___ none
34. Skin ___ normal
35. Varicose veins ___ none
36. Hernia ___ none
37. Hemorrhoids ___ none
38. Genito-urinary (nonvenereal) ___ normal
39. Venereal diseases ___ none
40. Feet ___ normal
41. Musculoskeletal defects ___ none
42. Abdominal viscera ___ Appendectomy 1943 scar firm.
43. Cardiovascular system ___ normal
44. Lungs ___ normal
45. Chest X-ray ___ x-ray of chest negative
46. Endocrine system ___ normal
   * When indicated.

47. Vision, without correction:
   (a) Right eye 20/ ___ 20
   (b) Left eye 20/ ___ 20
   (c) Both eyes 20/ ___
48. Vision, with correction:
   (a) Right eye 20/ ___
   (b) Left eye 20/ ___
   (c) Both eyes 20/ ___
49. Color perception* ___ normal
50. Hearing:
   (a) Right ear ___ 15/15
   (b) Left ear ___ 15/15
51. Height ___ 173 inches
52. Weight ___ pounds
53. Girth at nipples
   (a) Inspiration ___ 39 inches
   (b) Expiration ___ 36 inches
54. Girth at umbilicus ___ 32 inches
55. Posture:
   Good ☒   Fair ☐   Poor ☐
56. Frame:
   Heavy ☐   Med ☒   Light ☐
57. Color of eyes ___ blue
58. Color of hair ___ blond
59. Complexion ___ ruddy
60. Pulse, sitting ___ 88
61. Pulse, after exercise* ___
62. Pulse, 2 minutes after exercise* ___
63. Blood pressure
   (a) Systolic ___ 150
   (b) Diastolic ___ 80
64. Urinalysis:
   (a) Specific gravity ___ 1.013
   (b) Albumin ___ neg
   (c) Sugar ___ neg
   (d) Microscopic* ___
65. OTHER DATA:

ORIGINAL COPY   (Page 3)

25

SECTION IV.—PHYSICAL AND MEDICAL EXAMINATION.—Continued.

66. Other defects, diseases, and/or remarks _____ None _____

Do Not Use

67. Summary of defects: (a) Principal defect _____ None _____

(b) Other defects in order of significance _____

24

68. (a) I certify that the above-named registrant was carefully examined, physically and mentally, that the results of the examination have been carefully recorded on this form, and that, to the best of my knowledge and belief he is:

(1) Qualified for general military service ☒
(2) Qualified for limited service ☐ because of _____

(3) Disqualified for any military service ☐ because of _____

(b) Signature of medical examiner ____J. D. Purvis____ September 1, 1944
(c) Name typed or stamped ____J. D. PURVIS, M., M. C.____ (d) Title ____

SECTION V.—DISPOSITION OF REGISTRANT BY ARMED FORCES. Detroit, Michigan.

69. Type of examination: Regular induction ☒ preinduction ☐
70. Registrant's service preference: None ☐ Army ☒ Navy ☐ Marine Corps ☐ Coast Guard ☐
71. (a) I certify that the qualifications of the above-named registrant have been considered in accordance with the most recent regulations governing the acceptance of Selective Service registrants and that he was this date:

(1) Inducted into the armed forces ☒
(a) Service: Army ☒ Navy ☐ Marine Corps ☐ Coast Guard ☐
(b) Was ordered to report to ____Ft. Sheridan, Ill., 25 Sept. 1944____
(c) Qualified for: General military service ☒ Limited service ☐

(2) Found acceptable for limited service but not inducted ☐
(3) Rejected for service in the armed forces ☐ because of: Medical ☐ Moral ☐ Alien ☐
Other ☐. If other, specify _____

(b) Signature of Commanding Officer of the Induction Station _____
(c) Name typed or stamped ____G. G. CURTIS, , Lt. Col. Inf.____
(d) Place ____AFIS., CHICAGO, ILL.____ (e) Date 25 Sept. 1944

SECTION VI.—TRANSFER FROM RECEPTION CENTER.
72. Above-named man was transferred from Reception Center to: ____RRC CP ROBINSON, ARK.____

_____ (Place and organization, if known) _____ ____2 Oct. 44____ (Date)

SECTION VII.—FINGERPRINTS—RIGHT HAND (for only those registrants who are inducted).

1. THUMB	2. INDEX	3. MIDDLE	4. RING	5. LITTLE

26

Chapter III
FT. SHERIDAN, ILLINOIS
September 1944 – October 1944

I had breakfast in the hotel with the rest of the inductees and then marched (after a fashion) down the streets of Chicago to a building just like every other building in the area. We had roll call and all were present and accounted for. We filled out a few forms, and then had a physical exam by a dentist who thought he was a doctor. We all went up some steps to the second floor and entered a room and sat at desk-like chairs. The corporal in charge explained to us that we would be assigned to either the Army or Navy. One or two of the inductees asked if they could be assigned to the Air Corps, as they wanted to fly. The corporal responded by answering, "Go stand by the window and jump, because that's about the closest you will get to flying." Despite his answer someone asked about being assigned to the Marine Corps and the answer was just one word "No." At this time the Marine Corps was open only to volunteers. No more dumb questions were asked and I just sat there wondering what would become of me. Did I do the right thing?

We were to line up and follow the man in front of us as we were about to be assigned to either the Army or Navy. We did not have much of a choice. We were told that today they needed more men in the Army so it was going to be five men to the Army with one man going to the Navy. We had no way of knowing where we would be going. Some fellows really wanted to get into the Navy so they put up a fuss, but the corporal in charge said that it was going to be the luck of the draw as to who went where.

I said to Gordon, "Now would be the time for us to separate." We were nearing the counter where the officer in charge was stamping our wrist, Army or Navy. I looked for Mike Van Couwenberghe but he was quite a ways back in the line. Gordon was ahead of me and some fellow stepped in between us. ARMY was stamped on Gordon's right wrist as the next man's wrist was also stamped ARMY. Now it was my turn, ARMY was stamped on my right wrist also. The ones assigned to the Navy were directed to another doorway and we moved on to the next Army officer.

This officer assigned each of us our Army Serial Number with instructions to know that number backwards and forwards. We would not be able to go any place unless we knew that number. I was now 36-916-144. I looked for Gordon to see what number he had acquired and it was 36-916-142. Again, we just sat around waiting for something to happen. Mike came over to us as he was also from Detroit and we talked awhile about life in the big city. Mike was also inducted into the Army. His number was 36-916-210. No longer were we to be addressed as Kenneth or Gordon or Mike, but by our numbers.

Some of us looked out the window; we could see the Navy recruits being marched off to another building. We found out later that they were headed to the Great Lakes Naval Training Center. While we were sitting in this room, I noted that not one fellow was black. Another draftee wanted to know if he could smoke, the corporal in charge said, "Sure, go ahead and light up." We waited around for what seemed like hours, which we were to learn, was the way things were done in the Army.

Later a snappy female lieutenant WAC came into the room, the corporal yelled out, "Attention." Being in the ROTC, I assumed a military position with eyes to the front, arms to the sides, and heels together.

While standing at attention, we were told to raise our right hand and repeat after her the Pledge of Allegiance to the United States Army. "One step forward," was her command. We did just that. We had just taken our first step as soldiers in the United States Armed Forces. We were to be proud that we could serve in the Army. We were to wear our uniform with pride; when we got them.

She gave her second command, "Pick up all the cigarette butts."

One of the fellows said that no woman was going to tell him what to do, at which the lieutenant said, "Give me 25 push ups." I guess we had better learn early to do what we are told.

We ate lunch, boarded the Chicago Northwestern Railroad train and headed out of town. We were told that our destination would be Ft. Sheridan, which is about twenty miles north of Chicago. There were five carloads of draftees on this train, all heading toward new adventures. The first car was destined for Great Lakes Naval Training Center and as we approached Ft. Sheridan, our cars were dropped off and the first car went on to Great Lakes. The Naval Training Center was located about another fifteen miles north of Ft. Sheridan. The differences between the two camps were that Ft. Sheridan was just a Reception Center, while Great Lakes was a Training Center for the Navy. We knew that we would remain at Ft. Sheridan for a short time.

It was late in the day when we arrived and marched to our new barracks. We received a warm welcome from the fellows who were already in camp. Some encouraging words like, "You'll be sorry" and "Just wait till you get your shots" and "Barber bait". Did we really need these words at this time?

After being assigned to a barrack we picked out a bunk. The bunk beds had a firm mattress over springs. We received two sheets, plus a regular Army blanket that was very heavy and woolly. We were shown how to make the bed, the Army way, and then marched to the mess hall to eat. We were all very tired that night so after our meal, we headed for our bunks and quickly fell fast asleep.

The next morning, a crazy fellow blowing a whistle came through the barracks yelling it was time to get up. It was only 6:00 a.m. Where was I? Where was the toilet? Where was I going to eat this morning? What clothes was I to wear? Who was this fellow blowing that whistle? I had a hundred more questions but no time to think as fifty inductees were all running to the toilet (latrine) to get ready for the day's activities. There were no stalls, just twenty open commodes; fifty pairs of eyes were on us. We hurried to shave as formation was at 6:30 a.m. I really didn't have to shave, but did anyway just to be like the rest of the fellows.

Off to mess. It was here that I saw my first prisoners of war (POW) soldiers. These were German POWs, they were interned at

Ft. Sheridan keeping the grounds clean and working in the kitchens. We did not have kitchen police (KP) duty while at Ft. Sheridan. We would pick up metal trays and move down the food line at which time the German POWs put food on our tray. Most of the food was dumped on top of each other; green peas put right on top of our mashed potatoes or ice cream on top of our bread. When we complained, the POWs looked at us, as if to say, we don't understand English. We were told to *never converse* with a POW. I believe that most of them spoke English and were just antagonistic by putting the food on top of anything we had on the tray. I was really surprised to see that most of the POWs were young. I wondered just how long they had been in the States and from what city they were from in Germany. Later, I watched as the POWs played soccer and observed that they were having a good time. They seemed glad that their war was finished while my war was just beginning.

Next, we went to the barbershop for our military hair cut, one-inch length all over the head. Some guys had a good head of hair but not after meeting with the Army barber!

We went to the warehouse to be fitted out with all clothes that we would need. It was done like an assembly line; moving first to get measured for our shirt, then pants, later our jacket, shoes, underwear and even a tie. We were given the famous Army duffel bag. Everything we owned had to fit into that bag. If not, you didn't need it.

We were issued our dog tags, which we wore around our neck inscribed with our name, Army serial number, Tetanus shot (T-44, year shot was given) blood type, (A) and religion, (P) Protestant. This made it expeditious if we were killed in action, I still have my dog tags. Our civilian clothes were packed in the small bag we came with. The military saw to it that these were shipped home. That night we went back to our barracks wearing government issued (GI) clothes. We knew that we were in the Army now.

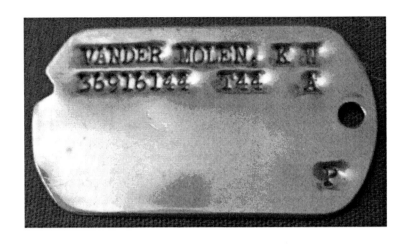

We spent the next three or four days filling out forms. We were given the Army General Classification Test (GCT). This test covered general education; vocabulary, arithmetic, and block-arrangement reckoning. Recruits were classified into five groups according to the test results. The higher your score the better chance you had for specialized training. The highest score possible was 163. I was in Class I, with a score of 120, which made me eligible to attend Officer Candidate School (OCS). I took a typing test and passed with a good score. I figured maybe that I would be a clerk. Finally, we were able to call home to inform the folks how we were doing. I'm sure they were concerned over our safety and well being.

It seems strange now but no one asked if Gordon and I were twins. I guess we all looked alike. We dressed alike; in fact, there were thousands of us at Ft. Sheridan who all looked the same. While we were growing up, my mother wanted Gordon and I to be exactly alike, even to the socks that we had on; now that we were in the Army, everybody else looked just like us. That would have made my mother very happy.

We were staying around camp until the time when we would go "bingo" meaning, shipped out to our basic training camp. No one knew when we would go; some guys who came in after we arrived were shipped out, but for some reason our group stayed longer. Of course, the post-exchange (PX) was open and we could get some goodies like ice-cream or better still, meet some of the young girls at the PX.

I was able to get a one-day pass on Sunday and left the post traveling to Des Plaines, Illinois, because I knew there was a Christian Reformed Church located there. I was invited to the home of Case and Nell Van Polen; formerly from Detroit. I was also expecting to see Lois Van Polen, who had been in my homeroom class at Jackson Intermediate High School. I found their place and went with them to church. I enjoyed a delicious meal; afterward Lois and I played a card game. I enjoyed their hospitality and returned back to camp.

It was boring just sitting around camp with no place to go. We could go to the post movies; the cost was only fifteen cents. I thought that when I got into the Army things would happen quickly. I recalled the ROTC uniform I wore while attending Southeastern High School. I had to polish the buttons on the jacket to make them shine. All the ribbons had to be just right and now I was in the Army with no shoulder patch, no markings at all on my uniform. The POWs had some markings on their uniform, even if it just said PW. My uniform was dull and had no life to it. We had been instructed not to sew any markings on our uniform.

Our routine required us to get up in the morning for formation, roll call, eat breakfast at the mess, and form up to police the area. To "police the area," required that all of us were to spread out in a line and look on the ground, move forward and pick up every piece of paper, tooth pick, nail clipping, or paper clip that we could find. If we had nothing to do that day, we would police the area again. It got so that we would throw paper on the ground just to have something to pick up. No matter how boring the time was, I didn't get to know a lot of fellows. It was difficult to make friends. Most of the guys would drink beer and smoke and I didn't do either one, but I was beginning to think that I probably ought to take up smoking, after all, I picked up their butts, why not my own?

It was at Ft. Sheridan that I attempted smoking. We were all called to the orderly room. We were introduced to a civilian who was from the American Tobacco Company. He said that he had something FREE to give each of us; two packs of Lucky Strike cigarettes. He told us how good the cigarettes would be for us while we were serving our country and by smoking we were really cool. I didn't know what to do with my packs. A couple of the fellows gave their cigarettes to others that smoked. I figured that now was as good as any to start smoking. I put the packs in my pocket and went back to the barracks.

I read the bulletin board and noticed I was on fireguard that night. It meant that I walked around a certain area of the camp; if I saw any smoke, I was to yell "Fire" and get all the guys out of the building. Well, just walking around with nothing to do, I remembered the cigarettes and matches in my pocket so why not smoke now. What I really did was to suck in smoke and blow it out of my mouth. In about 20 minutes, I had the whole two packs finished. If that was all there was to smoking, I couldn't see any enjoyment in it, so I quit smoking the day I started.

Another instruction related to smoking was called field stripping. After smoking a cigarette, we were required to roll the butt into the palm of our hand until all that was left was the paper around the tobacco, which we then threw on the ground to be picked up by someone later.

Finally we were told to get ready to move out. We were not allowed to make phone calls home, but have our duffle bags packed and ready to move out. The best news was that we were leaving Ft. Sheridan.

Chapter IV
BASIC TRAINING
October 1944 – January 1945

On Monday, 2 October we are ordered out of Ft. Sheridan, Illinois for places unknown to us. There was no time to call home, besides we did not know our destination. Only the sergeant in charge knew and he wasn't talking. After boarding a troop train we passed through Chicago and traveled past many small towns, not knowing where we were headed. Going slowly by one of these towns we yelled out to ask the name of the city, the answer was "Joliet". We were still in Illinois but heading south. Maybe we would go to Florida and spend our winter months in training there. The Army provided us with a boxed lunch. At one time we went through the dining car and used our mess kits to hold our meal. We slept in the seats assigned to us. It was a long, long trip. Traveling farther and farther south we entered another major city, and discovered that it was Memphis, Tennessee. After some time our train pulled into a large railroad siding, we could tell by all the soldiers around that this was an Army Post.

Friday evening, 6 October we were told to get our duffel bags, put them on the ground and get over to the mess hall for something to eat. The first thing we noticed was there were no POWs here. American soldiers served the food and soldiers in the kitchen did the cooking. A few of us seemed to have gotten into the wrong mess hall. We were in the top three-grade mess hall, meant for sergeants only. We did eat well and no one said a word to us until we returned to pick up our duffel bags. Sergeants do not like to eat with us lowly privates. We were sternly "chewed out" by our sergeant.

We had arrived at Camp Robinson, Arkansas; this was an Infantry Replacement Training Center (IRTC) that trained soldiers for the infantry. After roll call, we were assigned hut numbers. I located my new home and was introduced to the other five GIs with whom I would be sharing sixteen weeks of basic training. They were Mike Van Couwenberghe, (the older fellow from Detroit) my brother Gordon, and Charles Reynolds from Gobles, Michigan.

Chuck just got married the day he entered the Army and spent most of the time calling his wife and writing letters to her. Also in this group was a GI named Rothe. I don't remember his first name. He was somewhat different from the rest of us. He never seemed to associate with us. He always went to bed in his birthday suit, that is, stark naked. When the weather was below freezing, Rothe still would strip off all his clothes and jump into bed. The last of our group was a soldier from Menominee, Michigan named Donald R. Twork, Jr. He claimed that he was married but Mike told us later that he didn't believe Twork was married because he had all his insurance made out to his mother. No one in the hut let him know that we knew he wasn't married. Later, when we shipped out he confessed this information to us. He also had a real bad dental problem; his teeth just didn't seem to line up right. He also turned out to be a gold brick soldier, that is, lazy.

Let me describe our new home. It was about twenty by twenty feet. In the center was a gas stove, which was lit with a match. It really could throw out the heat. The cots were placed around the room on the outside walls. These were not like the soft beds that we slept on while at Ft. Sheridan. These were canvas cots. The windows around our hut had screens but no glass. We had only one door. At night we would go around outside the hut and drop the shutters making it cozy. One large light bulb hung above the stove. We each had a shelf above our cot; under the cot we found a trunk, which held our clothes, writing materials, and maybe a book or two. It was nice in our hut because Charles Reynolds had a radio with him and we could listen to local stations. He had the radio set to turn on at 5:30 a.m. and the very first noise we would hear was Roy Ackhof singing, "Top Of The Morning, It's a Bright And Sunny Day." In the south all we heard was blue grass music or, as we called it, hillbilly music.

On Monday, 9 October my sixteen weeks of basic training would begin. That morning the bugle sounded over the loud speaker and we were up and ready. We formed into squads of twelve men each, with three squads making up a platoon. We then met our platoon Sergeant named Stripmaster. He was 39 years old and had been in the Army for twenty years. He saw service in the Aleutian Islands and right away I liked him. At least he wasn't yelling all the time like the sergeant of the first platoon. We were in the second platoon. Three platoons form a company, three companies form a battalion, three battalion's equals a regiment, and three regiments together created the Infantry Division. So I was now in the second platoon, "B" Company, 128th Battalion, 81st Infantry Regiment.

We had no shoulder patch for this unit, only after finishing basic training would we be allowed to wear the Replacement Training Command patch. This patch was a vertically striped blue, yellow and red disk. The blue is at the left and the stripes are equally spaced. The colors indicated the three training branches of the Replacement Training Command. The blue denoting Infantry, yellow the Calvary and red indicated the Field Artillery.

Shown below is my immunization register. For some reason they used the "V" on my medical records. It records all the shots that I received while in service including Japan. Last shot was in October 1945 for Plague and Influenza.

36916144

IMMUNIZATION REGISTER

LAST NAME	FIRST NAME	ARMY SERIAL NO.
Vander Molen	Kenneth V.	

GRADE	COMPANY	REGT. OR STAFF CORPS	AGE	RACE
			18	W

SMALLPOX VACCINE

DATE	TYPE OF REACTION	MED. OFFICER
Oct 14-44	Vaccinoid	[illegible]

TRIPLE TYPHOID VACCINE

SERIES	1ST DOSE	2D DOSE	3D DOSE	MED. OFFICER
1st	9-27-44	Oct 14	Oct 21	[illegible]
2d	18 [illegible]	[illegible]		
3d				

TETANUS TOXOID

INITIAL VACCINATION	DATE	MED. OFF.	STIMULATING DOSES	DATE	MED. OFF.
1st dose	Oct [illegible]	[illegible]			
2d dose	[illegible]	[illegible]			
3d dose	[illegible]	[illegible]			

~~YELLOW FEVER VACCINE~~

DATE	LOT NO.	AMOUNT	MED. OFF.
Plague	[illegible]		
Influenza	3 Oct '45		

OTHER VACCINES

DISEASE	DATE	TYPE OF VACCINE	DOSES	MED. OFF.
Blood Type - A				
CHOLERA	FEB. [illegible], 1945		0.5cc	[illegible]
Cholera	Feb [illegible] 1945			
TYPHUS	FEB. 15, 1945		1cc	[illegible]
Typhus	Feb [illegible] 1945			
PLAGUE	FEB. [illegible] 1945		0.5cc	[illegible]
Plague	Feb [illegible] 1945			

[illegible], M. C.,
U. S. Army.

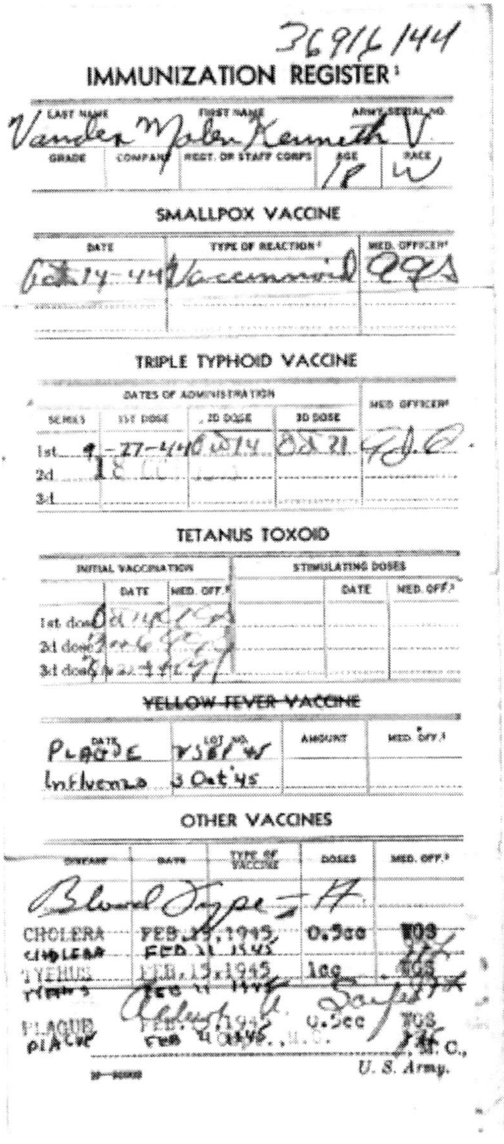

During this first week of training we received a new piece of equipment called a helmet liner. When in combat we wore a steel helmet but because it doesn't really fit our heads, it required a liner to support the steel helmet. In basic, we wore this plastic helmet liner printed with our name on the outside. Mike Van Couwenberghe had such a long name that it went completely around the back of the helmet liner. He said that he would never get shot in the war because no bullet was large enough to have his name printed on it.

I never took many pictures while at Camp Robinson. The photo on the right is of Mike Van Couwenberge in the middle and Gordon and Kenneth protecting him. I believe that these pictures were from Mike. Note the windows with wooden supports holding them open. When it rained we had to run outside to drop these "windows".

On Saturday, 14 October we were all ordered to wear combat boots, helmet liners and nothing over our skin except our black rubber raincoat! That Saturday must have been the hottest day the State of Arkansas ever had. We were marched over to the infirmary where we were to be given our smallpox immunization shots. It was getting hotter and hotter every minute and sweat was running down our backs and also under our helmet liners. We dare not touch the fellow in front of us because when our hand touched his back; it was like a sizzling iron. We stood outside while the other platoons went in first.

Our turn came when our name was called. We went inside where it was cool. I walked down the corridor and was told to take my raincoat off and to move down the hallway, as a medic struck a needle into my arm. Not only on my right side, but another medic from the opposite side would jab his needle into my left arm. It didn't hurt going in but I'm sure they had a hook on the needle when they pulled it out! We got three different shots that day. We were told to take a shower and to stay in bed because these shots would easily knock us out. Some fellows passed out when the shots were given. On Monday we were all back to our regular routine of basic training. For about two weeks, no one slapped anyone on the arm.

A dentist also checked our teeth. Records indicate that I had my teeth checked 13 November 1944 and again on 11 January 1945.

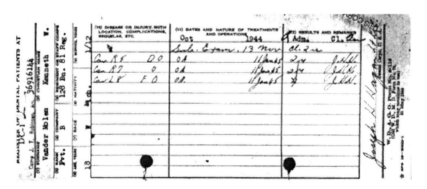

The second Sunday, 22 October I thought I would sleep in and miss going to Chapel. I was far away from Detroit and no one would ask if I had attended church on that Sunday or not. WRONG. Just as I was turning over for forty more winks, there was a knock on the front door and a voice from the other side asked, "Is Private Vander Molen here?" Gordon had left so I said sleepily, "My name is Vander Molen."

He came into the hut and said, "My name is Private Hunderman from Byron Center, Michigan." He had obtained my name from the Young Calvinist membership list and was also a member of the Christian Reformed Church. He invited me to go to Chapel with him.

What was I to say, "Sorry, no I want to sleep in this Sunday morning?" So I quickly got dressed and walked with him to the Chapel. Even when away from home, the Lord moves in mysterious ways.

We did a lot of PT (physical training) in camp. We called it physical torture. Sergeant Stripmaster told us that we had to run three miles and in the near future we would be marching twenty-five miles. These were the two things we had to accomplish before we could ever hope to leave Camp Robinson. We all said no way, at which time we all had to get down and do twenty push-ups. When we were in Ft. Sheridan, all we had to do were five push-ups but now every morning we had PT first thing. We would walk about ¼ mile, then run ¼ mile, and the next week we would run ½ mile, walk ½ mile. You can understand that at the end of ten or twelve weeks, we were easily running three miles every day. My weight was 173 pounds when I got into the Army, but now I was really getting in shape. We did a lot of marching and PT. Another one of the exercises was a real killer, the telephone pole carry. Our squad of men would pick up a thirty-foot telephone pole and extend it over our heads; we would swing it to the left, then to the right, and overhead again. That really developed muscles.

Once again we were required to line up with helmet liners, raincoats and combat boots. We already knew that meant more shots. So on Wednesday the 25th we had our tetanus immunization. This wasn't quite as bad as the first shots we received. Most of us were getting tougher each day.

We were now part of the Infantry; we were issued rifles. We practiced cleaning them, taking them apart, and most importantly, how to fire them. We even slept with them! It was exciting at the firing range. We were given live ammunition and had to fire at a fixed target. If we missed hitting anyplace within the target area we would get a "Maggie's Drawers." This was a red flag, which was displayed on the target area to let us know that we didn't hit anything. We also fired other pieces of equipment, such as the mortar, the machine gun, the Browning Automatic Rifle (BAR) and the carbine. We would fire the mortars at barrels located about 1,000 yards from our firing point. Each of us was to fire three rounds to get our "shell" into the barrels. We fired blanks, not the real shells. We were trained how to be prepared for gas attacks using a gas mask, and of course, first aid. We were also instructed in squad infantry tactics.

The smallest infantry unit was a squad consisting of twelve men. The squad leader plus nine others were armed with M1 Garand semiautomatic rifles; one with a Browning Automatic Rifle and one with an M1903 Springfield rifle fitted with a sniper scope. The squad generally operated as a two-man scout section, a four-man fire section and a five-man maneuver and assault section. The squad leader customarily advanced with the scout section and held the rank of staff sergeant.

At this point it would be a good idea to tell how I was involved in the squad formation when overseas. In combat the squad was formed along the line we learned at Camp Robinson except we had more firepower. We had a two-man scout section with a technical sergeant as the squad leader. Instead of one, we had two four-man fire sections with one assistant staff sergeant section leader. Each four-man fire section had a BAR plus the three M1's. We usually didn't have the M1903 Springfield rifle with us. We called these rifles 03's and I did use one of these in actual combat. During the war I was the first scout and carried a sub-machine gun. The following are the weapons that we in the Infantry had to be able to operate effectively.

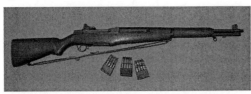
The basic rifle was the M1 Garand. This was a .30 caliber, gas-operated, semi-automatic weapon, weighing 9.6 pounds, loaded with an eight round clip. Effective range was 550 yards to over 3,000 yards. The rate of fire was twenty rounds per minute.

The Browning Automatic Rifle, called BAR, was a gas-operated, fully-automatic which only weighed 21 pounds loaded. Ammunition was fed from a twenty round, detachable box magazine. Effective range was approximately 875 yards with a maximum range of 3,500 yards; the rate of fire was 550 rounds per minute.

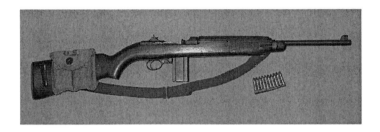

The M1 Carbine was a gas-operated, semi-automatic weapon weighing six pounds with a 15-round .30 caliber magazine. Effective range was approximately 300 yards with a forty round per minute rate of fire. Mostly officers, not the enlisted men used this weapon. We used to say that you couldn't hit the broad side of a barn using a carbine, even if you were inside the barn. The enemy usually would aim for soldiers carrying a carbine knowing it was an officer. In combat we made sure we never carried a carbine, even if it was lighter to carry.

The M1 Thompson submachine gun was a .45 caliber delayed-blowback weapon capable of selective fire. It weighed twelve pounds with a twenty round magazine. Effective range was about 600 yards with a rate of fire up to 100 rounds per minute on full automatic. A good Infantryman could fire one round at a time. This was a weapon that I used for about a month in combat. I never could pull one round off at a time. It was an easy weapon to clean and didn't have much of a kick, but on automatic it tended to

43

rise. To correct our field of fire we usually held the gun sideways and fired.

The M1911 pistol or "45" was recoil-operated and fed by a seven-round magazine that fit in the grip. The eighth round could be loaded in the breech. It weighed 2.5 pounds. The gun was not accurate and it had considerable recoil. It was a very powerful weapon because a single hit anywhere on the body would most often stop a person. These weapons were usually carried by troops assigned to the Artillery; I did see a couple of the medics wear them.

We carried at least two or more M3A fragmentation grenades. These had a smooth cylindrical casing and weighed only .84 pound. It had a ring-shaped safety pin and handle. After pulling the pin the grenade was safe so long as the handle was depressed. Once the handle flew off the grenade, we had to get rid of it as it had a four-second fuse.

You have to remember that the contract for making the hand grenades were given to the lowest bidder. Never trust a four second grenade. Just throw it..........

Another weapon, which was available to combat troops on the frontline, was the flame-thrower. The standard M1 flame-thrower used two fuel tanks holding four gallons of fuel and a pressure tank that was strapped onto a man's back. It weighed about seventy pounds and projected a stream of flame some twenty-five yards. If you were assigned to be a flame-thrower, two riflemen were assigned to go with you, as you had no protection. You had to get in close to use this weapon and your two buddies were to pin the enemy down while you crept close enough to release your flame. It took about eight seconds to release all of the fuel and weight from off of your back. Only a volunteer could be a flame-thrower. I saw it being used at least five times against the enemy in pillboxes and believe me it does the job.

Mortars were an Infantry weapon and could be taken apart and carried as a backpack. The standard mortars were the 60-mm and 81-mm. These were muzzle loading, high-trajectory weapons and were very effective weapons because of their accuracy and mobility. The 60-mm fired a thirty-one pound round to a maximum distance of 1,985 yards. The  81-mm mortar used a ten-pound high-explosive round that could discharge its projectile 3,290 yards. The 60-mm mortars weighted forty-two pounds ready to fire while the 81-mm weighted in at 132 pounds. Both mortars had a sustained rate of fire of eighteen rounds per minute.

We were very busy at Camp Robinson during the fifteen weeks of basic training. We had to learn so many ways to survive. I had never fired a weapon before going into service. I learned that there were other Christians in service and I wondered if they, like me, could kill another person. The Chaplain at camp told us to trust in the Lord and obey the higher military authority. When the time would come, could we really kill one of God's creatures? We were being trained to kill.

November was a month of marching, and *more* marching, of PT and *more* PT! Each day we would be introduced to a new skill in Infantry training. We did map reading; going out into the field and then try to find our way back using the compass. We had hours of first aid training. Our company would go out and stay overnight, sleeping on the ground or in our two-man pup tents. Sergeant Stripmaster would just roll up in his shelter half and sleep. How could anyone just fall asleep lying on the ground without a soft pillow? We were getting trained for something big!

Payday was once a month. On the fifteenth of the month we signed the payroll, on the thirtieth we got paid. Payment was distributed according to rank so the sergeants got paid first and finally the lowly privates. We were paid alphabetically in each rank. Being a private, with a name like Vander Molen, I was near to the end of the line for my reward. We always got paid in new money. Since the sergeants were paid first, they would go to the Orderly Room and cover our pool table with a green cloth. This was the table where you could play poker. Somehow the sergeants always seemed to win. Other tables were set up to play dice or other games of chance. It was a real temptation to play, but I watched some of the new recruits lose all of their month's pay in one throw of the dice. This is not what I wanted to do. My fifty dollars per month was hard earned money to me. I always set aside $18.75 each month for a war bond. Four dollars each month was taken out for the laundry service. Once every two weeks, we would send our dirty clothes to the supply room, they would be cleaned and returned the next day. We had to mark all of our clothes with the first initial of our name plus the last four numbers of our service number. All my clothes were marked V-6144. My monthly payment after expenses was in the neighborhood of twenty-eight dollars a month or more like seven dollars per week.

On 23 November my parents came to visit us at Camp Robinson. They came down on the Greyhound Bus, stopping in Little Rock and then to our camp. They were put up in the guesthouse on the grounds and had dinner with us. Mother didn't think much of the food. The weather was damp and cold while they were with us. Father didn't have too much to say. We did get a few days off; we showed them the camp and they also saw the hut that we lived in. I believe that my folks did meet Mike Van Couwenberghe at this time. Gordon remembers that Mother was surprised to see me on guard duty. It was cold and I was wearing this heavy issued overcoat. I had taken a towel and wrapped it around my throat using it as a scarf to keep me warm.

After returning home, Mother shipped a white scarf to me. She informed me that a towel was not the item to keep you warm. I guess mothers are the same all over the world. I used an Olive Drab colored towel because it was Government Issued. I said thanks to my mother about that gift, but never wore a white scarf.

46

On 25 December we all were given the week off to celebrate the Christmas Holiday. Gordon and I went into Little Rock to see the big city. We registered at a local hotel and since we were not heavy drinkers, or interested in girls, we stayed mostly near the hotel. I do remember that we filled a balloon with water and dropped it out of the hotel window. It landed near a couple of soldiers with their "girl-friends." They ran into the hotel trying to find the fellows who had tried to "bomb" them. The Military Police (MP) were called and came knocking on every door to locate the culprits. They rapped on our door and I opened it and claimed that I had been sleeping and didn't know anything about anything. They must have believed me. There wasn't much going on in Little Rock, so we returned to camp earlier than most other GIs.

When I returned to Camp Robinson, I heard the news about the Battle of the Bulge. The combat in Europe was not going too well for the Allied Forces. We were shown pictures of the battle in Europe, mostly of the snow. We saw quite a few pictures of the fighting in Italy, and of the mud and mountains there.

During the last two months of basic training we acquired a new Company Commander, a full bird Colonel; he was from the Americal Division. He wore the blue shoulder patch, with four white stars that formed the Southern Cross. We went into a different training program; instead of doing things as a squad, we started to do things more or less by ourselves or with one other fellow soldier. We practiced more hand-to-hand combat, crawling around on the ground and digging in the dirt. We did a lot more night marches in silence. We would take off across fields instead of following the roads, which we always had done previously. The speed of conquest was bogged down in Europe because of the set backs with the Battle of the Bulge. Our training seemed to be heading more toward the Pacific Theater of Operation (PTO).

Some of the soldiers in camp wanted to go to Little Rock every weekend, if possible. I really had no interest in going there. When these fellows had Kitchen Police duty on Sunday, I would volunteer my services to work their KP for them. Sunday morning breakfast usually consisted of cold cereals or pastry. Normally eggs were not prepared on Sunday mornings. For lunch the menu was cold cuts with lots of fresh fruits. You can see by the menu that there weren't a lot of dirty pans that had to be scrubbed clean. I also got a little extra pay from the GIs who wanted to be in Little Rock. Sunday KP duty was a snap.

We were still faced with the twenty-five mile hike that was required of all men before leaving Camp Robinson. Private Twork said that he wasn't going to march for twenty-five miles; he would find a way out of marching that distance. Doing the hike was like being on jury duty, no way would you be excused. Well, the day finally arrived; I should say the night arrived. With full field packs on, we started out down the road for twenty-five miles. Twork was marching in the column behind me and I kept looking to see if he was still with us. He was, with a big smile on his face; I knew that his plan of operation would soon take place. I saw an ambulance going by me and there was Twork, sitting on the back of that ambulance, heading back to camp and the hospital. I knew there wasn't anything wrong with him, but I couldn't stop wondering how he pulled this one off.

We kept marching for the rest of the night and arrived back at camp, dog-tired. The weather was cool, and rainy; we knew that when we returned to our hut we would have to light the fire in the stove and wait for the room to heat up. When we got to our hut, we opened the door and believe it or not, the stove was lit, the room was nice and cozy and Twork was sitting on his bed. He had prepared hot coffee and had gotten an apple pie from the kitchen for the five of us. We had a little party, even though we were flat out tired. How did Twork manage not to march twenty-five miles? He had pulled his heel off the shoe and no way will the Army let you march missing a heel. We really had a good laugh at that one. Twork went to all the other huts that night and lit their stoves also, so he wasn't such a bad fellow after all.

While in Arkansas we were required by the Army to attend several classes. We had to hear the Articles of War read to us every six months. This deals with the law that governs us while in service, such as if we are AWOL (Absent, Without Official Leave) and what punishment we would get when convicted. For being AWOL we could get three months at hard labor, forfeit all the pay received and then be dishonorably discharged from the Army. If we disobeyed an officer, we could get maybe three months and forfeit all our pay for six months. It was explained that if the enemy captured us, all we had to give was our name, rank, and serial number. If we gave anything else we could be considered a traitor, which meant that we would get shot against a wall.

Another very interesting class we attended was Sex Education. First they showed us graphic movies on what happened when you got VD (Venereal Disease). It showed an airman who had spent the night out with a call girl who contracted VD. Later, he was flying his plane in combat and just as he had his sights on an enemy plane to shoot it out of the sky, he passed out because he had VD, the plane crashed into the ocean and he died! Then they showed some guys in a mental institution. They were insane. They had dribble running out of their mouths. We also saw some horrible pictures of guys infected with VD. It almost made me throw up and I wasn't the only person in that condition. Then the Chaplain got up in front of us and told us not to go out with girls who had syphilis or gonorrhea. He said that it was morally wrong and that was a sin to be with a woman unless you were married to her. The church didn't go for that kind of activity. After the Chaplain left the podium, the medical officer was next; explaining that if you wanted to go out and have a good time with a woman, make sure you wear a condom. Now when you leave the post you were to report to the medical officer and get a Prophylaxis Kit, which included a condom and a wet-nap. When returning from your visit in town, you signed in and reported if you had any contact with a woman and if you used the PK or not. This was against my religious principles and was probably the reason that I didn't go into Little Rock as often as the other fellows did.

19 January basic training was finished. I survived!

On 25 January we reported to the company headquarters and were given our orders where we were to report next. Most of us were given a fourteen-day delay on route, which meant that we could travel home, then report to our next camp in fourteen days. The name of that camp was to be TOP SECRET so we were told not to tell anybody about our destination. We were given our travel papers. Some fellows were to report to Ft. Dix in New Jersey so they knew that they were headed for the European Theater of Operation. I opened my papers and read that on 9 February 1945, I was to report to Ft. Ord, California. Most of the men in our hut and company were to report to Ft. Ord; we would be going to the Pacific Theater of Operation.

We prepared to go home. The Army gave us money to spend for travel. We also had to arrange for our own transportation to California. The cheapest price was by rail, but flying allowed us to spend more time at home. Since I really didn't have a lot of extra cash, I decided to travel by rail. Mike had traveling papers to Ft. Ord as well as did brother Gordon. We put all of our belongings into the now famous duffel bag and headed for the railroad station to board a train going north. We finally arrived in Detroit. I believe that we attended at least one church service. Things sure have changed since we departed from our home in Detroit. A lot of people were working in defense factories making equipment for war. My cousin Ken (Dutch) Zylstra left Grand Rapids and came to Detroit to work. He was staying at our place and now that both Gordon and I were home, he made his bed in the living room.

I was now qualified to sew a shoulder patch on my left sleeve of my uniform. I felt like a real Army guy.

I had one medal for MARKSMANSHIP.

Infantry Replacement Training Center
Camp Robinson Arkansas
December 1944

51

Chapter V
HOME AND THEN WEST
January 1945 – February 1945

My folks insisted on having our pictures taken so we went to a photo shop near our house, called John's Studio. Mother also wanted us to have our pictures taken together. I would have liked my picture taken alone. Gordon is shown on the left because he has more medals then I did. I counted three on his uniform. At least we had a good shoulder patch that indicated we were real soldiers.

The time at home seemed to just drag on. All of my friends were in service. I didn't even make an effort to see Mary Margaret. Gas was rationed, food hard to get, people working many hours in defense plants. I could hardly wait for the days to pass when I would be back with my comrades. I did find the time to visit Southeastern High School. I located and watched the ROTC unit in action. It seemed to me that these kids were really young.

I went to the Michigan Central train station and made arrangements to arrive at Ft. Ord on 8 February. That would be at least one day earlier than I was to report. If we were late in reporting to Ft. Ord, California we could be charged with being AWOL.

On returning home, I told my parents that I was going to California. My parents thought that I was going for more military training.

While home at 2662 Manistique for our delay on route, we took a couple of pictures. The flag in the window, on page 54, has two stars meaning, that two members of this home were in the service.

On 5 February, we left by train for California along with Mike Van Couwenberghe. The train was loaded first with service men; the seats left were for civilians. On boarding the train, we all decided that each one of us would sit by a window to see who would be sitting next to us. We were going to be traveling to California for at least three days. We all had coach tickets requiring us to sleep in our seats.

We were hoping of course, that some nice young, good-looking girl would sit next to us and we would have a pleasant trip out west. Well, the first one in our coach was a very large woman, with a small crying child. This woman sat next to Gordon. Both Mike and I were having a good laugh at this one. Another fellow came on board and sat next to me and he didn't have much to say. No one sat next to Mike so I decided to sit next to him. At least we didn't have a large person next to us with a crying child. Someone said that there was room in the last car and the large women and child  left and went to the rear car. Gordon had a smile on his face and an empty seat next to him, which meant that he would be able to stretch out his legs while we could only lean back in our seats.

Just then a young, attractive girl came in and asked in a loud voice, if there was any empty seats in this car. Gordon, without hesitation, jumped up and said he had an empty seat next to him. He carried her bag and put it in the overhead storage and began to get a conversation going with this beauty. She sat next to him the whole trip to California. When it came time to sleep, she put her head back and went off to sleep. This was about the only time that Gordon left his seat, because he knew that if he left even to go to the bathroom, one of us guys would jump right in and take his place. We would have done it too! It was really funny as I think about it now. We went through Kansas City, and had a four-hour lay over so we went to a steak house and had a very big steak. Everywhere servicemen went they were given first class service.

I remember going through Salt Lake City and San Jose, California. The train stopped at Monterey and we stayed overnight there. The next day we arrived in San Francisco. We had an extra day before reporting to camp so with Mike in tow; we three guys took a bus ride around San Francisco. We went down the famous street often shown in the movies, with police chasing a bad guy down this steep hill. The cross streets level off, which made it feel like we were going on a roller coaster. We returned to camp the next morning, reported for duty and were assigned a barrack. The following morning, we had many forms to fill out, mostly insurance papers and next of kin information. I was able to get GI insurance for only $6.40 per month. This was a $10,000 death claim.

There was a very large swimming pool in camp and one morning we all had to swim across the pool. When we got to the other side, they told us that if we couldn't swim across the pool, we would have to stay until we learned how to swim. Of course, they told us this after we swam across the pool. The weather in California was just wonderful and it would have been nice to stay there at least until the end of the war. While here at Ft. Ord, we were issued some new suntan uniforms. We were headed for the tropical climate to be sure.

THE UNITED STATES OF AMERICA

VETERANS' ADMINISTRATION

WASHINGTON, D. C.

National Service Life Insurance

DATE INSURANCE EFFECTIVE ___SEPTEMBER 27, 1944___

CERTIFICATE No. N 17 523 757

This Certifies That ___KENNETH W. VANDER MOLEN___ FN___

has applied for insurance in the amount of $___10,000.___, payable in case of death.

Subject to the payment of the premiums required, this insurance is granted under the authority of The National Service Life Insurance Act of 1940, and subject in all respects to the provisions of such Act, of any amendments thereto, and of all regulations thereunder, now in force or hereafter adopted, all of which, together with the application for this insurance, and the terms and conditions published under authority of the Act, shall constitute the contract.

Frank T. Hines
Administrator of Veterans' Affairs.

Countersigned at Washington, D. C.

October 11, 1944
(Date)

H. L. Kibile
Registrar.

Mrs. Martha Vander Molen
2662 Manistique Ave.
Detroit, Mich.

Insurance Form 350

57

Chapter VI
PACIFIC PASSAGE
February 1945 – March 1945

Official Photo, U.S. Navy

AP-113 GENERAL H. W. BUTNER

The AP-113 was classified as a Navy Transport. The maiden voyage was on 23 February 1944 and she supplied the troops in Casablanca. On March 19 she made another trip to Casablanca. This ship made port in Durban, South Africa, Kenya, Bombay, Melbourne and Los Angeles. The overall length was 622 feet with a speed of nineteen knots. A total of 74,134 passengers were transported aboard this ship. During the war the General H. W. BUTNER steamed a total of 166,951.7 miles at an average speed of 12.5 knots.

Early on 17 February, we were taken by truck to the harbor area and boarded the GENERAL H. W. BUTNER. We had breakfast on board ship. What a nice meal it was! We even got to sit down and eat out of bowls and plates. Around noon the ship left dockside and proceeded to another pier area to take on more men. There were some black troops but they were mostly truck drivers and engineers, in other words they worked on road construction. Our bunks were on the first deck below the main open deck.

This Navy ship pulled out into San Francisco Bay heading toward the Golden Gate Bridge. It was 5:45 p.m. on Saturday as we steamed under that famous bridge. What a wonderful sight to look up and see many people-waving farewell. We all waved back. The ship continued along very smoothly until we HIT the Pacific Ocean.

As the coastline of California disappeared my thoughts were of home, my parents, my church, and my classmates at Southeastern High School...what was I doing here! It was very quiet on deck as everyone on board were probably thinking similar thoughts of loved ones. It was good to be home for even a few days visiting with some of my school buddies. They were very envious of how I looked in my uniform and they wanted to get into the action before the war would end. It was going to be hard for my parents to have two sons in service at the same time, but Clarence was exempt from service.

I was aboard this Navy ship along with 5,261 other GIs, yet I felt alone. I had faith that God would never fail me, as He would be at my side wherever I went. I was not afraid.

I don't believe that anyone on board figured we would be going into combat. Our chances of fighting on the front line were getting slimmer and slimmer each passing day. The war was going good for our side so why would they need more fighting men? I speculated that we would all be in the supply line doing things like typing or assisting in unloading ships. Yes, that's what we would be doing, so let's get on with this war! By the way, where are we going?

I was trying to adjust to this new environment aboard this ship heading for some place in the South Pacific area. We are now, so to speak, in the Navy and will be doing things the Navy way. One rule the Navy has; if it doesn't move, paint it, and if it does move, salute it.

There were five decks on this ship, since we were replacement infantry troops; we were placed on the first deck below the main deck. There were four more decks below ours that were reached by going down a steel ladder. The farther down in the ship, the classification of the troops changed. Infantry was given high priory, while troops in maintenance and truck drivers were placed in the lower decks of the ship.

We were all issued colored meal tickets and my color was yellow. These indicated which deck we were assigned to and were also used for identification. Meals were served by calling off the color of our tickets. It was very important to keep this card handy because without it, we didn't eat.

There were other things about the Navy that I could never figure out which has to do with food. Why does the Navy serve beans for breakfast every Wednesday and Saturday morning? At least in this way we knew that it was either Wednesday or Saturday. Navy coffee was always available served in large white mugs with no handles and very strong! We didn't eat from our mess kits but used Navy metal trays.

There were so many aboard that we had to stand to eat our meals. This also gave us better control of our trays. If we placed our tray on a table, the ship would shift to port or starboard and so would our tray. We were served only two meals a day, once in the morning and again at night. The food was good and very hot.

When an announcement would come over the loud speaker calling, "Yellow deck to the mess hall," all holders of yellow cards would move quickly to the mess deck. We would get into the mess line, or as we called it the chow line, and were given table utensils. These included a spoon, knife, but no fork. They had just come out of the dishwasher and were almost too hot to handle. We placed these quickly into our pocket to cool off. Next we were given a metal tray, which was also very hot. We soon learned to take a towel or handkerchief with us to handle our hot trays. It was important to keep our eyes open as the food was placed on our tray; gravy was never placed over our potatoes but usually over our slice of bread. Beans were repeatedly placed on top of potatoes. This reminded me of Ft. Sheridan. If we complained, the answer was always the same, "Go see the Chaplain."

During the first few days, some of us had what is called "sea-sickness." We would look at our food and our stomach would turn as often as the ship went up and down. Since we could not run to the nearest exit and over the railing, we just let it all spill out. There was no cure for "sea-sickness" and we were not allowed to be on sick call for this complaint. I never became seasick but will admit that I was a little green behind the ears.

The greatest thrill a sailor could have was to make a soldier ill. This was accomplished by looking for the soldier who was somewhat weak in the knees and green behind the gills. As this seasick soldier came to the serving table the sailor would ask if he would like a greasy pork chop. That would be enough to cause problems for the soldier and laughs from the sailors. What a mess! This is probably why the Navy eats in a mess hall!

We were given Mae West life jackets to wear at all times, I repeat, we were to wear them at *ALL TIMES*. We had an "abandon ship" drill; our compartment was assigned to the top deck, the second deck was to go to the deck that we had just vacated. The third deck was to move to the second deck, the fourth and fifth decks were to stay where they were, as they were expendable. If our ship was torpedoed in the Pacific, the soldiers in the bottom two decks didn't have a prayer to get out.

We were allowed to be on deck about one or two hours each day. This enabled everyone on board ship to get some sun exposure. While on deck we noticed that the ship was painted light gray and had some large guns near the front of the ship. We could not wander around the ship but stayed mostly in the forward section. Orders prevented us to be on deck at night. The officers on board stayed in cabins topside. They did not have to wear the bulky Mae West jacket, but instead were given a small inner tube, which went around the waist. It was not as bulky as ours but I guess rank has its privileges.

We spent most of our time on our bunks. Bunks (beds) were virtually our only living space. A canvas sheet was stretched between tubing to form a bunk. They were six feet long and about two and one half feet wide. They could fold up against the supporting rack so that the bottom bunk was just three inches from the bottom deck. When lying on the bottom bunk face up, we had about one foot of space between the bunk above us. Just imagine six more bunks on top of that bunk! Across a three-foot aisle the same set-up was repeated. If all the soldiers in the area were to get up and stand in the aisle; there would be fourteen soldiers standing in a three foot by six-foot aisle. Don't forget everyone was wearing a life jacket. It was very crowded with no place to go. We had to keep our duffel bags and our newly issued steel helmets in our beds also. This was no place to have claustrophobia!

Author's Note: Many years later after the war, I subscribed to the World War II Magazine, there was an article written by a GI from the 24th Infantry Division. It told of his travels to the PTO aboard the General Butner. I wrote to him; his name was Larry Stuckenschneider. Larry was an artist and had sketched a number of drawings aboard this ship. The following four are of his sketches, which he sent to me. Larry was a Benedictine monk at St. John's Abbey in Collegeville, Minnesota.

I mentioned that we HIT the Pacific Ocean; well that is how it felt below decks at night. After leaving San Francisco the waves seemed to take over and continued for the entire voyage. There was only a dim light on while we slept in our cramped quarters located near a ladder leading to the main deck. This was the place where most of the smokers would gather for a last smoke before retiring. We were not allowed to smoke in our bunk area and after 6 p.m. the smoking lamp was turned off throughout out the entire ship. There were always some guys who just had to smoke and would light up near the stairwells. It was usually quiet while we were in our bunks, but the waves kept moving the ship this way and that way. Some fellows, who did not get sick in the chow lines, got sick while lying in bed. Nighttime would be the worse time to get seasick; you couldn't run up on deck because the top deck belongs to the Navy. Instead, you would aim into your steel helmet. Too bad for the guys beneath if you missed the helmet!

One of the cruel things that some one would do was to wait until everyone was quiet; then make a loud retching noise and dump water into a steel helmet, making the sound of someone throwing up. This usually started a chain reaction among the troops. We couldn't go on sick call with seasickness because there was no cure for it, just get over it the best way you can. One remedy was to eat a piece of bread. It was important to keep busy and think of other things.

On Wednesday the 21st our deck was called topside. It was going to be basic training all over again. Only instead of just helmet liners, raincoats and boots, all we had to do was to remove our shirts and come topside when ordered. We then were given our Typhus and Cholera Immunization shots. After that shot we were ready to head for our crowded bunk and hope that no one would touch our sore arm for a day or two.

A call came over the loud speaker asking for volunteers to help in the mess hall. In the Army you never volunteer for anything but I was now in the Navy so I volunteered. "Here I am," I said, "Put me to work."

I was assigned to the supply detail. My job was to go to the very bottom of the ship and put supplies on the small elevator that transported items to the kitchen. I worked about two hours per day. It was a very easy job but the worst part was to be in the very hole of the ship. I could hear the water as it went under me. However, there was also another advantage to working with the Navy; I got to eat at noon with the sailors.

I would load about eight pounds of tomatoes or fifty pounds of potatoes on the elevator then close the door and the food was transported to the upper regions of the ship. I would then go up to the kitchen and eat with the sailors that were on duty. They weren't so much different from the rest of us. Usually I was given a couple of extra loaves of bread to give to the guys on my deck. Sometimes when there was cold meat left over from lunch, they would give me a platter full of cold cuts, which I shared with the guys. It felt good to do something constructive rather than hang around or play card games.

On my many trips to the lower decks, I witnessed some of the troops that were assigned to the very bowels of this great ship. Most were truck drivers, construction persons and general labor troops. I often wondered what would happen to them if the ship were under enemy attack.

Every so often the Navy would have gunnery practice. They would release a large balloon and take turns trying to hit it with their four-inch guns, machine guns or whatever other weapons they had on board. I was up on deck one time and watched them try to take out that balloon. They couldn't hit the broad side of a barn. I sure hope that the Japanese Air Force would not attack us because they could easily get through to us without any damage to their planes. Could it be possible that some of these sailors were in training at Great Lakes the same time I was at Ft. Sheridan?

Eventually I needed to take a shower because of my hard work aboard ship. I did a lot of sweating and was beginning to smell awful! I entered what the Navy calls "the head" and the Army called "latrine." There were about twenty stalls enclosed with a showerhead, fourteen soldiers were standing in line in front of one

shower stall. Now why would these guys all be in front of one stall and not using all the other empty ones?

So I went over and turned the water on in one of the empty stalls, the water was hot and the other tap was cold, so I turned both knobs and got a nice flow of lukewarm water, removed my clothes and entered what I thought would be a refreshing shower. The water was OK but a little salty to the taste, then all the other guys in line started to laugh and I realized why those other shower stalls were empty. Only one shower had fresh water, all the other stalls had saltwater. I had just taken a saltwater shower and there is no way that I could make any suds using ivory soap. There was only one option and that was to dry myself off and get in line with the other fellows and wait my turn to take a fresh water shower. Of course, while I am standing in line waiting for a fresh water shower, I begin to turn into a pillar of salt; my skin turns white, my hair gets straight and my skin tightens up.

While I'm standing in line another fellow walks up to an empty shower, do I yell out and say, "Hey fellow that's a salt water shower?" No, you do not; if I got hooked into a saltwater shower then he can suffer the same embarrassment that I had endured.

We spent most of our time on this ship waiting in lines. We stood in line to eat mess, use the head, and the line for sick call. No wonder they call these ships *ocean liners*!

We were not allowed to gamble while on this ship; everybody did in some form or another. Cards were the number one game. They used matches for money; most of us didn't carry any or very little money in our pockets. Dice games were always going on someplace, but a little more room was needed for that game. Dice was usually played under the ladders or by the lifeboats.

Another thing that passed the time was to take a half-dollar and with a spoon, hit the edge of the coin. You keep striking this coin using the steel deck as a base and keep hitting until the coin would flatten out. By cutting out the center we had a nice ring. It sounds like it would take forever to make one, but we had plenty of time. Boredom was enemy number one.

Rumors began to fly when we conversed with the sailors. They seemed to know where we were heading. On the last trip this ship went to India, so we had it figured that we were on our way to India. That was going to be a nice place, because nobody was fighting in India. Well, at least we were not going to the Philippines, because we would have been there by now. India would be a nice place to spend the rest of the war.

Just one week after getting our Typhus and Cholera shots, on 28 February we crossed the Equator and had a rendezvous with King Neptune. The mighty keeper of Davy Jones' Locker appeared and called his court to order. Hostages were charged with attempting to cross the Equator without permission and each were found guilty and sentenced to suffer oceanic tortures as pleased the King. A couple of the new sailors on board had all their hair cut off; nothing

was done to us soldiers. We were all granted safe passage over the hidden barrier, which separates the Northern and Southern Hemispheres. We were given a blue card, which identified us as shellbacks, and if we crossed the Equator again, we would not be endangered of the wrath of King Neptune. It was fun to see the sailors getting what they deserved for all the tricks they had played on us.

We were now in the Southern Hemispheres and if we looked up at the stars we no longer were able to see the Big Dipper, instead we saw the Southern Cross. We were now headed away from India; maybe we would go to Australia, or New Zealand. Rumors and more rumors are what kept us from going insane.

It was reported that a Japanese submarine attacked our ship and sent a torpedo across our bow. The torpedo came straight at our ship, then the GENERAL BUTNER's bow rose up out of the water just enough, so that the Japanese torpedo went right under the ship. Since our transport was so fast, we escaped by out-running the enemy. Later, we heard that every ship crossing has a story like the one you just read. It makes for good story telling!

Right above our deck was the space allotted to the Chaplain for church services. The Chaplain held church services every morning starting at 8:00 a.m. I did go to a couple of the Chaplain services. Sometime later I was to meet one of those Chaplains while in the hospital on Leyte.

After the worship service was over, the space was converted into a movie theater. This theater had enough seating for about forty to fifty GIs. I remember lying on my bunk, (I was third up from the bottom) and listened to that movie repeatedly. I never saw the movie, but I can quote every word of it. The name of the movie was "Cover Girl", starting Gene Kelly. He did some singing and great dancing. One of the songs was "Long Ago And Far Away." One of these days, I will rent the movie and try to match pictures to the sound. I'll know the songs but I won't attempt dancing.

The movie was one of the popular pastime activities. It was not so much as seeing the movie but getting into the theater. We were required to follow the same procedure used at mealtime. We had to show our colored meal ticket to enter the show. When our deck was called, I would rush to view the movie. Since only forty or fifty men could be seated in the movie area we had to move fast. We showed our colored meal ticket at the door and entered. A new game was being played out. The object was to get into the movie even if it was not your turn.

One of the best ways to get see the movie was to first attend the Chaplain services, because as soon as his service was over, the troops would leave and the moviegoers were then checked in at the door for the ticket check. If we ducked under the seats before every one had left, then the other troops would come into the room and we would quietly crawl from under the seats and take our place to see the movie. Once in awhile, the sailors would check our meal ticket card after we were seated. This would of course create a problem. First, we had the wrong color meal ticket and they would then throw us out of the movie. Secondly, they would take our meal card and hold it for one full day, meaning we were out of luck and couldn't eat the next day. Army troops stick together, so when it came time to show our "wrong" ticket, someone would always hand us theirs. It was always the Army trying to outsmart the Navy guys.

We could pull the "under the seat trick" for just so many times. We figured another way to get in. We would get one sergeant and about four enlisted men to go together as a cleaning squad. We would approach the sailors at the door, and while carrying mops and pails, tell them we were part of the Captain Troops and were to clean out the room before any soldiers could be seated. The sailors never questioned us and we would enter and make believe that we were cleaning. Shortly the doors were opened, the soldiers would come in, and we just sat next to them, saw the movie (again) and then left mops and pails behind. This worked for a few days but more soldiers wanted to become part of our cleaning detail. When there were too many soldiers on clean up detail, the sailors began to figure that something was wrong and finally asked for our orders to clean up the room.

I was able to see that movie more than any other person on board ship because of a little mistake one of the sailors made. I was sitting on the steps leading into the movie projection room; a sailor asked if I would get him a cup of coffee. I did and started to show an interest in what he was doing. One time he asked me to load the film into the projector and then to show the entire film. The sailor had other things to do, so I ran the films from then on. Every so often he would come into the room by a back door and check on me. I was having a ball and soon I was entering the booth by the same back door. It was really getting to be very boring on board ship.

Every night over the loud speaker we would hear, *"**Now hear this, now hear this.** Sweeper, man your broom, sweep all trash from the main deck to the fantail. At 0300 all clocks will be set ahead one hour. Set all watches. The smoking lamp is out. That is all."*

We would then turn into our small prison. They would lock the doors leading into our compartment. They turned on some low voltage lamps. Our hope was to get to sleep fast and trust that when we awoke, our ship was still afloat. We didn't do much to keep ourselves clean. We didn't take too many showers and never shaved. Some fellows even grew beards; all I could come up with was peach fuzz. We wanted off this ship.

What seemed like a lifetime after leaving San Francisco, I happened to be on deck when a PBY Catalina flew overhead. The Catalina's were flying boats that the Navy used for coastal patrols. I then knew we were close to land. What a great sight to see that aircraft flying around our ship with its large white star painted on its side. I felt safe now that we would be in port shortly.

Sunday, 4 March at 11:20 a.m. we docked at Pier #8 in Langemak Bay, New Guinea. It was very hot and humid in the harbor of Finschhafen. There were many oil tankers at the various dock sites. The smell of oil was in the air. We could hear strange sounds coming from the interior of the land. We could feel the muggy jungle heat as we walked around the deck that night. Most of the guys chose to sleep on the deck, as it was extremely warm and smelly below. They pumped in fresh water and it was wonderful to take a fresh water shower. At least the ship wasn't moving from side to side. I finally got a good night sleep.

No one got off the ship except one fellow who was so seasick that they removed him from sickbay on a stretcher. I peered over the railing and watched as they carried this poor fellow off the ship. I recognized him; it was Private Hunderman, that's right, the same fellow who invited me to church while at Camp Robinson, Arkansas. My understanding was that he stayed on New Guinea for some time and was put to work in the kitchens. After he had gained some weight, they shipped him home, by air.

The next morning, March 5, our ship slowly pulled up anchor and headed in a more westerly direction. The GENERAL BUTNER followed the coastline until the next day when we anchored in the harbor of Hollandia at 2:33 p.m. Again, we did not get off the ship. This was a very large harbor and there were a great many other ships at anchor. At Finschhafen, the ships were very close together but here the harbor was larger and all kinds of ships were seen around the horizon. We could make out many cargo ships, and some Navy Destroyers. Planes flew overhead, I really felt safe.

There was a gentle breeze blowing, it was cool on deck. I slept in comfort for another night under a tropical star lit night. They left the compartment doors open that made it easier for all of us aboard to move about freely. Supply vessels were moored along the side as the now empty compartments were being filled. There was a bustling of activities among the other ships in this harbor. I was told that my duties in the kitchen were ended. It was going to be a real vacation from now on. That is IF we were going to go to India.

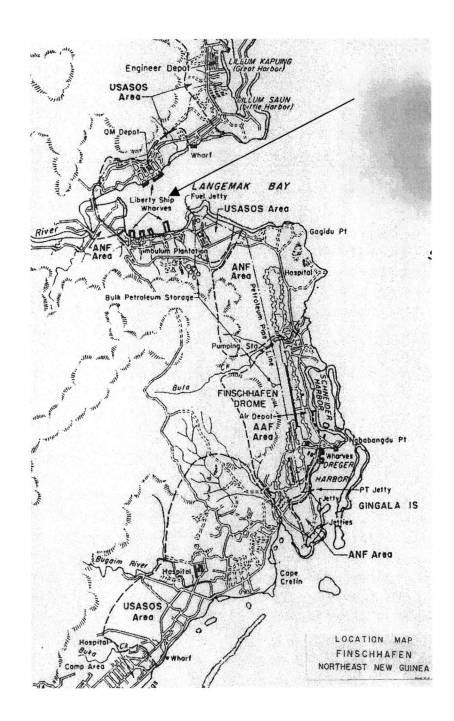

Engineer Depot

LILLUM KAPUING
(Great Harbor)

USASOS
Area

LILLUM SAUN
(Little Harbor)

QM Depot

Wharf

LANGEMAK BAY

Liberty Ship
Wharves

Fuel Jetty

USASOS Area

River

Gagidu Pt

ANF
Area

Timbulum Plantation

ANF
Area

Hospital

Bulk Petroleum Storage

Petroleum Pipe Line

Pumping Sta

Ck

Buta

FINSCHHAFEN
DROME

SCHNEIDER HARBOR

Air Depot

AAF
Area

Ngababangdu Pt

Wharves

DREGER
HARBOR

PT Jetty

Jetty

GINGALA IS

Jetties

ANF Area

Bugaim River

Hospital

Cape
Cretin

USASOS
Area

Hospital
Buta

Ck

Camp Area

Wharf

LOCATION MAP
FINSCHHAFEN
NORTHEAST NEW GUINEA

74

The slopes overlooking Hollandia were lush and green. We could make out a road cutting through the thick brush leading to the top of one of the hills. We were told by one of the sailors, who seemed to have all the answers, that this was the home of General Douglas MacArthur. Here is where I first heard the phrase "Dug-out Doug" and we called him that throughout the remainder of the war.

A native in his dugout canoe came along side our ship and sailors did some trading with him. He had bananas and coconuts in his flimsy craft and they looked appetizing to me. Over the loud speaker the order was given to the sailors to stop trading with the natives. They didn't seem to hear that command and so two shots were fired into the air; the sailors stopped their bargaining and the native canoe departed quickly.

While at anchor we were able to have our mess at tables, which was quite a change considering that the past twenty days or so we ate standing up. The food was excellent, as fresh supplies had been put aboard.

We had been in this safe harbor for just over two days but it seemed like much longer, however on Wednesday, 7 March the U.S.S. GENERAL BUTNER left the safety of Hollandia Harbor. It seemed like every ship in sight had fired up their boilers and were moving out to sea. Smoke curled into the sky from some ships while others moved gracefully toward the north. I could tell that a convoy was now being formed and we would not be alone. Our ship was one of the largest in port having crossed the Pacific without any armed escort. I was told that we carried more guns then most U.S. Destroyers. The captain on board our ship was in charge of this convoy. We flew the flag of a Commodore, since our ship was the fastest and the most heavily armed. Consequently, we went from one part of the convoy to the other to make sure every ship was in its proper line. Other ships flashed their lights and made turns as most convoys do. We still had no idea where we were going and what was to happen. As our ship cut through the blue Pacific the warm breezes soothed our sun burned skins. We watched flying fish jump from wave to wave. There were a few dolphins but the strangest sight was the neon fluorescent fish. The waters of the Pacific were very clear and it seemed that we could see the bottom. Maybe, just maybe, we were going to India. WRONG!

I don't remember much of this trip from Hollandia to our final destination except that the seas were somewhat calm and the waters very clear. The dolphins were with us most of the way darting into the waves from our ship. They were wonderful creatures and gave me a sense of calm. If God cared for his sea creatures, I knew He would care for me.

16 March Friday at 4:49 p.m., we finally dropped anchor in San Pedro Bay, off the Island of Leyte in the Philippine Islands. This was not India. We looked at the shoreline but remained on board ship for the night. We had spent twenty-eight days on board this ship. What will tomorrow hold for us? Few slept that night. The stars were in all of their glory. I felt closer to heaven than at any other time. It was quiet and I could see a few fires on the beach area.

I awoke to an early morning sunrise. What will this new day bring? I had my last meal aboard ship. Saturday morning at 11:55 a.m. on 17 March, I left the GENERAL BUTNER by going over the railing, down a cargo net and into waiting LCM's (landing crafts). It was tricky putting my feet into the thick rope ladder with men above and below all scrambling to get off the ship. The LCM's went around in circles and we headed for the nameless beach.

As we approached the shore the front ramp was lowered and we ran out onto dry land. I had the misfortune of getting my foot caught on the edge of the ramp and fell headlong into the soft wet sand. Before I could recover, I was hit by a wave from the Pacific Ocean and went down again into the sand only this time I was drenched.

Photo above from the National Archives and Records Administration.

The above photo shows infantrymen hitting the beach on Tacloban, Leyte.

I was not part of the above landing but it gives the readers an idea of how it was like leaving the troop ship, USS General Butner.

It was a very hot day so I got dried very quickly. The palm trees were a welcome sight to see, green and flowing gently in the breeze. What a relief it was to get off that crowded troop ship, welcome dry ground.

Chapter Vll
LEYTE
March 17, 1945 – April 1, 1945

On 20 October 1944, General MacArthur landed with over 202,500 troops at Tacloban, Leyte in the Philippine Island group. That is more troops than landed in Normandy on 6 June 1944. I too am experiencing an invasion but no one is firing any shots at me.

There was much activity going on as I approached the beach. Palm trees hovered in the breeze while dark-skinned natives were busy around their bamboo huts. There wasn't much to be said for this area. It was just a simple village located at the water's edge. I had expected to see bomb craters like you see in wartime movie. Instead the natives were just going about their own business ignoring us. Weren't we the conquering heroes?

We seemed to be waiting around for something to happen. I was glad to just stand around because my clothes were getting dryer every minute. I was also trying to get the sand out of my combat boots. Finally, trucks arrived and we were driven to the Fourth Replacement Depot. We arrived at 10:30 p.m. in an area brightly lit up for our arrival. We were now in a camp with many more GIs. Most of them had arrived just ahead of us. We were a young group of kids, most of us only eighteen years old.

We were directed to large tents. There were about forty of us in our tent. What a luxury it was to sleep on a cot instead of a ship's deck! We did not receive blankets or pillows; just an Army issued gray cot. We surely did not need any covering at night because it was hot and most of us slept in our underwear. My duffel bag was used for a pillow but during the day it was placed under my cot for safekeeping. These tents were open on all sides so breezes cooled us as we slept.

As mealtime drew near we would form a line with our mess kit in hand awaiting the mess sergeant's order to be served. It was usually a line of open kettles containing hot food. The first cook dished out potatoes; the next placed gravy on top, then our vegetable and perhaps a slice of bread. Hot coffee was dipped from a very large steaming pot. We sat on the ground to eat our meal sharing it with all kinds of strange insects. If it rained we returned to our assigned tent and ate inside.

After eating we proceeded to another area where we scraped our mess kits clean of uneaten food into large drums. What they did with this, I do not know. Maybe it went to feed some pigs. After removal we would then dip our utensils into a large pot of hot soapy water. We would use a brush to scrub it clean and then dip it again into another pot of hot clear boiling water. After a final rinse we would shake any water left on them. This was the way the Army did dishes. We followed this procedure after every meal on Leyte. Our drinking water was taken from a large canvas waterproof sack called a lister bag. We drank huge amounts of water because of the hot weather. Every day, water would be trucked into camp and used for our drinking and eating. I noted that the natives didn't drink water as we Americans did. They were probably accustomed to a different source of water.

Rumors started to spread. Maybe we were going to be assigned to MacArthur's staff. Perhaps we were going to stay on Leyte and help unload ships for the rest of the war. Or, we could be sent back home, as we were only eighteen. Some thought we were going back to Hawaii to relieve the troops there. (That was the rumor I liked the best!) It could be that we were still going to India. Were we going to have more jungle training here on Leyte? No one knew anything and the one who knew where we were going wasn't telling us.

We were issued our own Garand .30 caliber, M1 rifle, which is the infantryman's basic weapon. Our new rifle had a serial number on the stock and we were required to memorize that number. We were responsible for each piece of military equipment and if we lost it, we would have to pay for it. That's what they told us.

All new M1 rifles were packed in cosmoline, which resembles grease. We first cleaned off all grease then polished our weapon until it shined. I looked at my rifle (in Army language, it was called a piece) and began to wonder if I would have to use it in combat. An officer came through the hut area to inspect the condition of our rifles. If they were not cleaned properly we had to clean it again. My rifle passed inspection but we were not issued ammunition at this time. It seemed strange to me that we never had the chance to zero in (test fire) our rifle after it was inspected. We did not do any marching, just waited. What were we waiting for? No one tells you anything.

The water table was very high, so if we dug a hole, water would surface. It wasn't the best water to drink. To construct a latrine for use by the troops, they put barrels into the ground and all the waste materials from humans were contained in these barrels. When the barrels were full, they would put fuel oil into them and ignite them; all the human waste materials would be burned. An awful stench resulted when burning the latrines! They always tried to burn them when the wind was blowing into the island and not toward our living quarters. No one went swimming in the ocean. All kinds of ships were in the harbor being unloaded. There was much activity in that area.

We saw several poor starving children on this island. They would gather where we were eating and when we went to dump our mess kits, they were right there asking if we would please empty our leftovers into their tin cans. I would deliberately not eat a couple of things and give it to these poor starving kids. Other guys were doing the same thing, even when we were told not to. There is nothing so pitiful than to look into the eyes of a starving child.

The Filipinos were occupied with their daily routines. They did not seem to be in any hurry. Children tended chickens and other domestic animals while the men went out to sea on hollowed tree-trunk boats for their catch of fish. Women sat in the shade fanning themselves and tending their babies in this hot steaming atmosphere. You wouldn't think there was a war going on.

Many young girls hung around our camp area also. These were what we referred to as "working girls." The morality of these people was quite a shock to me. They had very little religious principles. Even young boys aged seven or eight would approach us and ask if we wanted some pom-pom. They would then point out their sister to us. Several of the GIs took "advantage" of the offers to have a good time. There were colored troops on Leyte, mostly truck drivers, who would tell these very young girls that they were true-blooded Americans. They would claim that they had dark skin because they were part American Indian. Most of the girls went for that claim and so it was not unusual to see these girls hanging around the motor pool to view these pure Americans. The white skin was more related to the Spanish people and these Filipinos had ill feelings toward white people going back to the time of Magellan.

I was beginning to wonder if we were going to sit out the rest of the war here on Leyte.

Finally, we were called to an assembly area to receive our orders. The Chaplain spoke to us first. He gave a short but serious speech encouraging us to put our faith in Christ. He prayed that God would see us all through the upcoming battle. The Chaplain issued a statement to all Catholics that he would be holding confessionals after this formation.

We now realized that something big was about to happen! We were given ten cartridges (clips) of eight rounds of ammunition, which we placed into our cartridge belt. These clips were later inserted into our 30-cal Garand Rifles. We were issued ammunition but never had the opportunity to test fire our weapons.

We all were issued two water canteens and instructed to clip them onto our ammunition belt. One was to be placed on our right hip and the other on the left. We also carried a first-aid kit on our belt. The last piece of warfare was the gas masks. I filled my water canteens and headed back to the Fourth Replacement Depot to wait again.

Later, as we assembled again, it was explained that we were to be assigned to a fighting unit somewhere in the Pacific. As replacements we would be going to a unit that needed us. Further instructions included removing any papers from our pockets. We were not to have billfolds, or pictures of our loved ones on our person. The only item we could carry would be a small Bible or religious item.

The Articles of War was read to us again and under no circumstances were we to surrender to the enemy. If we were captured, we were only to give our name, rank, and serial number. We also had to pack our backpacks with items to be used in combat. All other items were to be packed into our duffel bag. We carried these bags to a large enclosed area and our name and serial numbers were stenciled with orange paint on the outside. These were placed on a large pile. Our bags would be shipped to assigned units and we would be able to recover them there. <u>I never saw my duffel bag again</u>.

This was beginning to look serious. I wondered what was ahead of us. Where would we be going? No one explains anything to a foot soldier.

Chapter VIII
LST – 777
April 1, 1945 – April 3, 1945

The date was 1 April 1945, Easter Sunday, at 12:08 p.m. that I left the safety of Leyte Gulf aboard the LST-777 en route to Cebu, Philippine Islands. We were now part of the Navy Task Unit 79. This ship was combat loaded with five officers and 385 men of the United States Army, with seventy-two vehicles and 205 tons of miscellaneous cargo. I don't remember too much of the voyage from Leyte to Cebu. Next day at 6:20 p.m. we arrived at the Caldron Street Jetty and started to unload the combat cargo. I do remember watching the sailor unloading the equipment. It was fun just looking and not helping. Unloading was completed at 10:30 p.m. and we slept out under the stars. Early the next morning, we got underway and headed for the beach area. The LST-777 just headed for the beach and ran aground, opening its great steel doors and we just walked out. By 11:30 a.m. the disembarking troops were ashore. I didn't even get my feet wet.

It was at this point that I began to realize that we were now in combat. As soon as LST-777 had unloaded us, they were bringing aboard seventy-nine men for medical treatment and disposition. The LST-777 pulled itself away from the beach and that was the last that I saw of that ship.

The LST was the workhorse for landings in the Pacific Theater of Operation. Sailors referred to this ship as a *Large Slow Target*. American firms built 1,052 with only twenty-six lost to enemy action; another thirteen were victims of weather, grounding or accidents. The LSTs were 328 feet long and fifty feet wide; they carried 2,100 tons of cargo. There were two or six davits for landing craft.

The LSTs carried a number of fifty-foot landing craft mechanized (LCM) that transported troops right onto the beach. Soldiers descended into these crafts by use of the landing cargo net. In most cases the LSTs moored right on the beaches and unloaded their cargo. If the beaches were mined then the LCM's transported all the cargo to the shore.

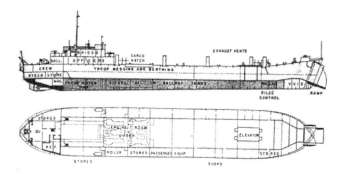

The first beachhead on Cebu landed on 26 March. The first wave were troops from the 132nd Infantry and the 182nd Infantry. The 164th Infantry was still on Luzon. The beaches of Cebu were mined and so LCM's were used to transport troop on shore. The LST-777 was able to transport our landing right up to the beach as most of the land mines were cleaned up by time of our arrival.

The above photo shows a LST unloading troops right on the beach. Please note this is not the LST-777, but only to give the reader what it was like for me to land on Cebu.

The next photos are from the National Archives and Reccord Administration. (NARA) These are photos of the landing on Cebu by the 132nd and 182nd Infantry on March 1945. I was not on these landings. I came ashore on 3 April 1945.

The first wave hit the beaches in good order, however the Japanesse had established a mine field. Twelve LCM's were destroyed in that first attempt.

A lot of coconut trees plus a great many hills to climb.

Once the beach head was established the wounded from the first wave were placed on the LSTs for medical treament. We take care of our own. (above photos NARA)

The following documents were issued 29 March 1945, from the Headquarters of the Fourth Replacement Depot, United States Army Forces in the Far East.

Special Order Number...86 Par 31...
300 Enlisted Men, Infantry are transferred on 3 April 1945 to the Americal Division, APO 716 from the 4th Replacement Depot on 3 APRIL 1945.

A true copy of the Special Order Number 86 Par 31 is listed on the next page.

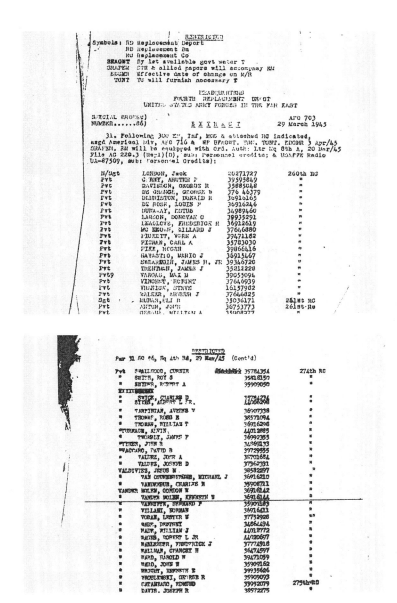

Symbols: RD Replacement Depot
RD Replacement Bn
RC Replacement Co
REAGNT By 1st available govt water T
SHAFEX STR & allied papers will accompany EM
EDCHG Effective date of change on M/R
TONT TU will furnish necessary T

HEADQUARTERS
FOURTH REPLACEMENT DEPOT
UNITED STATES ARMY FORCES IN THE FAR EAST

SPECIAL ORDERS)   APO 703
NUMBER......86)   E X T R A C T   29 March 1945

31. Following 300 EM, Inf, MOS & attached RC indicated, asgd Americal Div, APO 716 & WP BY AGNT. TON. TONT. EDCHG 3 Apr/45 SHAFNA. EM will be equipped with Ord. Auth: Ltr Hq 8th A, 20 Mar/45 File AG 220.3 (Repl)(D), sub: Personnel credits; & USAFFE Radio UA-87509, sub: Personnel Credits):

M/Sgt	LONDON, Jack	20271727	260th RC
Pvt	CARNEY, ARTHUR F	39595849	"
Pvt	DAVISIAN, GEORGE R	35885048	"
Pvt	DE ORANGE, GEORGE b	376 46379	"
Pvt	DEIRMISTON, DONALD R	36916165	"
Pvt	DE ROSE, LOUIS F	36916246	"
Pvt	DUNAWAY, LOTUS	34989460	"
Pvt	LARSON, DONOVAN C	39935291	"
Pvt	LEAGLOVE, FREDERICK R	36912629	"
Pvt	MC KEOWE, WILLARD J	37646680	"
Pvt	PICKETT, VERN A	39471182	"
Pvt	PIGMAN, CARL A	35783030	"
Pvt	PIKE, ROGER	39866416	"
Pvb	GAVASTIO, MARIO J	36915467	"
Pvt	EBBARNOLIN, JAMES R, JR	39346720	"
Pvt	TRENTMAN, JAMES J	35212228	"
Pvt9	VAROAG, MAX H	39055094	"
Pvt	VINCENT, ROBERT	37646939	"
Pvt	VISLRICK, STEVE	16157902	"
Pvt	WALKER, ARTHUR J	37646825	"
Sgt	MUGGS, ELI R	33056171	261st RC
Pvt	ANTON, JOHN	36753773	261st Rc
Pvt	GORDON, WILLIAM A	35008077	

Par 31 SO #6, Hq 4th Rd, 29 Mar/45 (Cont'd)

Pvt	SMALLWOOD, CURMIE	35784354	274th RC
"	SMITH, ROY S	35818150	"
"	SNYDER, ROBERT A	39909050	"
"	STICK, CHARLES D	17704974	"
"	STIKE, ALBERT L JR.	17706396	"
"	TARPINIAN, AVEDIS V	36007338	"
"	THOMAS, ROSS R	38571094	"
"	TROBAN, WILLIAM T	36916298	"
"	TURRAGE, ALVIN	44012885	"
"	TWOMBLY, JAMES F	36992355	"
"	TYNES, JOHN R	34869133	"
"	VACCARO, DAVID B	37729555	"
"	VALDEZ, JOCH A	35770184	"
"	VALDEZ, JOSEPH D	37367331	"
"	VALDIVIEZ, JESUS M.	38532297	"
"	VAN COUWENBERGHE, MICHAEL J	36916210	"
"	VANDENBUR, CHARLES R	35908711	"
Vander	BULEN, GORDON W	36916142	"
"	VANDER BULEN, KENNETH B	36916144	"
"	VANNUFEN, BERNARD F	35909189	"
"	VILLAME, NORMAN	36916411	"
"	VORABL, LESTER W	37752928	"
"	WADT, DWITNEY	34864494	"
"	WADE, WILLIAM J	44012772	"
"	WAGNER, ROBERT L JR	44020697	"
"	WALLENDER, FREDERICK J	37774928	"
"	WALLMAN, CHANCEY H	36474597	"
"	WARD, HAROLD W	39471059	"
"	WARD, JOHN W	35909182	"
"	WRIGHT, KENNETH E	39935626	"
"	WROBLEWSKI, GEORGE R	35909093	"
"	CATANZARO, EDMUND	33952079	275th RC
"	DAVIS, JOSEPH R	36572275	"

From the above list, these men will be assigned into different units of the Americal Division. Most of the men on this list were from Camp Robinson, which included brother Gordon, and Mike Van Couwenberge. The list is compiled by the rank of the EM. Hence the first EM on the list is Master Sergeant London, Jack. We will meet him later in this journey.

I have a copy of the Log Book of the USS LST-777. This Log Book keeps track hour by hour of what happens aboard ship. Hence, I was able to track my movements from the Island of Leyte to the shores of Cebu.

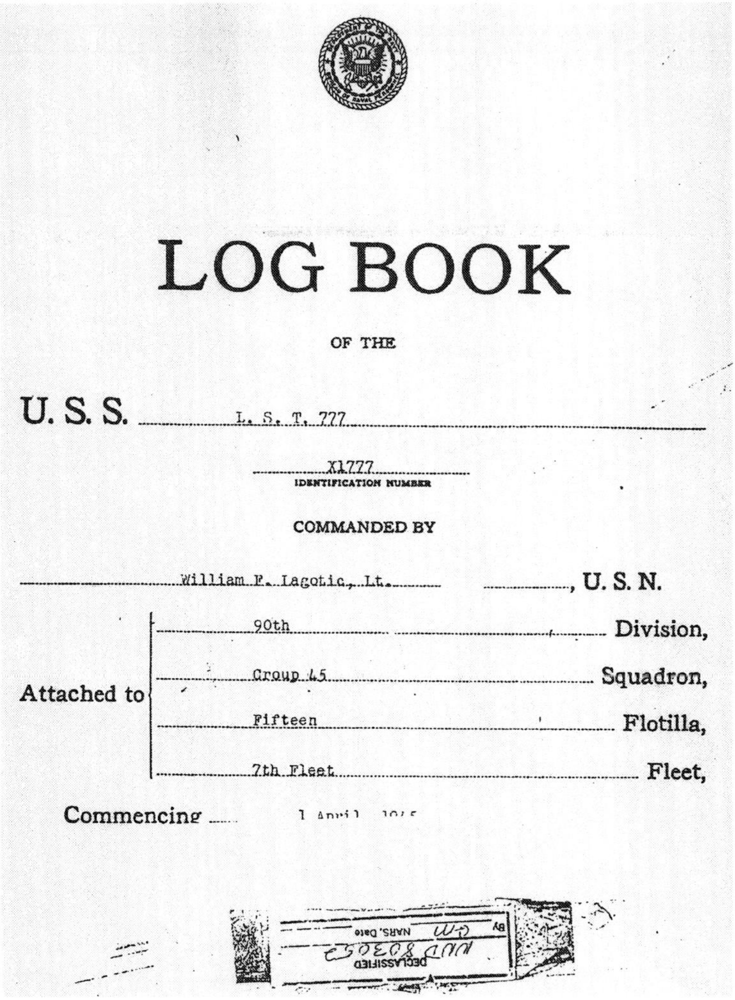

LOG BOOK

OF THE

U. S. S. _____ L. S. T. 777 _____

_____ X1777 _____
IDENTIFICATION NUMBER

COMMANDED BY

_____ William P. Lagotic, Lt. _____ , U. S. N.

Attached to
{
_____ 90th _____ Division,

_____ Group 45 _____ Squadron,

_____ Fifteen _____ Flotilla,

_____ 7th Fleet _____ Fleet,
}

Commencing _____ 1 April 1945

/PERS-134 (REV. 1-44)   DECK LOG—REMARKS SHEET

UNITED STATES SHIP_____LST 777_____   Sunday   1   April   , 1945
                                                                  (Day)   (Date)   (Month)

0000 - 0400

Anchored off Catman Hill, San Pedro Bay, Leyte, P.I. in 6 fathoms of water,
with 30 fathoms of chain to the bow anchor, on the following anchorage bearings; Old Fort 351 T; Capines Point 060 T; Various units of the U.S. Pacific
Fleet present. Auxiliary engines in use for auxiliary purposes. No further
remarks.

R. M. Kuhn
R. M. Kuhn
Ens., USNR.

0400 - 0800

Anchored as before. 0730 Pursuant to Ad Com 7th Phib Dispatch 311211 dated
March 1945, Lt(jg) H. L. Harrison MC USNR 394553, was detached from this vessel to report aboard USS Henry T. Allen PA-90, with necessary records and personal gear. 0745 LCM 808 secured for towing by stern anchor cable. No further
remarks.

R H Wehrmann
R. H. Wehrmann
Ens., USNR.

0800 - 1200

Anchored as before. 0900 Made daily inspection of magazines. Conditions normal.
1152 Set the Special Sea Detail; Made all preparations for getting underway.
No further remarks.

J. M. Derbacher
J. M. Derbacher
Ens., USNR.

1200 - 1600

Anchored as before. 1208 Underway from Leyte Gulf, P.I. Enroute Cebu, P. I.
In accordance with CTG 78.2 Operational Plan 3-45 Supply Echelon of 17 March
1945. In company with Task Unit 78.2.5, Captain on Conn; Navigator on Bridge.
Steaming various courses and speeds, assuming convoy position. Combat loaded
with 5 officers and 385 men of U.S.Army, with 72 vehicles and 205 tons of
miscellaneous cargo, LCM 808 being towed astern. Guide, Commander Stickley,
Com LST Group 70, in LST 597, in position 21, this ship in position 13, 500
yards astern LST 457. Steaming in Condition of Readiness 3. 1250 Took depart-
ure from Leyte Gulf, P.I. with Maraquitdaquit Light 020 T, at 7 miles, standard speed 7 knots. Steaming on course 150 T and PGC; 148 PSC; 156 P stg C;
1301 Changed base course to 155 T and PGC; 152 PSC; 159 P stg C; 1315 Changed
base speed to 8 knots 200 RPM. 1554 Changed base speed to 9.5 knots 245 RPM.
No further remarks.

S. H. Sunde
S. H. Sunde
Ens., USNR.

1600 - 2000

Underway as before. 1615 Changed base course to 180 T and PGC; 170 PSC; 179
P stg C; 1846 Changed base course to 175 T and PGC; 165 PSC; 175 P stg C; 1900
Exercised at General Quarters. 1954 Secured from General Quarters. No further
remarks.

R H Wehrmann
R. H. Wehrmann
Ens., USNR.

2000 - 2400

Underway as before. 2011 Changed base course to 215 T and PGC; 213 PSC; 220
P stg C. 2041 Changed base course to 245 T and PGC; 237 PSC; 234 P stg C. No
further remarks.

M Rome
R. M. Rome
Ens., USNR.

UNITED STATES SHIP _____ LST 777 _____   Monday   2   April , 19 45
                                              (Day) (Date) (Month)

0000 - 0400

Steaming on base course 243 T and PGC; 237 PSC; 234 P stg C. , at standard
speed 9.5 knots 250 RPM. Underway in accordance with CTG 78.2 Operational
Plan 3-45 Supply Echelon, dated 17 March, 1945. In company with Task Unit
78.2.5. Combat Loaded with 5 officers and 383 men of U.S.Army, with 72 vehicles and 205 tons of miscellaneous cargo, LCM 808 being towed behind. Guide
Commander Stickley, Com. LST Group 70, in LST 597, in position 21, this ship
in position 13, 500 yards astern LST 457. Steaming in Condition of Readiness
3. 0300 Changed base course to 272 T and PGC; 271 PSC; 264 P stg C. 0355 Changed standard speed to 8 knots 200 RPM. No further remarks.

                                    V. W. Davis
                                    V. W. Davis
                                    Lt(jg)USNR.

0400 - 0800

Underway as before. 0610 Exercised at General Quarters. 0700 Secured from
General Quarters. 0705 Changed base course to 310 T and PGC; 315 PSC; 304 P
stg C. No further remarks.

                                    S. H. Sunde
                                    Ens., USNR.

0800 - 1200

Underway as before. 0801 Changed base course to 340 T and PGC; 347 PSC; 338
P stg C. 0848 Changed base course to 020 T and PGC; 019 PSC; 021 P stg C; 0900
Made daily inspection of magazines. Conditions normal. 1137 Changed base course
to 010 T and PGC; 016 PSC; 011 P stg C. No further remarks.

                                    R. H. Wehrmann
                                    Ens., USNR.

1200 - 1600

Underway as before. 1235 Changed base course to 018 T and PGC; 024 PSC; 019
P s tg C. 1430 Changed convoy speed to 7 knots. 1530 Cast off Tow, maneuvering
on various courses and speeds, standing into Cebu Harbor, P. I. 1540 Passed
Lauis Light abeam to starboard, distance 500 yards. No further remarks.

                                    R. M. Rome
                                    R. M. Rome
                                    Ens., USNR.

1600 - 2000

Underway as before. 1600 Set the Special Sea Detail. 1615 Anchored in Cebu
Harbor, P.I. in 6 fathoms of water with 15 fathoms of chain to the bow anchor
on the following anchorage bearings. Capitol Tower 001 T. White Beacon2 051 T.
1643 Secured the Special Sea Detail; Set in port watch. 1715 Set the Special
Sea Detail; Underway from anchorage for Calderon Street Jetty, Captain on Conn;
Navigator on Bridge. Steaming at various courses and speeds, conforming to swept
channel. 1755 Moored starboard side to port side LST 1035 at Caldron Street Jetty.
Cebu City, P.I., with standard mooring in use. 1820 Commenced unloading cargo.
1825 LST 595 moored along port side. 1830 Secured the Special Sea Detail; Set in
port watch. No further remarks.

                                    R. H. Wehrmann
                                    Ens., USNR.

2000 - 2400

Moored as before. 2230 Completed unloading Army combat cargo. No further remarks.
                                    R. M. Kuhn
                                    R. M. Kuhn
                                    Ens., USNR.

UNITED STATES SHIP _____ LST 777 _____   Tuesday   April   3 __, 19_45
                                                 (Day)   (Date) (Month)

0000 - 0400

Moore d starboard side to port side LST 1035, Calderon Street Jetty, Cebu City, P.I., with standard mooring in use. Various units of the U.S. Pacific Fleet present. Auxiliary engines in use for auxiliary purposes. No further remarks.

> R. H. Wehrmann
> R. H. Wehrmann
> Ens., USNR.

0400 - 0800

Moored as before. 0745 Set the Special Sea Detail; Made all preparations for getting underway. 0756 Underway from port side LST 1035, Captain on Conn; Navigator on Bridge. Steaming at various courses and speeds, conforming to swept channel. No further remarks.

> G. M. Derbacher
> G. M. Derbacher
> Ens., USNR.

0800 - 1200

Underway as before. 0820 Anchored in Cebu Harbor, Cebu, P.I. in 6½ fathoms of water, with 100 feet of cable to stern anchor, on the following anchorage bearings; Beacon 4 - 042 T; Beacon 2 - 015 T; 0840 Secured the Special Sea Detail; Set in port watch. 0900 Made daily inspection of magazines. Conditions normal. 0910 Commenced disembarking troops, as per attached sheets. 1130 Completed disembarking troops. No further remarks.

> R. M. Kuhn
> R. M. Kuhn
> Ens., USNR.

1200 - 1600

Anchored as before. 1210 Commenced bringing casualties aboard. 1450 Completed loading casualties, having brought aboard 79 men for medical treatment and disposition. No further remarks.

> V. W. Davis
> V. W. Davis
> Lt(jg)USNR.

1600 - 2000

Anchored as before. No further remarks.

> S. H. Sunde
> S. H. Sunde
> Ens., USNR.

2000 - 2400

Anchored as before. No furthe r remarks.

> R. M. Rome
> R. M. Rome
> Ens., USNR.

This photo is a view of the Caldcron Street Jetty located at Cebu City, April 1945. This was taken from a New Zealand newspaper. You get a good view of the mountainous region. The Japanese had gun emplacements hidden in the caves of these mountains. It was over these hills that I was soon to be experiencing my baptism of fire. Magellan landed 491 years ago on this very island.
(27 April 1521)

Chapter IX
ORGANIZATION OF THE 182nd INFANTRY
MORNING REPORTS

The Japanese fight to die, ... The Americans fight to live.

The following notes were taken from the Americal Journal of January/March issue 2011. The author was David W. Taylor, ADVA WWII Historian.

"The Japanese soldier was small in stature compared to American and British soldier. His average height was 5 feet, 3-1/2 inches and his weight 116 to 120 pounds. Although rigorously trained, most soldiers were awkward and suffered from poor teeth and poor satiation habits when deployed in the field. This is primarily due to the fact most soldiers were of a peasant background with an early life of hard work and privation.

The Japanese soldiers humble background certainly helped in their training, where physical conditioning, arduous marches, and training in blistering heat or bitter cold, helped to make them accept the deprivations of war-time conditions.

The Japanese soldier was an expert at camouflage and considered it a military virtue to conduct deceptions and ruses. Surrender was considered a great disgrace not only to the soldier but it extended to his family back home. His religion taught him that it was the highest honor to die for his emperor.

Loss of officers was a great blow to Japanese units, for the enlisted ranks frequently failed to assert any self-reliance and initiative because their training failed to do so. Japanese soldiers on occasion were thrown into panic by an unexpected move by the their enemy during an attack or by the bungling of their own plans.

Their Army training emphasized hand-to-hand encounters and were indoctrinated with the conviction they were superior in this kind of fighting. Moreover they drew confidence in the length of their bayonets over Americans bayonets. This is especially true at night, which gave them a unique advantage in the dark. It was because of these kinds of attacks that fighting was so close-in against the Japanese, with levels of hand-to-hand combat not seen since the middle-ages. American artillery barrages were so massive in support of night ground attacks the Japanese suffered massive losses just getting to attack the American's main lines of resistance."

The above article will give the reader an idea of just what kind of enemy we were up against. You will learn more about them as my journey continues. There are many good sources for information about the campaign of the Philippine Islands. A few being, *MacArthur 1941-1951* (Willoughby), *Our Jungle Road To Japan* (Eichelberger), *Under The Southern Cross* (Cromin), *Pacific War* (Costello).

October 2005, while on a tour of Washington DC, I had the great opportunity of being able to get notes, journals, maps, special orders, battle reports and morning reports from the National Archives and Records Administration. It was here at the National Archives that I met David Colamaria from Vienna, Virginia. He was looking for information about the Pacific Theater of Operation. The strange part of our meeting was, Dave was seeking information on the Americal Infantry Division. Dave remarked to me that he couldn't find any information of the Americal Division. Seems he was looking under the title of American Division. I told him to look under AMERICAL. I helped Dave and he helped me get the information that I needed.

Copy of MORNING REPORT

MORNING REPORT ENDING 2400   3 April   1945
ORGANIZATION Co C   182d INF Regt
STATION OR LOCATION Crossroads 26 Cebu P.I.

NAME	SERIAL NUMBER	GRADE	MOS	CODE
Singerman Erwin M	36597513	Pfc		
Fr abs sk Co D 121st Med Bn Hosp				
this sta to dy eff 2 Apr 45				
Kalle John C	31032072	S Sgt		
Fr asgd not yet jd to jd (REF 14				
MAR 45 MIR)				

RECORD OF EVENTS

16 EM & 1 Off retd fr hosp
at last sta. 46 EM Repl
atchd for pai & qrs. Co
moved into Regt'l old area
at Crossroads 26 and set
up bivouac area.

	ASSD	ATCHD DEASED	TOTAL	ATCHD FR OTHER ORG'T	PRESENT FOR DUTY	PRESENT NOT FOR DUTY	ABSENT T D	ABSENT SK	ABSENT CONF	ABSENT LV FUR	ABSENT AWOL	ABSENT MISS INT
	1		1		1							
	2		2		2							
	3		3		3							
	1		1				1					
	4		4		3		1					
	10		10		7	2	1					
	12		12		12							
	6		6		6							
	93		93		77	15	1					
	126		126		105	17	4					

I CERTIFY THAT THIS MORNING REPORT IS CORRECT: PAGE 2 OF 2 PAGES

SIGNATURE _____

JOHN T MURPHY
Captain   Infantry
(GRADE)   (ARM OR SERVICE)

W. D. A.G.O. FORM NO. 1
1 MAY 1944   W. D. COPY THRU MRU OR SCU

97

Every day a Morning Report must be recorded. Each Company has its own typist with the rank of corporal who performs that task. I have copies of every Morning Report from 1 April 1945 to 30 June 1945, and 15 August 1945 to 30 September 1945. You will see copies of typical Morning Reports throughout this document. Also shown will be: Special Orders, General Orders, Company Orders and Medical Reports.

Information on Morning Reports include: promotion, demotion, being killed, wounded, Missing In Action, assigned to a unit or leaving a unit, and/or going to a hospital for treatment.

Morning Reports do not record medals and/or decorations.
Morning Reports are a great source of information and very helpful to me on this my journey.

The Morning Report as seen on page 97 is as follows:
3 April 1945, Company G 182nd Inf Regt.
Location Crossroads 26, Cebu PI.

RECORD OF EVENTS:
46 Enlisted Men, Replacements, attached for rations and quarters. Company moved into Regimental old area at Crossroads 26 and set up bivouac area.

The morning report also shows:

1 Captain	2 First Lieutenants	**Total:** Officers 3

1 Master Sgt	4 Technical Sgt	10 Staff Sgt	12 Sergeants
6 Corporals	93 Private First Class		**Total:** EM 126

Third column list **Present For Duty.**
It indicates 105 EM (Enlisted Men), so we are short 21 EM. These numbers change day to day as some soldiers are returning from the hospitals or other duties.

*See page 261 for abbreviations often found in Morning Reports.

The following are copies of Special Order #67 dated 3 April 1945, assigning me into the Americal Division, Company G. Several names listed will appear later in my story.

4. Having reported to this hq, fr Hq Americal Div., APO 716, pursuant to par 3 SO 67, Hq Americal Div., APO 716, dated 3 April 45, the following named EM (Replacements) are assigned as indicated: EDCMR 3 April 45.

ASN	NAME	RACE	GRADE	ASGD TO	MOO	OLD MOS
20271727	London, Jack		M/Sgt	Hq Co	055	502
39599935	Wright; Morgan B.		Pvt	Med Det	010	521
39595849	Corny, Arthur P.		Pvt	Hq Co 2d Bn	010	745
35885048	Davidson, George H.		Pvt	Hq Co 2d Bn	480	745
37646379	De Grange, George W.		Pvt	Hq Co 2d Bn	499	745
36916165	Denniston, Donald R.		Pvt	Hq Co 2d Bn	345	745
35833458	Schmidt, Bernard P.		Pvt	Hq Co 2d Bn	010	745
37644750	Schoonlau, George O. Jr.		Pvt	Hq Co 2d Bn	010	745
35909072	Simons, Henry W.		Pvt	Hq Co 2d Bn	050	610
35906837	Snyder, Jack J.		Pvt	Hq Co 2d Bn	590	610
35818079	Turner, Carl R.		Pvt	Hq Co 2d Bn	480	745
39729488	Casas, Frank L.	Mex	Pvt	Co "E"	302	745
39729191	Casillas, Benjamin	Mex	Pvt	Co "E"	179	745
42119980	Castellano, Rocco		Pvt	Co "E"	302	745
38618753	Chapman, Murray		Pvt	Co "E"	499	745
39425468	De La Cruz, Elias	Mex	Pvt	Co "E"	499	745
39597457	De La Cruz, Joe T.	Mex	Pvt	Co "E"	590	745
31436241	Dempsey, Gilbert O.		Pvt	Co "E"	480	745
36916246	De Rose, Louis P.		Pvt	Co "E"	195	745
34909460	Dunaway, Estus		Pvt	Co "E"	499	745
39425712	Hudson, Kenneth O.		Pvt	Co "E"	345	745
33663166	Hughes, Walter L.		Pvt	Co "E"	590	745
38573649	Langolf, Victor		Pvt	Co "E"	499	745
39935291	Larson, Donovan C.		Pvt	Co "E"	480	745
39425557	Laster, John M.		Pvt	Co "E"	113	745
36912619	Leadlove, Fredrick H.		Pvt	Co "E"	010	745
36846519	Lobal, Milton		Pvt	Co "E"	499	745
34999908	McKenzie, Elroy Jr.		Pvt	Co "E"	499	745
37646680	McKeown, Willard J.		Pvt	Co "E"	499	745
35908351	McKinley, Harold L.		Pvt	Co "E"	129	612

-4-

(SO 39 Par 4 Cont'd)
6 April 1945

ASN	NAME	RACE	GRADE	ASGD TO	MCO	OLD MOS
39935133	Pond, Richard D.		Pvt	Co "G"	480	745
39935431	Porter, Roland H.		Pvt	Co "G"	345	745
35780536	Powell, Troy		Pvt	Co "G"	010	745
39930807	Preece, George A.		Pvt	Co "G"	103	745
39524043	Prose, Lawrence A.		Pvt	Co "G"	499	745
44041018	Proffitt, Albert W. Jr.		Pvt	Co "G"	188	188
37751041	Radecker, Leroy O.		Pvt	Co "G"	499	745
39425221	Salazar, Donaciano A.	Mex	Pvt	Co "G"	251	745
35818092	Sanders, Roy G.		Pvt	Co "G"	499	745
36471721	Schaefer, Gord G.		Pvt	Co "G"	482	745
37752592	Schieffer, Lawrence H.		Pvt	Co "G"	499	745
35909053	Shively, Richard L.		Pvt	Co "G"	480	610
35909038	Showalter, Jay S.		Pvt	Co "G"	483	610
35908973	Sixbey, Robert W.		Pvt	Co "G"	499	610
35784354	Smallwood, Curnie		Pvt	Co "G"	010	812
35818150	Smith, Roy S.		Pvt	Co "G"	026	812
35909050	Snyder, Robert A.		Pvt	Co "G"	260	610
35784234	Swick, Charles D.		Pvt	Co "G"	483	745
4006298	Sykes, Albert L. Sr.		Pvt	Co "G"	499	745
38607338	Tarpinian, Avedes V.		Pvt	Co "G"	144	745
36571094	Thomas, Ross E.		Pvt	Co "G"	010	745
36916298	Troman, William T.		Pvt	Co "G"	302	610
44012885	Turnago, Alvin		Pvt	Co "G"	499	745
36992355	Twombly, James F.		Pvt	Co "G"	245	745
34869133	Tyree, John R.		Pvt	Co "G"	499	745
39729555	Vaccaro, David B.		Pvt	Co "G"	499	812
38701684	Valdez, Jose A.	Mex	Pvt	Co "G"	590	745
37362331	Valdez, Joseph D.	Mex	Pvt	Co "G"	499	745
38582297	Valdiviez, Jesus M.		Pvt	Co "G"	590	745
36916210	Van Couwenberghe, Michael J.		Pvt	Co "G"	129	745
35908711	Vanderbur, Charles H.		Pvt	Co "G"	480	610
36915142	Vander Molen, Gordon W.		Pvt	Co "G"	010	745
36916144	Vander Molen, Kenneth V.		Pvt	Co "G"	010	745
39935081	Price, Thomas R.		Pvt	Co "H"	010	745
39933426	Pubigee, Erven A.	AI	Pvt	Co "H"	251	745
39400349	Pulliam, Donald L.		Pvt	Co "H"	245	745
36700750	Sanbrano, John A.	Mex	Pvt	Co "H"	186	745
39935032	Sandoval, Celso		Pvt	Co "H"	480	745
44037794	Satterfield, Robert C.		Pvt	Co "H"	255	745
35909183	Vanhyfte, Bernard P.		Pvt	Co "H"	129	745
36916411	Villani, Norman		Pvt	Co "H"	590	745
37752928	Voran, Lester W.		Pvt	Co "H"	499	745
34864494	Wade, Dempsey		Pvt	Co "H"	499	745

By order of Colonel DUNN:

W. J. COTTER
Captain, Infantry
Adjutant

OFFICIAL:

W. J. COTTER
Captain, Infantry
Adjutant

100

Organization of the 182ⁿᵈ Infantry Regiment

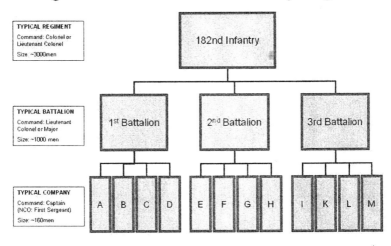

TYPICAL REGIMENT
Command: Colonel or Lieutenant Colonel
Size: ~3000men

182nd Infantry

TYPICAL BATTALION
Command: Lieutenant Colonel or Major
Size: ~1000 men

1st Battalion 2nd Battalion 3rd Battalion

TYPICAL COMPANY
Command: Captain (NCO: First Sergeant)
Size: ~160men

A B C D   E F G H   I K L M

January 1941, Task Force 6814 was headed for the South Pacific. Shortly after that a new Division was formed with the name of Americal Division. The name comes from the words America and New Caledonia, hence <u>Ameri</u> and <u>Cal</u>. The Americal Division was made up from three National Guard Units, namely, the 132ⁿᵈ Infantry (Illinois NG), 164ᵗʰ Infantry (North Dakota NG) and the 182ⁿᵈ Infantry (Massachusetts NG).

On page 100, you will notice Special Order #67 dated 3 April 1945. Looking at the Table above, I was assigned to Co "G", 2ⁿᵈ Bn, 182ⁿᵈ Inf. The Companies are broken down into three squads of twelve enlisted men. Most of my story involves around the second squad. Mike Van Couwenberghe and my brother, Gordon were assigned to the first squad.

Every division had its own postal service number. If you were assigned to the 32ⁿᵈ Division than your ARMY POSTAL OFFICE would be APO 32. Since the Americal did not have a number it was given APO 716.

I remember most of the fellows from the second squad, maybe not by their names, but most by their loyalty to each other. Some men by rank, such as Captain Murphy and Lieutenant O'Day. A majority of the men of the second squad were known by just a single name, such as: Sergeant Morton, Trippy, Schively, Smith, Trombly, Schaver and, yes, even a Private Ryan. I can't forget Templeton. Many of these men will appear in the following adventures on the Island of Cebu. It was an honor for me to call these men *my brothers*.

Chapter X
CEBU COMBAT
April 3, 1945 – June 4, 1945

I still recall the markings on the ship's bridge; it showed three sets of dice. The first pair showed an one/six combination, the next showed a two/five, and the last set pictured a three/four dice arrangement. The last view of that LST-777 has been imbedded in my memory forever.

The above photo shows LST-777 returning home to San Francisco in 1946. Wilbur Redlin of West Bend, WI was aboard this LST during the Pacific Campaign.

Did I keep a diary of events as they happened? We were not allowed to keep any record of events as they occurred. No one had a camera. For the next 62 days on this journey, I will have to depend on different sources of information that will refresh my memory.

We walked away from the waters edge in the shade of the many large coconut trees that lined the dirt road. There was a huge amount of debris on the beach and we could tell that there must have been a catastrophic encounter with the enemy at that spot.

103

I saw an overturned LCM and went to look it over. I wondered how many men lost their lives coming ashore here only a day or two earlier. Reality was setting in. This was not a movie. Something major was about to happen.

A sergeant appeared and stood on top of an overturned truck, his name was Master Sergeant Jack London. He informed us that, as of now, we were all members of the Americal Division. It seemed strange that while in basic training, one of our instructors was from that Division. Could it have been planned that most of the fellows at Camp Robinson were assigned to the Americal?

We all gathered close to Sergeant London as he called out our names. It took some time before my name was called and I began to wonder what company I was going to be assigned to. I recall hearing the name of Pvt. Mike Van Couwenberghe and later Pvt. Gordon Vander Molen. I answered "Here" when my name was announced. All three of us were still together and now assigned to Company "G" of the 182nd Infantry, Americal Division.

We gathered up our equipment, moved to the side of the road and waited for someone to take us to Company "G". Smoking was permitted and about every soldier had a cigarette in his mouth. We never worried about field stripping our cigarettes here.

When we hit the beach, we carried full field packs and that included rifles, steel helmets, extra ammo and believe it or not, gas masks. After we were gathered into our company groups, the first order we received was to get rid of the gas masks. Why, we just got them two days ago and they were brand new? I was hoping that maybe we could get rid of the steel pot for our heads. No luck...

Shortly, a young soldier came in view and asked if we were the replacements for "G" Company. His uniform was sweat covered and quite shabby. He wore his steel helmet and after instructing us to put ours on, we moved out heading in a northerly direction.

We moved along the dirt road and it surely wasn't in a marching cadence. There was plenty of talking and we were in a friendly mood as we moved along with our full field backpacks, ammunition and rifles. I think we were trying to look the part of real combat infantrymen. It wasn't long before we could hear machine gun fire and small arms fire responding.

I asked the leader of our group just where the front line was. He replied that we were on the front line at that very moment. He was directing us to where "G" Company would be defending a perimeter line against any sudden enemy attacks. We continued up the road while I wondered where I would be spending the night. When we landed on Leyte, I slept in a tent, on a cot. Surely they would have a tent shelter for us. Would we sleep this first night on the front line?

Our guide stopped and told us to move forward and join our company. I asked. "Where is "G" Company?" "Just keep going down the road and ask the first soldier you see," he responded and bid us a fond farewell. I think I heard him say something like, "You'll be sorry."

Here I am with forty-five GIs walking down a road looking for someone in charge. We saw a fellow with a heavy beard, who looked like he hadn't taken a bath in three months! He said he was the first sergeant of "G" Company. He didn't have stripes sewn on his uniform, but he talked like a first sergeant. He divided us up into a couple of groups, assigning our group to the second squad. Gordon and Mike went on to the first squad so we parted our ways at this time. The second squad leader, by the name of Jack Morton, told us to follow him to his section of the line.

On any war map, symbols are drawn to indicate unit locations. They show where the headquarters are located and even where the first aid station would be. To indicate the furthermost advance of any unit, a thin blue line is drawn. That thin blue line is where the Combat Infantryman stands to face the enemy.

With Sergeant Morton in the lead, we finally came within view of small groups of GIs just sitting around. Some were cleaning rifles, others were eating rations and a few were sleeping. They seemed to be a strange bunch of guys. Most were young with only a couple of older fellows. Their uniforms were really messy, while mine was nice and clean. Somehow, I just did not seem to fit in with these guys. They looked me over and called me "Junior." This is the name given to the youngest member of the group, a name I did not like to be called.

I felt a little awkward with these experienced veterans. In basic training you could read his name on the helmet liner, but these fellows were wearing steel headgear. Jack Morton introduced us replacements to the members of his squad, mostly as last names. Even to this day, I cannot remember anybody from that first group. You see, being called replacements, you are the lowest rank.

After a time looking at each other, someone will ask, "Where are you from?" "I was born in Detroit, Michigan," These fellows didn't care where you were from. I can understand the way they treated us at first. I was a replacement, meaning I was taking the place of one of their buddies who was killed or wounded. Nobody in those first few days trusted how you would react in combat. You had to prove yourself.

Most of the GIs in this outfit were from Massachusetts. These veterans had been fighting in Guadalcanal and Bougainville in the South Pacific. They were very proud of the 182nd Infantry Regiment and especially the Americal Division, of which I am now a part. Slowly I was able to bond with these fellows.

Morton told me to dig a foxhole for the night, as I was now part of his squad. I started to dig the foxhole as ordered. I dug the hole according to the way I was instructed in the states, that is, six-foot deep, and three feet across. It was hard digging and no one offered to help me. I discovered as I was digging that I didn't strike water, as I would have on Leyte. I was satisfied with the job I had done and a couple of the guys came over and started to laugh at my work of art. They informed me that when the Japanese shoot me, they wouldn't have to dig a grave for my body as I had already done the job for them. From then on, I dug a hole only as deep as necessary. I found out later that when the enemy started firing, even a small boulder gives good protection.

My first night of combat I shared my foxhole with Sergeant Morton. I was glad of that as he pointed out where the Japanese would probably strike our lines. He pointed out where the machine guns were located and gave me the password for the night. He spoke in a very low tone as night was coming on. Then Jack said I was to be on guard against the enemy attack. Jack fell fast asleep after saying, "wake me when the action get started".

Night came fast and I settled into my hole. I started to imagine shadows appearing before me and wanted to fire my rifle at them. No one else was shooting so I just kept seeing things. Strange sounds also were heard like, bird-calls, or were the Japanese calling each other in the eerie dark jungle? This was my first night on the front line and I didn't sleep a wink. I think that others were awake in their foxholes with the same feeling. I was glad to see the dawn of another day. I had survived my first night of combat.

Not much was going on that first morning so I decided to scout the area. Looking in front of our line of foxholes, I saw what seemed to be a pillbox. Since it was close to our perimeter, I was curious to view what was inside. I started down the slope toward the pillbox. I saw for the first time a line of strings across our front line. On these strings were hung empty shell casings. I hit the line and you could hear the sound of metal hitting metal. A voice from behind me yells, "Stay away from my picket line!"

At night, if the enemy crawled up, he would hit that line and make a sound that would warn us of approaching danger. After this experience, I never retired for the evening without stringing up a line in front of my hole. That pillbox still intrigued me.

Leaving the safety of my squad, I moved out cautiously down the trail to investigate that pillbox. After a few yards I had the funny feeling that I was being watched. I smelled something and then saw the reason for that stink. It was a decaying Japanese soldier lying by the side of the trail. By the looks of the body, he had been there a long time. I kicked the body just to see if he was really dead, he was! His face was no more; it seemed a bullet had entered his head. I am sure he died on the spot. I stooped down to look more closely at the body, looking for souvenirs. That eerie feeling that I was being watched was getting stronger. I decided to return to the safety of my fox hole and fellow comrades. I slowly started back up the hill and told no one where I had been.

I joined the other fellows for my first C, or was it a K Ration breakfast. One package was enough for ten men providing three meals (one day), we called it 10-in-1. The tins contained a variety of meals. They included: chicken & vegetables, frankfurters & beans, ham, eggs, potatoes, lima beans, meat & beans, and meat & spaghetti. There were also cereals, crackers, jam, powdered drinks and sugar. Coffee came in a little package, which we mixed with hot water, when we could get a fire going. We ate these rations either hot or cold. The dehydrated eggs had to be heated over an open fire.

We recalled our first meal on Leyte was great. The mess sergeant placed our hot food into our mess kits and even put the gravy on our potatoes. Seconds if you wanted them. On Cebu, meals were when you found the time to grab something. The C Rations were really for the troops in the rear area and not on the front lines. We enjoyed at least this first hot breakfast. We cleaned our mess kits in the local stream that flowed by our area.

The medic came around and gave every one an Atabrine tablet to swallow. We were instructed to take this pill every morning. It was a substitute for quinine that was in short supply. Atabrine did not cure but suppressed the symptoms of malaria. This was a yellow colored pill, which caused the skin to turn yellow after taking it for a number of months. Most of these veterans in my outfit had a yellow skin color.

It was important to know our medic, as he was the one who would assist if you were shot or wounded. In the Pacific area of fighting, the medic did not wear the large white helmets with the Red Cross emblem as in the European Theater of Operations. Medics were not allowed to carry weapons, only for self-protection. We were instructed not to call out, "Medic, Medic" when wounded. The enemy would fire at the first soldier that moved, knowing that he was the medic. Our medic was named Trippy, a terrific fellow. You will hear more about him later.

I rejoined my squad and found that some of them were wearing the steel helmets. These guys were experienced veterans and if I wanted to live, I had better learn fast on how to stay alive. Our Company just seemed to be dug in and we were waiting for orders to move out. Some mail was delivered to the front line. I didn't expect any mail, as I was sure no one knew where I was. It was surprising that mail delivery was a month in coming to these fellows. Shortly after these few lucky fellows had received their precious letters, we had to hear about what was going on in their hometown. One thing that I missed most was not getting any mail. All the time I was on Cebu, I received very few letters from home. Main reason being that most of our mail was tied up in Leyte.

There were a number of Japanese pillboxes in front of our perimeter. They seemed to be empty. Morton told us to keep our eyes open and listen. Seems to me that Jack had a second sense as to when the Japanese would attack our line. I could hear the movements of the enemy, as they seemed to be creeping close to our line. Someone or something hit our forward picket line and then I knew that danger was in front of our area. Then it happened; the enemy was trying to break through our lines to determine our strength. The squad on our left flank had to bear the brunt of that attack. The Japanese came in full strength at around 1:30 a.m. We could hear the sounds and see the gun flashes of that action. I had my M1 rifle ready to shoot, but Morton told me to stay quiet and not give our position to the enemy. I wonder if my brother Gordon was on my left flank? Were any of my buddies wounded or even killed?

MORNING REPORT – 5 APR 1945 - RECORD OF EVENT

This is the report that every Company has to fill out showing the actions of that day. It shows the location of our Company, at the Crossroad #26. This report has some valuable information on my activities while on the Island of Cebu. Note the two patrols that went out and I was a member of one of those patrols.

ORGANIZATION Co G   182d Inf Regt   Inf
STATION OR LOCATION Crossroads 26 Cebu, P.I.

NAME	SERIAL NUMBER	GRADE	NOS.	CODE
Brooks Gene A	20724738	Pfc		S
Dy to AWOL 1600				
Kemp Henry L	37620697	Pfc		
Dy to MISSING IN ACTION eff				
28 Mar 45 Add Bay Comb Inf Badge				
Duty 745 Not dropped fr rolls				

RECORD OF EVENTS

3 enemy shot & killed while
trying to infiltrate through
our perimeter during night.
Enemy blew-up an unoccupied
pill-box 12 yards infront of
perimeter at 0130. 2 15 men
patrols sent out infront of
perimeter - both made contact but not casualties inflicted.

	ATCHD UNASGD (3)	TOTAL (4)	ATCHD NOT JOINED GR'S (5)	PRESENT			ABSENT				
				FOR DUTY (6)	NOT FOR DUTY (7)	T D O S (8)	SK (9)	CONF (10)	AWOL (11)	(12)	MFSS (13)
	1	1		1							
	2	2		2							
	3	3		3							
	1	1				1					
	4	4		3		1					
	11	11		10		1					
	13	13		12	1						
	6	6		6							
	105	105		94	3	1	5		1		
	2	2		2							
	142	142		127	4	4	5		1		

I CERTIFY THAT THIS MORNING REPORT IS CORRECT: PAGE 4 OF 4 PAGE

SIGNATURE _____

JOHN T MURPHY
Captain   Infantry

Another item of interest is the PRESENT FOR DUTY. That is column three, which shows how many men are engaged in active combat. The total should be 142, however, only 127 are Present For Duty. Company "G" was short fifteen men for combat.

Morning Reports are one of the best sources to refresh your memory of events as they happened. I will be referring to MR as I continue this my journey.

That morning Morton told me that I had just volunteered for a patrol. This meant I would go out in front of our perimeter and investigate the pillbox that was in front of our line of fire. I would be the twelfth man in the squad. This first patrol was for my education. Our patrol proceeded down along the trail that I had taken the previous day. Maybe I could get a peek into that pillbox. I still could smell that decaying dead soldier, something that I would soon get accustomed to.

Morton checked on every man who had survived his first night in combat. He spoke words of encouragement to each of us new recruits. Helmets were required, no questions asked, and we just followed orders. I made sure that I had extra hand grenades with me.

As Jack Morton lead his squad down the trail, I took up my position as the last man. I believe I said things like, "see you all later" or "leave something for me to shoot at". To be quite honest, I was scared.

Just then bullets started to pass over our heads. This was not the time to be a hero; I fell on the ground and crawled for the nearest cavity. I was not the only one to seek cover; the whole patrol went down like tin soldiers trying to avoid being hit. There was no use in me running back to tell the company that we were in trouble, as they could see us sprawled around on the ground. Where was this firing coming from? We could hear and see the bullets as they struck the ground. We were the target of a sniper but where was he? Another patrol was sent out to locate the hiding place of this enemy. They informed us that the soldier was firing from a pillbox ahead of us. Could this be the same pillbox that I had explored yesterday? The other squad got around behind and with a well-placed hand grenade, disposed of the enemy. We then proceeded to finish our patrol mission. I was terrified, but the other fellows seemed to take it in stride; that gave me some encouragement. Buddies were there to help and they did. I may not remember the names of these fellows, but we fought as a unit and formed a bond that could not be broken.

The copy of Company Order Number 8 dated 9 April 1945, *(shown on the bottom of this page, and continued on page 113)* indicates under the provision of AR 615-8, as amended by Par II, Circular 110, Hq USAFEF, dated 16 December 1944, the following named enlisted men are promoted to the grade of PRIVATE FIRST CLASS, effective this date. This included brother Gordon and Mike Van Couwenberge. Why did I get a promotion? The enemy took a shot at me.

COMPANY "G", 182d INFANTRY
AMERICAL DIVISION
APO 716   JTH/kop

                                          9 April 1945

COMPANY ORDER
NUMBER 8

1. Under the provisions of AR 615-8, as amended by Par II,
Circular 110, Hq USAFEF, dated 16 December 1944, the following
named enlisted men are promoted to the grade of PRIVATE FIRST
CLASS, effective this date:

Private	Hugh, Fredolph	39480290
Private	Kirchner, Harry W.	35784151
Private	Larsen, Leo	39425328
Private	Zasick, Erwin G.	37752700
Private	Lawrence, Bob H.	34348695
Private	Lawson, Everet J.	39734496
Private	Lee, Bobuie K.	37647338
Private	Mc Keven, Thomas L.	34935245
Private	Mc Leod, John A., Jr.	39480863
Private	Moore, Harvey D.	39933433
Private	Pittenger, Marshall D.	37600955
Private	Pond, Hubert H.	37734428
Private	Pond, Richard D.	39935135
Private	Porter, Roland H.	39935431
Private	Powell, Troy	35780536
Private	Preece, George A.	35930907
Private	Prass, Lawrence A.	39824043
Private	Proffitt, Albert W., Jr.	44041012
Private	Radecker, Leroy O.	37751041
Private	Salazar, Demasiano A.	39425221
Private	Sanders, Roy G.	35818022
Private	Schaefer, Gerd G.	36471721
Private	Schieffer, Lawrence H.	37752592
Private	Shively, Richard L.	35902055
Private	Showalter, Jay S.	35909058
Private	Sixbey, Robert W.	35908973
Private	Smallwood, Curnie	35784254
Private	Smith, Roy S.	35818150
Private	Snyder, Robert A.	35909050
Private	Swiok, Charles D.	35784234
Private	Sykes, Albert L., Sr.	44008299
Private	Tarpinian, Avedes V.	36907539
Private	Thomas, Ross E.	30671094
Private	Troman, William F.	36918290
Private	Turnage, Alvin	44012808
Private	Twombly, James F.	36992368
Private	Tyree, John R.	34869133
Private	Vaccaro, David D.	
Private	Vargas, Jose S.	37701580
Private	Valdez, Joseph D.	37563351
Private	Valdivies, Jesus H.	38195307
Private	Van Couwenborghs, Michael J.	36918210
Private	Vanderbur, Charles R.	36805711
Private	Vander Molen, Gordon W.	36518145
Private	Vander Molen, Kenneth V.	36718144
Private	Bell, Auble	34501709
Private	Shirley, Everett L.	37732435

John T. Murphy
Captain, Infantry
Commanding

I am now a Private First Class; my pay has been increased by 5%, which gives me an extra $4.00 per month. I can now put PFC as part of my address. In Army slang, PFC stands for Praying For Corporal. I also received the Combat Infantryman Badge award that entitled me to an extra $10.00. I am making $66.70 per month, which comes to about $2.22 per day. When I first started to work for Holbrook Super Market my pay was $2.50 per day. I seemed to have taken a cut in pay, but I was seeing the world.

MORNING REPORT - 6 APR 1945 – RECORD OF EVENTS
2 Small security patrols sent out in front of Co Perimeter 0700-0800 & 1700-18-- -- No enemy contact OP sighted 2 Nips to the front – No action taken for security reasons.

Things became scarier for me the next few nights. Seems the Japanese were testing our defense line. At about 3 a.m., the wired picket line in front of our perimeter was tripped, right in front of my fox hole. The GIs in the next fox hole started shooting. I really couldn't see any movement but the noise that the enemy made was out of this world. Then the whole front opened up firing all kinds of weapons. I will have to admit that I got into the action as well. My M1 rifle worked well. I didn't know what I was aiming at, but I don't think the other fellows knew either. I guess that is what's called hindsight. I even threw two hand grenades. Somehow our front line held and at morning light, I saw three of the enemy who had died during our firefight. Captain Murphy was not too happy because we had used up so much ammunition for only three dead enemies. You can't make everybody happy. I know that my rifle works and that God was still with me. I somehow couldn't figure out why these Japanese soldiers would attack our strong defense line.

That morning we got chewed out from Sergeant Jack Morton. Seems Morton got chewed out from Captain Murphy. Murphy got chewed out from Colonel Dunn! Somebody has to be the fall guy for that action. It was decided that maybe the privates (now privates first class) were wasting too much ammo for only three of the enemy. We had to turn in all of our grenades and were only to have one. We were limited to ten clips of ammo. Besides all of that, we had to make sure the grounds around our fox holes were

114

kept clear and open for any attack from the enemy. That afternoon all sergeants were to check every man's rifle to see if it was cleaned according to the manual. Now that was real over-kill.

As evening came upon us, Jack Morton came over to me and handed me three hand grenades to add to the only one I had. He then told me not to worry; the Japanese would not attack tonight. It was going to rain. I unrolled my poncho and put it on and within a few minutes, it poured. Rainwater now poured into my newly cleaned fox hole. When it rains in the Philippines, it really rains. At least Noah had an ark to keep him dry.

Author's Note:

The picture on the left was given to me by Ed Gekosky. This picture was taken on 4 March 1945, on Bougainville.

It shows standing, L to R; Sgt. Gekosky, S/Sgt. Farino, Sgt. Egler and kneeling, Sgt. Jack Morton. Ed Gekosky is the son of Sgt. Gekosky.

Sgt. Egler was killed shortly after this picture was taken. Jack Morton was just behind Sgt. Egler when a Japanese knee mortar went through his chest.

MORNING REPORT – 8 APR 1945 – LAUUG AIR STRIP

Co moved from bivouac area in the vicinity of Crossroad #26 and moved to new location approx 300 yards SE of Watts hill at 1030.

Company "A" of the 1st Battalion was on our right flank when there was an explosion that shook the whole side of the hill. It seemed like the Japanese had filled some caves with all types of explosives and then detonated them with the use of a timed fuse or remote control. Company "A" suffered heavily that day and withdrew from the area. When I saw that cloud of white smoke ascending into the sky, I figured that the enemy had blown up our ammunition dump. We later learned that one of our Sherman tanks had fired point blank into that cave; not knowing it was full of ammunition. This resulted in the blowing off the top of the hill. Lieutenant Colonel John Watt died with his men. The engagement was later called the Battle for Watts Hill.

On yet another patrol, we were sent out to scout the movements of the Japanese, but we were not to give our position away. We were to hold our fire. Our destination was the local racetrack, which was pointed out to us by some local natives. They told us that the Japanese were making plans to move out of the foothills and relocate into the hills overlooking Cebu City. We again moved out in single file, very quietly, I was the last man in line. We came upon a hut and crawled under it. We could see in the distance what appeared to be a racetrack and assumed that we were in the right place. It was here that I saw my first live enemy soldiers. In fact, I saw about seven persons running across the track and they seemed to be going up into the hills beyond. Most were carrying water canteens and it was assumed that these soldiers were supplying water for their comrades. We did not open fire, although we were all given the opportunity to sight them down our rifle barrels. We spent three hot hours under that hut, watching and remaining silent. We returned to the company area to give our report. I'm glad that I didn't have to give a report because I really didn't know what we were doing out there.

Co lines remained un-changed, 2 hot meals sent to troops in field. Van Couwenberghe, Michael J. 36916210 SLIGHTLY WOUNDED IN ACTION………..

I remember while in basic training Mike had said, "There wasn't a bullet large enough to print his name on it." I was informed that Mike was walking down a trail when an enemy soldier threw a hand grenade at him, which exploded and wounded Mike. The name Van Couwenberghe *can* be printed on the side of a grenade.

Mike was with Gordon and I from the very first day when we were all on the same train heading for Chicago. We were all together at Ft. Sheridan, thru basic training and landing on 3 April on Cebu.

Mike was with Gordon in the first squad, in combat for just six days. After a short hosptial stay, Mike was later transferred to the Anti-tank Company of the Americal Division.

Every day of World War II, whether in training or during the most explosive warfare, a 3 ¼" by 7" Morning Report was issued from each company to higher headquarters. They are still preserved at the National Archives in College Park, MD.

When you see a soldier "dropped from rolls" due to evacuation to a hospital, he will sometimes be found in a later report when he rejoined the unit.

MORNING REPORT – 10 APR – LAHUG AIR STRIP

The records for this day are very interesting. Troman William T, 35916298 Pfc, SELF INFLICTED WOUND (Accidental discharge of B.A.R. while cleaning weapon Left large toe)

We had no idea as to what day it was; later on we didn't even know what month we were in. We just kept advancing everyday. War is not what you see on TV, that is, one fellow running forward into battle throwing hand grenades, killing twenty enemy with every shot, waist deep in water and carrying a wounded buddy to the nearest aid station. No way! We were just a group of fellows trying to do a job. A job which none of us really wanted. We did everything we could to stay alive so we could eventually return home. We really didn't know why we were on Cebu and what the rules of the game were all about. We wondered sometimes if the guys in charge knew what they are doing! We just followed orders and did what we were told to do. That is the only way to survive this whole mess.

As darkness approached, we teamed up with a buddy and dug a trench to spend the night. The size and placement of our evening lodging would depend on the condition of the soil and the nearness of the enemy. As we approached the hill country, we would use available tree trunks for cover. Our perimeter was set up so we would be very close to the other members of our squad. By forming this line we would try to prevent the enemy from passing

118

through and striking our supply lines in the rear. If there were not much danger at night, the distance between groups would be farther apart. At dusk, usually around 9:00 p.m., we would slip into the safety of our hole. We would wrap a poncho (raincoat) around us as we slept.

I usually holed up with a fellow named Shively. He carried the BAR. Richard Shively was from Wabash, Indiana. He was Christian Scientist. He was very faithful in his belief of the scriptures as taught to him by Mary Baker Eddy. We usually stayed on guard for two hours and then slept for two hours. If three fellows were together, then it was two hours on and fours hours of sleep. The only fox hole that had three fellows in it was usually where the machine gun was placed. I would take watch from 9 to 11 p.m., then I would awake Shively; he would watch from 11 to 1 a.m., then it was my turn to watch from 1 to 3 a.m. Rich would then take over from 3 to 5 a.m. and again he would wake me and I would go from 5 to 7 a.m. We didn't get a lot of sleep, so the nights seemed very long. This was followed by all of us during combat. One activity that Schively did faithfully every night was to brush his teeth. He never failed to do this even when we couldn't locate water. He would use coconut milk.

No one smokes on guard because the enemy easily sees the glow from the cigarette. If you shared your watch time with a GI who smoked, you were in real trouble. Most smokers wanted to have a drag on their cigarette ten minutes before going on watch. That meant that you didn't get your two hours of sleep. They also would wake you before their time was up because they always wanted a smoke before they went to sleep. You never could win with a smoker.

Why would we stay awake all night? What were we watching for? What could we see if it was so dark? Were we afraid? The answers to these questions were that we wanted to stay alive.

We were to watch and listen for the Japanese trying to get through our lines at night. We always strung wire in front of our foxholes, hoping that the enemy would hit that line first so we would hear them coming near our position. Our reasoning was to shoot first and ask questions later. With that rationale we never, NEVER got out of the safety of our foxholes at night. If we had to relieve ourselves, we did it in our foxhole. If we left our shelter, our own people would likely shoot us. If we snored at night, we were telegraphing the enemy where we were. That is why we always had someone else in the foxhole with us; he was to keep us from snoring. If we heard snoring in the hole next to us, pick up a rock and throw it into that hole as most likely both were asleep. If we heard a noise in front of our position we quickly but silently, woke our buddy. Two of us would look into the dark space ahead and would hope and pray that there would be nothing there. Sometimes, if we were really sure that someone was out there, we loped a hand grenade in front of us. The next morning, we would go out and see if we had killed any enemy soldiers. Usually we didn't. Once a stray cow hit the wire and the GIs in the nearest foxhole let go with his BAR, that cow didn't stray again.

If a soldier fell asleep on guard duty and his buddy got killed, that death would be on his conscience for the rest of his life. I know of some cases where one fellow refused to sleep with a buddy who could not stay awake at night.

Nights were long, scary and full of strange noises. There were those weird birds that would whistle at night. We could almost make out a song from their birdcalls. There were lizards that crawled into our holes. These lizards were large creatures, very ugly, but harmless. They moved slowly across our sleeping bodies. If awakened by their movement, we remained quiet. We tolerated lizards because they ate centipedes. Centipedes were everywhere and most were poisonous. If bitten, you would have a ticket out of the front line. I knew of one fellow who let a centipede bite him so that he could get out. His arm swelled up and we could see his blood vessels turn from blue to red. There were no snakes in the Philippines, so we didn't have to worry about them crawling on us. There were always monkeys traversing up and down the coconut trees, yelling and screeching most of the night. At times we wanted to take a shot at those creatures to shut them up but we knew better.

We usually had a code signal to identify us each night. It was a password that only our buddies knew and they had to give the counter-pass word. It went something like this; if you happened to be moving around at night and was approaching a gun emplacement you would whisper softly "Mickey" and the GIs would respond with the word "Mouse". We always used code words with lots of "L's" in them. The Japanese could not pronounce the letter "L". Hence our code words would be: "Lopping" and "Lulu" or "Late" and "Later" or "Love" and "Lois" were also a good combination to use.

Filipino guerrillas reported that the Japanese Army had around 3,000 troops on the island of Cebu. Our information was that over 10,000 enemy troops were on the island. Therefore, we never took much faith in what the Filipinos told us. We knew that the Japanese had the 102nd Division and a few thousand seasoned troops from the 1st Division that crossed over from the island of Leyte. Also, the 33rd Special Naval Base Unit had units on this island. These soldiers were a very elite unit, many of these men being over six-feet tall. We located some of these soldiers later and found that one fellow had blue eyes. The Japanese soldier usually wore an insignia on his collar that identified the unit he belonged to. We never wore any markings on our uniform.

I was becoming more and more a veteran like the other fellows. I no longer was called "junior", but just "Van." No one was called by their first name; it was mostly our last name or a nickname.

At one time we spotted a Japanese sniper in a group of trees. He wasn't causing us any trouble, so we left him alone. Somehow this news got back to Headquarters that an enemy was spotted in a tree. A couple of the GIs from the rear area wanted to get into the action and become heroes. They somehow got a sniper Springfield rifle and started to take pot shots at this fellow who was about 4,000 yards away. That is too far away for accuracy. This rear area would-be hero aimed and fired, while his buddy stood next to him looking through field glasses, directing the fire. Finally, that Japanese soldier just had enough and returned the fire. He had the advantage, holding high ground. He proceeded to fire off about six rounds into our positions. That was enough for the "Headquarter heroes" who turned and ran to the rear where they belonged. The two rear-area GIs had made that sniper angry because they probably ruined his afternoon nap. Every so often the Japanese soldier would fire a few rounds into our position just to keep us honest. We had to stay buttoned down in our holes, which is what we did not want. Finally, someone asked the Weapons Company to bring up their 37mm field artillery piece. They made short work of that guy in the tree. They may not have killed him, but they sure did move a lot of shrubbery. So ended another exciting day on the fighting front.

I was walking behind our squad leader Morton, moving in single file. Sergeant Morton would point out things that I should know. Morton had a lot of background on tracking the enemy, as he was one of the guys who served on Bougainville. Morton pointed out things like human waste along the trail. The diet of the Japanese was mostly rice so the end results were usually a small soft pile of human waste. This enabled us to know just how far ahead the Japanese soldiers were. He told me about the types of booby traps, which were used, and how to disarm them. I believe that Sergeant Morton was interested in me and showed concern.

As we were scouting this trail, around 3 p.m., it was getting quite warm. On our left was a steep slope with a deep valley on our right. Without any advance warning, Morton spotted two Japanese soldiers ahead and to the left of us upon the slope. There was not much coverage for them and we could see them very clearly. They just seemed to be daydreaming and were very relaxed. Why were they there and what were they doing?

As the sergeant raised his hand to caution us, we all froze in our tracks, as the enemy had not seen us as yet. Morton then ordered me to shoot them. Why, I wondered, they didn't do anything to me? They were just sitting there, minding their own business. I have to admit that I just did nothing.

"Shoot, Shoot," yelled Morton at me, so I put my rifle to my shoulder, aimed and let go with about three rounds. I was aiming over their heads. The sergeant then took aim with his rifle and fired at them. He must have hit one of them, but they disappeared over the crest of the hill. Since the slope was so very steep, it was decided not to follow them. Morton looked at me and said, "Don't worry, you WILL get the next one!" I knew what he meant and what I had to do.

The Japanese had taken a 90mm anti-aircraft gun and hauled it into the hills and placed it in a cave. They had leveled this weapon and were firing it like an artillery piece. We finally located that gun in the mouth of a cave and radioed the Navy for some ship-to-shore firepower. I could look into Cebu harbor and see the Destroyer fire off a couple of rounds. I could even see the shells passing over my head and watch it strike the target. That Destroyer's gun crew was really good, because they had that gun zeroed in and shortly the cave was no more. It was shortly after this the Navy Force steamed out to sea. We wondered at the time where they were going, maybe they would return with more replacements.

The Japanese were especially good with their mortar. The largest mortar we had in the field was a 81mm but they had a 90mm. They also had another small mortar that we called a knee mortar because of its size. This had no sights or aiming devices, they just placed the tube against a tree or on the ground, dropped a shell into the tube and by dead reckoning; they could land that shell into your back hip pocket. Using a rifle, they couldn't hit the broad side of a barn but give them a mortar and watch out.

The Japanese rifle was a 25mm caliber and ours was a 30mm caliber. Our M1 Garand Rifle was clip-fed and we could fire eight rounds without reloading another clip. Theirs had a bolt-action rifle, that is, he had to pull back the bolt to eject the spent round and slide the bolt forward to put another round into the chamber. If we waited after they fired, we could hear that click, click, then you knew where he was and where to direct our shots. We were told in basic training to look for the flash fire as the bullet left the gun. We were then supposed to know where the enemy was hiding. However, the enemy used a flame-less powder and we never saw their gun flash. We could, if need be, use their cartridge in our rifle but they could never use our shells in their weapon.

Attached to the Japanese rifle was a very long knife or bayonet. They had a hook on the handle of the bayonet that was used in hand-to-hand combat. They were trained to use that bayonet hook.

When they got close in combat, by using that hook they could grasp your rifle; twist it and you to the ground. Once you were on the ground your time on earth was limited. He had that bayonet stuck into your throat.

The Japanese hand grenade had to be struck against a rock or against his helmet before he threw it in our direction. The timing device would go off about five seconds later. When we hear the tap, tap, tap, as he struck it against a rock we yelled "grenade, grenade" and hit the ground. Most of the time that grenade wouldn't go off, but it was better to be wrong than to get struck by flying metal. Our grenades had a pin, which we pulled out and about four seconds later we threw that missile as far as we could. Our grenades were suppose to have a six second timing device but they had been known to go off before that time, so we usually pitched them shortly after four seconds.

During a heavy exchange of fire, the enemy seemed to throw everything at us. I stayed low in my fox hole. I could hear the metal flying over my head. The Japanese were using a 90mm mortar at us, one exploded very close to my hole. I was covered with rocks and dirt; my ears were ringing because of the impact of fragments so close. It was then that I noticed that a piece of mortar shell had hit my shoe and cut a hole on the side. My skin was cut and I was bleeding. I did not report this incident and didn't even bother to call Trippy as I was able to control the bleeding.

One of Trippy's jobs was to see that we all had taken the pills he distributed. We had one pill to prevent malaria and another the salt tablets. The salt tablets were taken because of the heat as we perspired a lot in the tropics. Our clothes were stained with sweat. Of course, we never took a bath while in combat, except when it rained and that was considered a bath. We never shaved. Our feet were in water quite a bit and since we did not have the time to keep our feet dry, jungle rot resulted. This fungus caused skin to decay and the only cure was to keep changing your socks or have Trippy apply penicillin. We never took our shoes off at night so we didn't know the condition of our feet, consequently infection spread. The Japanese usually attacked our lines at nighttime; we needed our shoes on to be prepared for action at all times.

MORNING REPORTS indicate that we are still in the area of the Lahug Air Strip. Map reading is important while in combat. Most of the time, if not all of the time, the infantryman had no idea where he was or where he was being sent. Hills are given numbers instead of names. After the war the "hill numbers" will be given names. Changing the name doesn't affect the out come. We still lose men.

12 April (Hill 22) was the Battle for Babag Ridge. The only way I knew it was 12 April was because this engagement was recorded in the book "UNDER THE SOUTHERN CROSS," and I quote:

"After dark, Captain John T. Murphy, commander of the 182nd Company G, took the situation in hand. Moving quietly up the hill in the blackness of the night, the company commander and his men crept to within a few yards of the Japanese defenses and halted. Then, with startling suddenness the company lunged forward the last few yards with a daring night bayonet attack. The brazen maneuver caught the Japanese completely off balance; it would seem that the enemy had had a patent on this type of attack – no Americans had ever done it before to their knowledge."

Yes, this engagement happened, I know, I was there. I did not know where my brother was at this time as he was in the first squad while I was in the second squad. We had not made contact with the first squad. Every time we went forward, we kept getting knocked off the hill by enemy fire. The Japanese had firepower coming at us from every direction. We had causalities and our numbers were getting smaller. There are times when we couldn't see the enemy. We knew they were there because we could hear the noise of battle and the sound of bullets as they sped past our ears. We heard buddies crying out for help.

We continued our slow advance until night came. I was in a trench near the top of the ridge. This must had been a trench dug by the Japanese. I could see that quite a few of us had made it to the safety of this narrow trench. Then the order came through the line that we were to fix bayonets. Fix bayonets? Are you crazy man! The order was issued again; "Fix bayonets!" I figured that if I couldn't hit them with my bullets, no way was I going to stick them with a bayonet. I remembered the training we had in Arkansas. We were supposed to stick our bayonet at the throat, not in the chest as the chest muscles will close up on the point and we would not be able to draw it out. These thoughts were going through my mind as I put the bayonet on the end of my rifle. It was getting very dark. Would I really stick this bayonet into a human being? It's one thing to fire my rifle into a pillbox, knowing I might be killing someone but I couldn't see the enemy. He was always shooting back at me. If I saw him face to face, would I kill that man? To fix bayonets and charge would be like TV or a movie, but this was for real! The signal for the attack was to be a parachute flare shot in the air, when that happened, we surged forward. I saw the signal and charged as ordered.

I reached another foxhole the Japanese had dug, it was empty, so I jumped into it and so did Shively. We sat there in the darkness with shots going over our heads and grenades going off right and left. Another GI crawled into the hole with us. Were we the only three to make it to the top of the ridge? Were we truly alone? We sat back to back, looking down the slope that we had just come from, hoping and praying that none of the enemy would come crawling back into their foxhole. I kept my hand grenades close by me in the darkness. We held out all night. We could hear the injured, yelling and screaming. Someone shouted, "J" Company over here!" I knew that was the enemy because there is no such thing as "J" company in the US Army. The Japanese would try anything to expose where we were located. After a long night, I welcomed the morning light and I had survived another day.

At dawn, we were able to reinforce our lines. We were instructed to remain on top of the ridge for a few days. We were informed that hot food would be sent up to us very shortly. We watched the trail coming from the base of the hill and sure enough, there was a long column of Filipinos carrying food up the trail. Two men hauled large kettles with a pole across their shoulders. As we observed this development, with anticipation of a hot meal we heard shots. Japanese started to fire at our food column. One of the rounds hit the side of the hill dislodging some topsoil. This debris came down on the road forcing some of the Filipinos to drop

126

the food and retreat down to the bottom of the hill. A few brave fellows did make it to the top of the hill. We devoured the hard-boiled eggs and chocolate cake, which was what remained of our hot meal for that day.

While sitting on this ridge top, the Air Force came to give us some air support. They were supposed to bomb the ridge and knock the Japanese off the top; however, someone forgot to tell the Air Force that *we* had control of the ridge. Here comes three P-38s, with guns blazing right along the top of the ridge shooting at us. Quickly, we ignited our red signal flairs; these were the signs that ground forces use to inform the Air Force that we were friendly. It seems these flyboys are colorblind. They made a wide circle and came at us again, only this time we shot back. I am sure that we did not hit them, but if we did, they would have been surprised to see bullet holes in their planes. We always said that the war would have ended six months earlier, if only the Air Force would have stayed out of the action. Only kidding, of course!

MORNING REPORT – APR 13/15 – LAHUG AIR STRIP

The Record of Events noted on the 13 April "Co attacked hill #22. Advancement was slow and casualties were heavy". The Morning Report also mentions PRESENT FOR DUTY on the 13 April was 132 and the next day the count was 119 enlisted men. We had lost thirteen fighting men. Our medic was very busy that day and night.

However, not all of our injuries were caused by enemy action. It is recorded on 14 April "Uhlar, Leo 33758557 PFC SLIGHTLY WOUNDED IN ACTION (Strained leg result of fall in fox-hole. atched det pts 58th Evac")".

MORNING REPORT – APR 15 – CROSSROADS #26

On 15 April we were attacking Hill 21. The day was another one of those very hot humid days. I knew something was in the works as we were told to make sure that we had plenty of ammunition and especially hand grenades. The hills in front of us looked overpowering. We all knew that the Japanese were just waiting for us to move. You could feel in your body that something was going to happen.

The first squad started up the hill using the ridgeline as a guide to the top. These are called "fingers." Battles usually are not fought as a large group but with small units of maybe six or eight men. If we ran into the enemy, we acted as a unit and either surrounded the enemy killing them, or we kept up some firepower against them until another unit came to our aid. Our squad followed behind the first squad.

This was a very steep hill to be climbing. Most of the time we had to use our hands on the ground in order to push ourselves upward. This area was thick with trees and foliage on our side that gave us cover as we pressed upward. The Japanese must have had this hill zeroed in because all kinds of small arms fire were coming in at us. We heard the call for Trippy so we knew that someone ahead of us had been wounded or even killed. Our advance came to a stand still. All was quiet. The Japanese had stopped their engagement. What was happening?

Then to my surprise, I saw Gordon, going down the hill on his backside. Our eyes met and I surmised that he was wounded. I felt helpless. Orders were to keep going forward and upward but it was difficult. I was concerned about Gordon but was required to climb upward through the thick vegetation. Just then another GI came down the hill, who was shot on his left side. As he clenched his side, I could see blood coming from between his fingers. His name was Charles Vanderbur, also a member of the first squad. A short time later another wounded soldier was being carried down the hill on a makeshift stretcher. This staff sergeant was seriously wounded. Later we were informed that he had been hit through both elbows and couldn't move his arms. Eventually he lost his arms. In just a short period of time three wounded soldiers had left the field of battle.

We were at a standstill here because no one was moving up and we hoped that the Japanese didn't have us lined up in their sights. Trippy found me and said that Gordon had been hit in the shoulder.

He informed me that the wound wasn't serious and that Gordon would be flown out of combat.

Lieutenant O'Day the platoon leader told me to carry the radio, which Gordon had been carrying. I put it on my back, it weighted around 45 pounds but it seemed to me that it weighed around 80 pounds. I was told to follow close behind Lieutenant O'Day as we continued to the top of the hill. The radio was the only contact we had with the rest of our unit. I had no idea how to operate the radio. At one time I was told to send a message to Captain Murphy, our Company Commander and inform him of our progress. I clicked the button on the side of the radio and relayed this message. "This is G Company and I want to talk to Captain Murphy." Within a split second Sergeant Morton came over and told me in plain English that I could not address my Company Commander as Captain Murphy. We were to use a code for

129

officers and his was Count Murphy. Nobody told me about any officer code name, now everybody knew!

We finally did get to the top and dug in for the night. That night sleep eluded me even though I was very tired. It was a rough battle and my concerns were for my brother. I was comforted in the fact that he was out of here and most likely receiving medical care.

We had reached the high point of the battle. From this height, we could see the beachhead below us and beyond the airstrip to the north of Cebu City. The Japanese had taken off and started to move in a northerly direction. I carried that radio for another day and then was told to return to my squad. I was glad to get that load off my back.

Jack Morton sent one EM and myself to locate Battalion Headquarters to check and see if there was any mail for Company "G". On the way down to the beach area I noticed the remains of a Japanese airplane. It was stripped bare of all types of souvenirs. A large strip of aluminum was torn from the side of that plane. Not much left of the Japanese Air Force. Who would want a piece of aluminum from that plane? I found out later that some GIs were making watchbands from that medal. Most of our watchbands were cloth and sweat from our bodies would cause those bands to break. Some GI set up a real good business on medal wristwatch bands.

Souvenirs were everywhere around us. Most of our squad carried Japanese pistols. These were taken from the bodies of dead soldiers. When an enemy is shot and it is safe to approach the body, we are to see what he had been carrying on his person. We look for markings on his uniform to find out his rank and also the unit he might be from. This is information that G-2 can use. We also looked for sabers, as an officer most likely carried them. Some Japanese units had a flag; on this flag they would record their unit and battles they fought. If and when, the war was over, and we had secured a battle flag, it would be a valuable souvenir. There were other flags that the Japanese carried into battle that did not have any writing on them. We would get a couple of these "no value" flags; copy some Japanese words from a bottle of beer onto that flag. After a time we would sell it to Junior as the real thing. Can you imagine much later, after paying $50.00 for a flag, he finds out that the writing said, "Don't drink and drive!"

The Japanese were great at finding caves in which to store supplies. Our job was to remove the enemy or supplies he had stored there. Sometimes we would bring in flame-throwers to spray the caves with liquid fire to eradicate the enemy. Most of the time we had to seek and destroy. This was not always the best job to be assigned to. Sometimes, we had Filipinos with us and would send them in first. I remember telling a Filipino to go into a cave but he would go only if he had a rifle. We didn't have an extra one so he wanted a flame-thrower, I said no way, to that idea. Someone had a flashlight so I gave it to him. He said a little prayer, crossed his heart and with his flashlight went into the cave. We waited and within a few minutes he returned after capturing one Japanese prisoner of war.

Once we uncovered a cave filled with boxes of tin cans. We couldn't read Japanese so we opened a couple of the cans and it looked like tapioca. On the side of these cans it read, "San Francisco, California, United States of America," so we figured that these cans were either from the states or going to the states. This food must be safe. We ate the contents of these newly found treasures. They contained fish eyes and didn't taste too bad. We could eat anything when hungry enough.

On 18 April part of the 182nd Infantry was assigned to cross over the Island of Cebu while other units are sent back to Cebu City. There they would board trucks and travel around the northern end of the island on Highway One. The objective would be the city of Toledo on the western side of Cebu.

Company "G" was selected to go on a new adventure by trekking across the middle of Cebu. The plan would cut off the escape route of the Japanese from this island. We knew the enemy were heading in a northerly direction, so "G" (George) Company's mission was to climb the hills and cross over to the other side of the island and establish a base camp near Toledo. (We kind of hoped they were talking about Toledo, Ohio).

131

We loaded up what supplies we could carry and started over the hills. We decided to change our name to GOAT Company. We were told that we would shortly make contact with the 82nd Division of the Philippine Army and to be on the look out for them. We came across these guerillas and stayed with them overnight. They were short of statue and it seemed that every one of them smoked. They didn't have much in the way of equipment but they had a radio and informed us that President Roosevelt had died on 12 April. Harry Truman was now our Commander in Chief. Harry who? How could we believe such a story as that? Roosevelt was going to live until the war was over. The Filipinos were always telling us things that were not true. They knew where the enemy was but never would go with us to hunt them out. We were now in the hills and disconnected from our main force. We did have radio contact but could not use it too much because the enemy listened in on our radio signals.

We moved early this morning and back to Babag Ridge. You will note on page 133, that at this time we had only 95 EM ready for that action.

There were times on a clear night, we could look up into the heavens and see a great number of stars. They were so close; we could just reach up and grab one or two. These stars reminded me of God's nearness.

Just then, my thoughts were interrupted; coming into view was a very strange airplane. It looked like a P-38 called the Lockheed Lighting. Later, I was to find out that what I had seen was the new P-61 called the Black Widow. It was a night fighter and was using radar. It carried a three-man crew and had four nose-mounted 20-mm cannon and four .50-cal machine guns in the top turret. They were an awesome sight but not quite as beautiful as the stars that night.

By this time we were not connected to any food supply line; we had to eat off the land. There were plenty of coconut trees. We would eat onions that grew wild. Rice was a main item at every meal. Rice was easy to carry and quick to prepare. There were a few apples, which were good, but nothing like Michigan apples. We figured the worms were a good source of protein. As we entered some villages, we were given fresh fruits and more rice. Once a small Piper-Cub plane flew in some rations. This plane dropped our supply of dry socks right in the middle of the only stream in that area, so much for clean dry socks. On another occasion the supplies were dropped right on our red signal panels.

133

We had a Filipino guide with us named George. George was real good at climbing trees and getting the coconuts for us. He would cut open these large nuts with his bolo knife. We drank the milk from the coconuts as our water supply was usually polluted. George also supplied us with "Tuba." This is the juice, which comes from the top of coconut palms; it is very dark red in color. If left to stand for a while, it gets lighter and lighter in color and it becomes an alcoholic beverage. It's like drinking 100% proof gin; so I'm told. We would use George as an interpreter when talking to some of the islanders. He knew at least 100 ways to prepare rice and I tried every one of them. No wonder I don't care for rice to this day.

Whenever we crossed a stream, we would fill our canteens. Trippy issued us tablets to purify the water but it still had a foul taste. Once we found a cow wandering in the field. It was decided that we were going to have steak for dinner that night. We tied a rope around the cow's neck and tugged it behind our group as we made our way along the trail. Trippy said no way would he allow us to kill this cow and eat the meat. It would probably be full of worms and other things. So what should we do with a cow?

We later came upon a small village. Morton and George went into the village and asked if any enemy soldiers were around. The answer is always the same: "The Japanese were here, but they left and are now two kilometers down the road." Morton then would tell the villagers that we would burn their huts to the ground unless we were given the correct direction the Japanese had taken. This would usually bring results. He made a deal with them; we would give them our cow, if they would give us eggs and fresh fruits. We received chickens and more rice. We rid ourselves of our cow. Now what do we do with eight live chickens?

We had some bacon with us so we built a fire using our steel helmets as the pot. We fried the bacon until it was all grease. We removed the feathers from the chickens and placed the meat in the bacon grease. When we thought the chicken was cooked well enough, we ate it. If it was too tough, we put it back into the grease and cooked it a little longer. We finished the chicken in a short

134

time. This was as good as Colonel Sander's Kentucky Fried Chicken.

We came across a hut in a remote area and as we started down to investigate the small building; one of our forward soldiers approached the hut and suddenly the door opened. A Japanese soldier with pistol in hand fired and hit our man in the stomach; he fell to the ground. Someone ran forward, disregarding his own safely to pull his comrade to safety. We all kept rifle fire on the hut and tried to get close enough to set it on fire. We knew that the Japanese was still alive because ever so often he would return fire. I happened to have four tracer bullets in my rifle and aimed at the roof of the hut, one of the tracers started a fire in that shack. The hut was soon ablaze because it was made of bamboo and dried palm leaves. While this was happening the wounded soldier was carried back behind our lines. We made camp for the night while he cried repeatedly for his mother. None of us got much sleep that night. A stomach injury had to be the most serious place to be wounded, as he was not allowed any water. In the morning, this brave soldier died. We wrapped him in his poncho and dug a shallow grave covering him with soil. His dog tags were removed and given to the medic. He was a staff sergeant squad leader from Boston. I never did know his name.

As our rag tag outfit moved from one hill to the next searching for the enemy, we would wonder who was in control. Every one dressed alike and no one ever wore his rank on the uniform. As we walked along the trails, someone would approach us and tell us to keep moving. We never really knew if he was an officer or not. Most all the guys were addressed by their last names. We never saluted anybody, if there were any Japanese in the area and saw our salute; they would immediately fire upon that unlucky fellow. Officers were issued carbines instead of rifles, after a very short time, many officers disposed of their carbines in favor of the Garand rifles.

Along the trails we often came upon a small gathering of people. They constructed huts of bamboo and used palm leaves for the roof. What they did for a living was hard to tell. Most of the older folks would just sit around and smoke cigars or cigarettes. Maybe they were just hiding from the enemy. Every time we came to a group like that, one of us would have to investigate if any Japanese had been there or if they had seen any. Most of the time we got a negative answer. We were always offered some rice.

Two Filipinos met our unit on the trail and informed us that they knew where there were Japanese hiding out. They took us to another clearing about four miles away. They pointed out the clearing, then left us to fight it out with the Japanese. Morton and I headed very cautiously into the clearing. All the time while we walked through the hills, we kept our weapon with the safety on. As we approached the enemy, the first two men have their weapons with the safety off. Only when either of the first two men opens fire, do the men behind click off the safety. Even during war safety is practiced.

As we headed into the clearing, the rest of our squad took cover in the under brush. We moved very slowly into the village to make sure that there was no enemy around. Very suddenly in front of me, a Japanese soldier appeared and raised his rifle to shoot me. I raised my rifle and fired off about three rounds. He never had time to shoot as he fell backward, dying instantly. I moved quickly to the back of the dwellings to see if there were any more around the area and found none. He had no markings on his uniform and Morton said that he believed this soldier was a deserter. However, that did not make me feel better, as I just shot another human being. I felt ill the rest of the day.

V-E Day occurred and we did not even know that the war was over in Europe.

We should have at least three first scouts. Each first scout carries a sub-machine gun. It is a very excellent weapon with extensive firepower. It fires a .45 caliber bullet instead of a .30 caliber bullet. This is a volunteer position as no one in their right mind would want to be a first scout. Morton said that since I had kept my cool when he and I entered that village, he was appointing me to be first scout. I believe he said that I was "volunteering" to be first scout. I was handed a Thompson submachine gun.

What is the job of the first scout? He is to walk ahead of the column and draw the fire of the enemy. The second scout walks behind and as the enemy is shooting at the first scout, he observes where the fire is coming from. The first two men are supposed to inform the men following as to the position and strength of the enemy. One way was to locate the source of firing is by observing the gun flash. The enemy was using powder less shells so we could not tell where the shots were coming from. If we kept our ears open we could hear the enemy as they pulled back on the bolt of their rifles. We heard that click when the bolt was driven home into the chamber. Our rifles were automatic; therefore as long as we pulled on the trigger we were firing shells at them. After eight rounds, our clip was empty then we reloaded. We also needed a good sense of smell, as we could sometimes locate their hiding places by their scent. We had to know our enemy to survive.

If a person could survive at least five days in combat, he was considered a good scout and also very lucky. One thing about being first scout, no one wanted your job. I had job security. Our unit had only three first scouts so that way I would get two days off and one day on. A soldier by the name of Ryan was one of the other first scouts and Gord Schaefer was the other. Ryan would lead the company at a very fast pace and at times would get caught in cross fire. I would proceed at a slower pace, as I was probably overly cautious. The guys behind could always tell who was leading the column.

As I came over the top of a hill, I saw five Japanese crossing an open field. I signaled the squad leader and pointed this out to him. He then ordered the rest of us to take cover on the crest of the hill. We all waited until these enemy soldiers were well within rifle range. They really were just walking across the field without any knowledge that within the next few seconds their lives would be wiped out. The command was given and we all opened fire and all five soldiers went down. Another soldier and I were told to go down and check out these dead troops. We were to look for any information that could be of importance.

We made our way down and cautiously came up to the lifeless bodies. One of them was not dead. Suddenly he got up and ran away from me. I fired out of instinct and hit him in the back of the neck. The bullet went through the neck and came out the front, causing his brains to be blown out. His whole face just collapsed. I was the cause of another man's death. The horror of taking a person's life remained with me for a long time. It's one thing to stand on top of the ridge and shoot down at a group, knowing that maybe one of your bullets might kill someone, but to go down and know for sure it was I who put an end to one of God's human creatures is traumatic. After removing the markings off the collar of a couple of them, I reported back that we were successful in performing our mission. We just left the bodies in the field. With the knowledge that these were soldiers, no doubt there would be more in the neighborhood. We had to be extra careful for the next few days. We didn't have to wait much longer to find out where the others were located.

The next morning I was in the lead as we proceeded toward our objective of reaching the western shores of Cebu. I maneuvered over the knoll of a hill with Templeton, my second scout close by my side but slightly behind. I could feel danger in my bones and mentioned to Templeton to be ready as I had a premonition that there was danger ahead. The third man to come over the hill was the sergeant. Just as he appeared over the knoll, the Japanese opened up with fire from a machine gun. Those bullets came very close to hitting me. In fact, I was thrown to the ground because of the velocity of those bullets. I had a ringing in my ears but knew enough to just lie on the ground and not move. I was hoping that the guy behind that gun would think that he hit me. Sergeant Morton yelled at both Templeton and myself, "Did anyone get hit?" Just then Templeton got up and started running for the protection of the other side of the knoll. That machine gunner had him zeroed in, but Billy was faster than a speeding bullet that day. I really can't believe how fast he ran! I just remained as quiet as I could; I was not about to inform the enemy that I was alive. Every time Morton would stick his rifle above that crest, the machine gun would respond with a hail of bullets. Somehow they must have forgotten about me.

Finally, after some time just lying there, I decided that I had better do something. I could just make out where that machine gun was

138

located. Slowly I reached for a hand grenade, I pulled the pin out, waited four seconds, and threw it in the direction of the machine gun. I got up and ran faster than Templeton did minutes before. When you have to move, you can move fast, if you have the right incentive. My desire was to stay alive.

Shortly after, I heard the fire of small arms and knew by that time the other guys had gotten behind the machine gun nest and finished the culprits off. We heard those guys yell that everything was safe and that we could come over and see what was holding up our advance. I went with Billy Templeton to view what was left of the enemy. We discovered three soldiers wearing the insignia of the Japanese Navy. We found out later that there was a detachment of Marines on Cebu and we had just run into three of them. These fellows were from a very elite guard unit.

The radio operator made contact with the small Piper Cub that was keeping in communication with us. We used the small plane to drop needed supplies to us. This pilot relayed to us that he had just crossed over an open field and had seen so many dead enemy soldiers that he couldn't fly any lower than 2,000 feet because of the decaying smell. We were then told that we should locate that field and count the dead. We were given the general direction and started off with our noses at the ready! Somehow a map was drawn for us and we all went off to look for this field of death. One question; if a plane couldn't fly any lower than 2,000 feet because of the smell; you can well imagine what that odor would be at ground level!

We were fairly sure that we were in the correct location but somehow couldn't seem to locate any decaying enemy bodies. We did locate four bodies, but these had died many days ago and were decayed. After a few more hours of searching, we returned to our outfit. We reported only four dead enemies. The sergeant got on the walkie-talkie and informed company headquarters that we had counted ten dead soldiers. The sergeant added a few more to the death count to make our scouting mission more believable. I would bet that every time our report went to a higher headquarters that the amount was increased. That's how our body count was reported.

So don't believe everything you read unless you know somebody who was there.

We came upon a very large rubber plantation. Located near the center of this plantation was a large Spanish style home. The family living there were very cultured people, they spoke Spanish. They had three young daughters, all of them very beautiful. We had not seen such attractive young ladies in a long time. For that reason we were told not to enter the house, but were ordered to set up our perimeter around the house. Later in the afternoon one of the girls came out and supplied us with some rice. This was served to us on glass plates. Why does everyone want to serve us rice? This was probably the first time I ate rice while enjoying the scenery. We were treated royally. They had a deep well and it was great to drink fresh water. I do believe we were able to attempt a makeshift shower.

It was amazing that not once during the war was this rubber plantation bombed. They even had a small runway along the rear of their homestead. Our small Piper Cub used that landing strip to supply us with ammo and much needed supplies. About three of my buddies were flown back to Cebu City as a result of contracting jaundice, another for having malaria. One time a P-38 Lockheed Lightning aircraft used the runway for emergency repairs and it was my duty to protect that plane while it was on the ground. I wished that I could have taken a ride with him, but a P-38 is only a single seated aircraft.

There was also a large building on this plantation that contain a great many cases of Japanese Sake. We were instructed to destroy that booze. We stayed about three days longer as some of the cases were hard to open.

Our life of luxury was soon coming to an end. We saddled up and moved on. We were getting closer to the western shores of Cebu because the hills seemed to be getting lower and lower. In the evenings we could feel a breeze coming off the Tamon Strait. Our movements were more rapid now, except when I was leading.

140

On this occasion, while I was in the lead, a newly appointed second lieutenant complained that we were going too slowly. "Can't we pick up the pace and move ahead faster?" he grumbled impatiently.

I was a bit agitated by his remark and responded, "I'm the first scout, and if you want to take over my job, be my guest."

Very sharply he ordered, "Move out, I don't see any enemy movements ahead."

"I can smell the enemy, SIR."

"That's crazy," he smirked, "No one can smell the enemy." As he passed me he added, "I'll show you how to lead."

His radio carrier followed him down the trail. These two were a pair of real eager beavers. They had gotten about fifty feet in front of me when a Japanese soldier opened up on them with rifle fire. This new "90-day wonder" turned tail and ran right past me to get to the rear of the column as fast as he could go. I was never again challenged by anyone after that.

On 10 May, Thursday, we emerged from the tangled underbrush on the other side of the island. It had taken us twenty-two unforgettable days. We were now heading for Toledo, but not Toledo, Ohio.

The above photo should give you an idea of what it was like to trek over the top of Cebu and stand on level ground. Steel helmets were required so you can tell that we are in enemy territory. Boxes were searched to see what could be used or taken. Note the GI on the left loaded with newly acquired ammunition and a poncho in his right arm. There seems to be an entrance to a cave located just on the right of this photo. I wonder what is in the package wrapped so tightly in the foreground. You can see a lot in the photo.

Chapter XI
CEBU CITY RETURNING
June 1945

We came within view of the Tamon Strait. Making our way down to the roadway we joined other troops already on the coastline. These were members of the 132nd Infantry and the 182nd Infantry who had made the trip around the island by truck. It was great to see these men. These were our Americal buddies. We were located just south of Toledo, not at all like Toledo, Ohio! It was a community of bamboo huts along the road. What they did for a living, I have yet to figure out.

I assumed that we were in for a short break but that was not to be. Some fellows from the I & R platoon came over to our group and selected us to go on a patrol mission with them. The I & R stands for Intelligence and Reconnaissance. These guys were really GUNG HO for their job. Everyone of them carried a submachine gun with an extra knife in their belt. They intended to move in and collect intelligence then get out. I was glad they were with us as they usually led the way. We were used for back up. These fellows had to make a report after every mission. Part of that report is very informative and is recorded as follows.

"There are some signs indicating a possibility of the enemy in the general area in-groups of 4-5 but this information is difficult to determine accurately because of civilian activity in this area. As soon as civilians observed the patrol they fled.

The terrain in the entire area with the exception of the ground along the coastline is very difficult to travel due to the fact that there are no connecting ridges in the area but all individual hills. The terrain is semi-mountainous with scattered vegetation and a few coconut trees growing in the deepest ravines. There is no water to be found in the entire area. Patrols operating in this area for more than one day must carry their own water supply with them. The few civilians who live in this area obtain their water supply by catching rainwater and draining the sap from banana trees. There is an abundance of coconut trees paralleling the entire W coastline."

This report gives the true picture of what it is to go out on patrol. I believe that I went on one more patrol with them. We never saw any enemy troops by the highway. These patrols usually lasted one day.

Military discipline was very loose so no saluting or calling person by their rank, even if you knew his rank. Everyone was on last name bases. It was now time to just relax and catch up on the latest rumors. We heard the rumor again that President Roosevelt had died. This was the second time we heard this report and now believed it was true. I was saddened even though I never voted for him.

We expected that the mail had caught up with us but no such luck. Without mail, life is boring. With very little to do, we explored the area. Most of these people live in huts built on bamboo stilts. There is plenty of room under each hut. You have to be careful at night, under which part of the house you crawl. There are usually two rooms; one is the general living quarters, which at night becomes the bedroom. The other room is the kitchen and latrine, or toilet. The flooring in the living area is usually solid, but in the kitchen area, the floor is laid out with small slits in the boards. If they have a chicken bone left over it was pushed through the floor unto the ground underneath. If they have to use the bathroom facilities, just let it go between the cracks in the flooring. That is why we had to be careful at night where we slept.

We didn't have to dig fox holes. It seems that the enemy is mostly to the north and has not ventured to the south. In the evening, we selected a soft spot and rolled into our poncho as a covering. There are no electric lights when it gets dark everyone turns in. Only the barking dogs could be heard in the silence of the night. We could hear young people talking and parents telling the kids to be quiet. I think that is what they are saying, as we could not understand the language. The stars are very bright and the air is clean, even with the smoke from the huts. It was wonderful to take a deep breath and not smell death.

144

At the crack of dawn the rooster crows and the small village begins to move about. The men squatted on the front porch, and lit up their cigars or cigarettes. They have their bolo knife tucked in their leather belt. There are usually several coconuts on the porch and before long these are cut open and the husks are used for fuel. Little children stand around waiting to eat the white coconut meat inside. There is always a dog or two on the porch. The young ladies go to the stream to do their washing. They wring out the clothes and beat them with a stick to get all the water out of the fabric. Younger children gather water in gasoline containers.

The only way to travel is on foot or in a horse drawn cart. The horses are very small and underfed. We felt sorry for them because of the loads they have to haul. There were carabao or water buffalo working in the rice fields near by.

Since we were in a relativity safe area on the coastline, we did not have guard duty, as it had been necessary for so many days and nights only a short time ago. Everything seemed very relaxed because there was little for us to do.

We were getting bored. Some fellows started to drink tuba, and a few drank too much! We watched the natives go out in the evening to fish. They would use lighted torches and came back in the morning with generous catches. We did not get the opportunity to eat any of the fish caught because Trippy had warned us not to do so. Some fish in that region were known to be poisonous. We noticed that supplies were being trucked in daily with more and more C and K rations. Perhaps we would be moving out of Toledo.

One evening I found a quiet place on the shore to relax, I watched the stars come out. A beautiful moon came into view reflecting over the water and I was reminded again of God watching over me. He created such a beautiful world but I had just experienced the ugly ravages that humans bring about. The enormous full moon seemed so close that I could almost reach up and touch it. Days would come and go, but we had no idea to the day or month.

145

The Red Cross was establishing a station near where we were located. I asked one of the guys driving the Red Cross truck if they had anything to eat. At this time he could not offer me anything because the supply truck had not come around with provisions. He said the only thing in the back of the truck was one bottle of Coke syrup. He claimed it wasn't any good because I would need soda water to give it the fizz to make it taste like Coke. I told him I wanted some; he said to help myself and repeated that it would be no good without the soda water. We always carried two canteens full of water. One was on our right hip and the other on the left. We usually drank out of the canteen on the right, keeping the one on the left for reserve. I emptied the water from the left canteen and filled it with that sticky Coke syrup. As time passed, I forgot about it.

We had arrived on 10 May and it is now Thursday, 17 May. We have been in this utopia for only one week, but it seemed to me a lifetime. The days were long and the evenings were relaxing.

We received orders to move out. Company "G" was to return to Cebu City not by truck but rather by the same route we used to get to the city of Toledo. It sure would have been nice to return by truck along the coastal road.

Saddle up men! I was not going to be first scout on the return trip so I gave my sub-machine gun to a fellow by the name of Schaefer. He wore glasses and was a very nice fellow to talk with. Maybe they wanted someone who would walk faster than I did to take us back. I was hopeful that the return trip would be a little easier on all of us.

We were a tired, smelly, grubby, sickly group of soldiers as we hit that trail back up into the surrounding hills. We carried everything on our backs, including food, water and ammunition. We were going back into the hot, humid jungle once again. When the sun shone, the heat was devastating. Trippy, our medic, continually reminded us to take our salt and atabrine tablets.

At night we would be able to sleep three fellows together. In that way our watch at night would be one hour on and two hours off.

146

Digging holes at night was also stopped, however, we still would put out our booby traps. We continued to set up the "alarm system" so we could hear that jingling and know that someone was approaching. Since we didn't dig any foxholes on this return trip, we would roll some large stones in front of us. If any one started to shoot at us the small rocks became a thick wall of protection.

On one early evening stop, a few of us craved fresh meat for supper. We had seen some chickens running around in the underbrush, with permission, we started out on the hunt. It wasn't very long when we came upon four or five chickens pecking and scraping around making noise. Since I discovered this game, I had the honor of taking the first shot. With my trusty M1, I drew a bead on the largest bird in the flock and slowly squeezed off one round as the bullet found it's target. The round had completely severed that chicken's head and a good share of his body as well. There wasn't much left to eat. The other chickens ran in every direction. Next time we will use a carbine instead of an M1. No meat that night! How about a large bowl of rice?

I do remember that we encountered one Japanese soldier on this return trip. We had located a level area for the evening and just as we were about to eat, I heard a sound of something banging against a stone or helmet. Not taking any chances, I yelled "grenade, grenade" and hit the ground. Sure enough, a Japanese soldier had set off his grenade. However, he did not have the strength or time to throw it. The explosion from the grenade ripped through his body, it looked like he had committed hara-kiri. One of the fellows pumped a couple shots into him, but he was already dead. He did have a pistol on him and a buddy grabbed his gun. It was a great souvenir for him. We all decided that maybe he was not the only Japanese around so we posted a double guard that night, just in case. Thankfully, it was a very quiet night after all.

It was not unusual for us to come upon a small village in an open clearing. We observed the usual huts, busy women, sociable men and playful children. The chickens scratched the ground while a cow or two kept the grass at a perfect height.

As in all villages, there was a local chief. His job was to keep the peace. This chief was no different and he was eager to please us. All of us were invited to join his village in the butchering of a cow and to join them later in eating their roasted animal. Trippy had warned us not to eat any animal meat but what if the meat was roasted over a fire? We must have been hungry so we stayed to observe this festive occasion. I had never seen the slaughtering of a cow so this was to be a new experience for me.

Four Filipinos proceeded to tie a rope to each of the cow's legs, and then they would pull on the ropes in opposite directions. That poor cow couldn't move. The chief proceeded to cut the throat of the cow and extracted the blood as it poured out of the wound into a bowl. They did not really kill the cow it bled to death. The blood was carried into a hut and mixed with flour or grain. This mixture was placed in a pan and baked over the open fire. They shaped the mixture into small cakes. After watching how they had killed the cow, I decided I would not eat anything baked by the locals no matter how hungry I was. I would rather eat rice, as much as I disliked it!

As we were getting closer to Cebu City, we began to recognize some of the places that we had been earlier. We located the burnt out house where the sergeant was killed. We also located the gravesite where we had placed the body but it had already been removed. Soldiers from grave registration had found the remains and relocated them to the cemetery somewhere on this island. Whenever we buried a comrade, we would usually stick a bayonet into the ground with a steel helmet on top so that the grave registration team could locate the remains.

While sitting under a coconut tree next to Templeton, our conversation turned into the direction of food and drink. Billy had his rifle across his legs and mentioned that he would give anything, *anything* for a Coke! The stars in my brain lit up. I had a Coke in my left canteen! Would Templeton give anything for a Coke?

"What would you give for a Coke, right now?" I asked.

"I would give you my right arm for a Coke right now," was his quick response and I believe he meant it.

With a smirk on my face I told Templeton to cut off his arm because I had a Coke for him. I opened my canteen and poured the sticky Coke syrup into his cup. We mixed some water with it and sure enough, we had Coke! I then had to share my Coke with every other fellow within our hearing. I actually never tasted it myself.

I was hoping I could take a shower or at least get some of the sweat off my weary body. We hadn't had a change of clothes since we were on this island, which was now almost two and a half months. Some of my clothes were stuck to my skin. I was having trouble with my feet; when I tried to pull off my sock, ulcer scabs would bleed. The combat boots had a strap around the ankle to give our feet support, but this tight fitting band didn't allow our feet to dry completely. Jungle rot was the result of wet feet. Trippy continued to apply penicillin to my feet. Now he was beginning to bandage my hands as jungle rot had started in my right hand. What good was I with my right hand in bandages? Trippy told me that as long as I could pull the trigger on my M1, I would remain in combat. I was also having problems keeping food down and at times had a very high fever. I was feeling miserable!

That night our camp was set up on the top of the hill overlooking Cebu City. I sat there with my rifle between my legs. I was all alone feeling sick and miserable and actually threw up. I wanted to die on that spot. I stayed on the crest of the hill all night.

The next morning, while still in this miserable state, I saw an American soldier coming down the trail into our perimeter. I had a strange feeling that I knew him and sure enough, as he got closer I recognized my brother Gordon. He had been released from the hospital and was now rejoining our company. What a difference between us now. He had a brand new uniform and seemed to weigh at least 200 pounds. He was clean-shaven and was carrying a new rifle. I was a mess, unshaven, sickly and weighed 143 pounds. We were no longer twins in appearance! It was good to see Gordon again and to know he was well.

Gordon and I talked for about an hour, as later he had to report to the company commander for assignment into our unit. He mentioned that he had written home to inform our parents about his wound and I am sure they were glad to hear from him. He said that he couldn't tell too much about what was really going on because the censor would cut out anything that had to do with Army activity.

I pointed out where the command post was and he reported in for duty. Gordon later rejoined me and we set up our outpost for the night. There wasn't any fear of an attack because we were very close to Cebu City. No guards were posted for the night. I gathered my poncho around me and prepared for sleep. Gordon wanted to know where he could pitch his tent and I had to remind him that we didn't sleep in a tent. I'm sure he had difficulty falling asleep on that hard ground.

The next morning Gordon reported to another squad assignment. He had been wounded on 15 April and it was now 4 June. I had not seen my brother for 49 days. There were many questions I needed to ask him. What had happened since he left our outfit? How was he treated in the hospital? Had he seen or heard anything about Mike Van Couwenberghe? Did he receive any letters from home? Unfortunately, these questions were never asked because that same morning I checked in with Trippy.

My bandages needed to be changed again. As Trippy was applying penicillin to my infected hands and feet, he asked if I was seeing things in a different color. I mentioned that items in the distance seemed blurred and took on a yellowish tint. I also said that my urine was very yellow. He informed me that I had contracted hepatitis. Drinking polluted water that infected my kidneys causing everything to become yellow. My eyeballs were no longer white, but yellow, so I had a true case of yellow jaundice. Trippy assured me that I wasn't going to die, but I was a casualty of war. I was done with war for the present time. I left that very hour and reported to the 2nd Battalion Aid Station located near Highway One.

I wanted to locate Gordon to inform him that I would be leaving but couldn't find him. I did have time to talk with Billy Templeton. Templeton was my second scout on our adventure across the hills and we had become very close. My only regret is that I didn't get Billy's address so I could contact him after the war. I surely would like to have met him. I was also looking for Shively, but he also was nowhere to be found. Taking my rifle and feeling very weak I headed down the trail toward Cebu City. Finally, I could leave behind all the memories of combat, destruction and death. Maybe I could begin to act like a human being again.

Finding the 2nd Battalion Aid Station was easy because it was well marked with the Red Cross symbol. I gave my name, rank and serial number to the medic on duty and was given a routine physical. I was told to go to the mess tent for something to eat. The smell of that food made me nauseated. They put food into my mess kit but I really wasn't hungry. The best thing they offered me was water. I was able to drink as much as I wanted to and it was WONDERFUL. After drinking polluted water, now to be able to see clear to the bottom of the cup was overwhelming. Water is something that we too often take for granted.

Leaving the mess area with all that food still in my mess gear made we wonder about the many times I was without food. Now I was about to just throw this good food away! As always, hanging around the Army mess kitchens were young children begging for food. I'm sure most of them were homeless and they seemed to be under ten years old. I scraped the food from my plate into a tin can of one of those starving children. He had a smile on his face. The mess sergeant took another view of what I had done. He did not want all of these starving kids around his area and kept yelling at them to leave. I told the sergeant that it was my food and that I could do with it whatever I wanted. These children needed it more than I did. The sergeant suggested that I find another mess tent to eat in the future.

I returned to the Regimental Aid Station and located my assigned Army cot. What a luxury! As night drew near, I slept on that "luxurious" cot, it was the first time in months that I was not

151

sleeping on the ground. I was going to enjoy this but that was not to happen. Shortly after nightfall, someone yelled that there were enemy soldiers in the area and everyone was to evacuate the tent. I crawled under my cot with my rifle and fell fast asleep. I decided to let someone else stand guard for the night. I don't know if any enemy troops appeared in the area or not, I didn't care. Consequently, this first night was not spent on an Army cot but on the ground.

I refused breakfast the next morning. I still couldn't keep anything down. My vision was getting worse. I had no pep. My mind was on my buddies and I was deserting them.

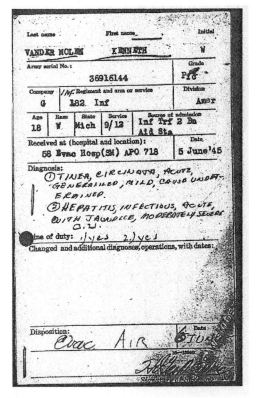

This is a tag that was attached to me as I left Cebu. It indicates that I was at the 2nd Battalion Aid Station and later would be transferred by air to the 58th Evac Hospital. I was diagnosed with Tinea, circinata, Hepatitis, and jaundice. These occurred while in line of duty.

Early on the morning of 6 June 1945, I left the combat zone as a casualty of war. No, I wasn't wounded but when a soldier leaves his duty, he is reported as a casualty just as if he had been shot. A C-47 was waiting on the Lahug airstrip that was located just north of Cebu City. A number of ambulances had already placed their wounded soldiers inside the

152

aircraft. It was a gray painted ship with the Red Cross Emblem affixed to the side.

My identification tag was secured around my neck with my name on it in very large lettering. There were a couple of Filipino soldiers flying with us as well as four nurses attending to the wounded. Soon all the stretchers were on board, then the walking wounded were instructed to board the C-47. The stretchers were stacked along the side of the plane, one on top of the other. The most seriously wounded were placed about the third tier from the bottom. This way they were in more direct contact with the nurses. A bench along the one side about ten feet long is where I was to sit. There were no seat belts. One of the Filipino soldiers sat next to me and I tried to say something to him but he seemed not able to understand English. The motors turned on, warmed up, and we took off. I tried to look out the window but there was a thick cloud cover and so my last view of Cebu was obscured. It was quite chilly in this plane and most all of the stretcher cases had covers over them. The nurses were attending to the needs of these wounded buddies. Fortunately, it was a very short flight.

The one who I really missed the most was Richard Shively. He had been with me from the very beginning in Cebu. He and I had shared the same fox hole together. Rich was a Christian Scientist and at night as I would be reading my Bible, he would be reading, "The Key to the Scriptures", by Mary Baker Eddy. We would have some very interesting talks about the Bible. He was one great fellow even if our thoughts about the Life of Christ were different. You learned to stand up for your beliefs but also to respect what the other person believed as well.

Shively's father owned the local theater in Wabash, Indiana. He would send Rich a copy of what was playing in the theater for that week. Whenever the mail got to us, we would ask Shively what was playing at the local theater on Saturday. Even when we did not get any mail, the other guys would yell out, "Shively, what is playing this Saturday at the show?" Rich would make up a double feature story, like Roy Rogers in, "The Trail of The Lonesome Pine," or "Abbott and Costello in Hollywood." He did not forget to mention that every Wednesday night was "Free Dishware

Night." This allowed us time to dream about the movies and enabled us to take our minds off the reality of war.

One of the things that made Shively unique was his habit of brushing his teeth. No matter where we were, every night we could hear Rich faithfully brushing his teeth with his toothbrush and canteen cup of water. Sometimes he had to use coconut milk. These are fond memories.

Our destination was Leyte. I was beginning to feel like MacArthur saying, "I shall return." I suddenly realized I had left my rifle behind on Cebu.

Chapter XII
LEYTE RETURNING
June – August 1945

The Filipino soldier next to me did not like flying. This trip must have been his first on an airplane. He began to turn green behind the ears and had a very shallow look on his face. The other Filipino soldier said something to him. The soldier next to me put his hand over his mouth and kept it there.

Thankfully the trip was short and soon our plane lowered its wheels as we approached the airfield at Leyte. We landed but the pilot missed the landing strip resulting in the roughest landing any pilot had ever made. The landing strip was made from steel sheeting welded together to form a solid base. The hard landing did not help the sick soldier next to me. One of the litter patients let out a loud cry and was quickly taken care of by one of the nurses. The door of the plane finally opened as the ambulances started to back toward the open doorway. My companion Filipino soldier couldn't wait any longer. He got up from his seat and made a dash for the open door, just in time to let fly everything he held inside him right into the arriving ambulance.

The ambulance driver was not happy to have this happen to his clean vehicle. Both of the Filipino soldiers were placed into the vehicle and headed out toward the city. The walking wounded were then told to enter one of the other ambulances and we were driven to the 117th Station Hospital.

This was quite the place. As I walked between these large white tents, I noticed that everything was bright and clean. There were wooden pathways leading from one building to the next. As I walked toward the tent assigned to me, I noticed some 50-gallon drums that seemed to be filled with arms and legs. In fact, these were the Plaster of Paris casts, which were cut off after broken limbs were mended. What a relief it must have been for the GIs to have those heavy casts removed in this place. I was grateful that I could walk into this hospital instead of having to be carried in on a stretcher.

155

They showed me a bed that had clean white sheets on it with a white pillow. I did not take my clothes off but just climbed into all of that clean whiteness and immediately fell fast asleep. I slept for thirty hours and did not remember a thing.

When awakened I was wearing white pajamas and my shoes were gone. I was at the mercy of unknown persons who stole my clothes! Even on the front line, my friends never stole anything that was mine. I was in unfriendly territory but I was soon to find out that this was the best place for me.

An orderly finally came with chart in hand and started to ask me a lot of questions about my general health. He wrote all these things down. I inquired about my clothes and was told that they had burned them. I asked the orderly, "How long am I to be in the hospital?" "The doctors will soon review your chart and will answer your question," he responded as he handed me a couple of pills to swallow and instructed me to just take it easy.

A doctor came by later and asked more questions about my illness. I mentioned to him that the soldier seated next to me on the plane trip over was being treated for tuberculosis. He used his stethoscope to check my breathing and ordered an X-ray of my lungs. I was to be checkout for chronic cough and tuberculosis.

There weren't too many female nurses around. I was receiving daily shots of penicillin for jungle rot. The disease was on my legs, feet and hands, and yet they insisted on giving the shots in my butt! My temperature was taken every day.

Life was good here. I was able to walk to the mess hall for meals. My appetite was improving. Food tasted better than on the island of Cebu. No one carried weapons. Instead of a metal cup, we had coffee mugs just like the Navy. I could go into the mess hall and have a cup of coffee any time, day or night. This was real living.

Form 55 A
MEDICAL DEPARTMENT, U. S. ARMY
Revised May 31, 1939)

CLINICAL RECORD
BRIEF

WD# 72

Register No. _15272_ Hospital _117 5TH Hosp_ _A-001001_
Name _VANDER MOLEN, KENNETH W._ Serial No. _36916144_
Grade _____ Co. _____ Regt. and Arm or Service _____
Age _____ Race _____ Nativity _____
Service _____ Date of admission _____, 19___
Source of admission _____
Station _____
Ward _____ Previous admission _____
Religion _____ Home address _____
Name and address of nearest relative _____

(Initials of admitting officer)

Disposition _Con Hosp_ Date _____, 19___

Final diagnosis:

(1) _Hepatitis, infectious with jaundice, acute, moderate, Cause undetermined, non effective ab 8 ¶_

(2) _Epidermophytosis, acute generalized, moderate_

Additional diagnoses (Complications, special treatment and operations):

Line of duty _1 + 2 y_
Condition on completion of case _1 + 2 improved_

Transfer diagnosis confirmed or not confirmed _____
Autopsy _____

DEC 15 196

I noticed an Army Chaplain walking down the length of beds talking with the various soldiers and trying to cheer them up. Finally he came next to my bed and picked up my chart, which was at the end of the bed. He looked at me and said, "Vander Molen, are you from Michigan?"

I was somewhat surprised that he said Michigan because it was not on the chart. "I'm from Detroit."

Then his answer surprised me even more. "I thought all Hollanders came from Grand Rapids". Looking over my chart he asked, "What is your Protestant preference?" I said, "Christian Reformed."

He broke out in a very large smile and said, "I am Chaplain Cornelius Schoolland, also Christian Reformed." He sat down on the bed next to me and we started to talk in earnest. I mentioned that my father's name was Cecil and he said that he knew of him. I just couldn't believe that a minister from the Christian Reformed Church was talking with me. We got on real great after that. Another coincidence, he had come over on the same ship, the USS General Butner, as I had. He wanted to know if I had attended any of the Chaplain Services, which were held aboard ship. Of course I said "yes".

TEMPERATURE--TREATMENT--NURSE'S NOTES

Date	A.M.			P.M.			St.		
	T	P	R	T	P	R			
June 4-5	97								Adm. amb to wd 12
6-8	99	84	18	98	80	18			Dx Tinea circinate
									② Hepatitis ac.
6-9	98	76	18						Multi vit cap ⅱ
6-10	98	78	18						
6-11	98	84	18						
6-12	98	80	18						
6-13	98	78	18						Chest X-Ray for Chr Cong
6-14	98	80	18						
6-15	98	73	16		80	18			

LABORATORY REPORTS

It was while recuperating, that I had become aware that on 8 May, the war in Europe ended. Every morning I would look out into Leyte Bay with the hope that the European troops would soon be coming to the Pacific Theater of Operation. I was receiving great food and the beach was just a few hundred feet from our ward. It was fun just walking along the shoreline. The sores on my hands and legs were getting better and every once in awhile I would rub some sand on the sores, to make them inflamed.

On 18 June, I was transferred to the 1st Convalescent Hospital. Now this is the last stop before you are considered well enough to get back to your unit. You have greater freedom to move around the Hospital area. This is where all the USO shows come to cheer up all the wounded servicemen. We even got a beer ration.

We would get four bottles of beer every three days. Sometimes we received ale from Australia and occasionally a Pabst Blue Ribbon Beer from America. There was no place to keep them cold, so we would go to the ocean, walk out a ways and bury them in the cool wet sand. A couple of days later, we would retrace our steps and try to locate where we hid our treasure. We seldom found our own but usually someone's "catch." Later we would see soldiers, knee deep in the water with bamboo poles prodding the sands for hidden beer.

Mail finally caught up with me and ultimately I received several letters. I first sorted out the mail of importance. I also checked the dates when these letters were mailed. Some mail took as long as three months to get to me.

Most of it was old news but it was great to hear from home. I finally got a letter and picture from Mary Margaret Liddane. She told me all the latest news as to what was going on at Southeastern High School.

I would write mostly to Mary Margaret Liddane. I enjoyed getting letters from her, because she talked about interesting things going on at school. She wrote about the fun we would have when I returned. I believed that she was falling in love with me. I was hoping it might be true, but I knew down deep in my heart that it could never be. She was Catholic and I was Protestant. I did keep writing to her, however, maybe some of my letters did encourage her somewhat.

160

Letters from my parents were mostly about events going on in the church. I did get a fruitcake from my parents at one time. They said that they had sent many packages to me but I never received any except one box of fruitcake. Believe it or not, that cake was OK to eat as it was about the only thing that could be sent and kept so long. Some guys received cookies and cake from home and by the time they got them they were moldy and turning green.

I remember getting a letter from my dear Aunt Lou; she was wondering if I would please get in contact with her son Robert (my cousin) who was attached to the 32nd Infantry Division in Manila. MacArthur had said the war was over so she wanted me to drop over and visit with Cousin Bob. I don't think people had any concept of where Manila was in relationship to either Leyte or Cebu. The war was still being carried on in Luzon and other islands of the Philippines.

My neighbor Mrs. Hawkins from Detroit sent me a whole sheet of postage stamps. She folded the sheet and placed it in an envelope and addressed it to me. The letter finally arrived but with all the wet weather and high humidity the stamps were stuck together. In a following letter she asked if I had received the stamps she sent the month before. I told a lie and said that I never got them. She wrote the Post Office Department and wanted her money back for the stamps *that* I never received. I thought that everyone knew we didn't use stamps as soldiers had free mail service.

I received a letter from my dad, he enclosed an article from the local paper dated 21 April, saying that General MacArthur claimed that the fighting was over in the Philippines and so why didn't I write home more often now that the war was over. He never realized that on that date, I was with other Americal soldiers trekking across the island of Cebu and the end was not in sight for me.

Japs on Cebu Wiped Out

MANILA, April 21 (INS)—
Complete liberation of Cebu
Island today signalized the end
of the central Philippines campaign.

Gen. MacArthur announced liberation of Cebu in his daily communique: American forces, the communique reported, surprised the main force of Japs on Cebu in a wide enveloping movement and routed the enemy remnants to the hills. Jap losses in the final mass battle were set at 5,000 dead.

The communique pointed out that virtual conclusion of the Visayan or central Philippine campaign leaves the enemy with organized resistance only on Mindanao on the south and upper Luzon on the north.

When soldiers have nothing to do, we tend to chat more with each other, not so much about home and girlfriends, but about our Division. Of course your own outfit was the best. Our division spent the most days in combat, our Division took the most prisoners, our Division made more landings than any other outfit, etc, etc, etc. As always happens, there would be one fellow who would not get into any conversation about how great his outfit was. I remember that on this occasion a fellow soldier had the last bed in the row and he would make no comments about his unit. We asked him, "Hey buddy, what outfit are you from?"

He replied, "I'm from the best outfit and never brag about my unit, I'm making more money just lying in the hospital than any one of you fellows." He was from the 11th Airborne Division and makes an extra $50.00 a month more than us GIs because he was a paratrooper. Those guys were a real elite unit and we never wanted to get into an argument with them about which was the best Division; they already knew and we didn't argue with them.

There was a Red Cross unit in the hospital that supplied us with writing materials so we could write home. If we couldn't write because of wounds they would assist us in that task. We could get just about anything from the Red Cross including toothbrushes, shaving creams, razors and combs. Mail was arriving more often but most of the mail was very old news. We couldn't write about where we were, the censor would cut out anything that would help the enemy.

The Red Cross would serve hot coffee and usually showed pictures in the evening. I was becoming a regular visitor to this Red Cross tent and so I asked them, "Could I assist in making coffee or perhaps in some other task?" They replied, "Could I operate a movie projector?" I answered, "No problem!" I had operated the movie projector on board ship coming over, but all I did was to turn the light on and off. That was the extent of my experience using or operating a projector. Well, I learned fast.

I would make fifty gallons of coffee and also distribute the toothbrushes, shaving creams, razors and combs to the guys. At night I would thread the films through the projector, turn the switch on and enjoyed the movie. I was being paid one centavo (50 cents) a day by the American Red Cross. I never signed the payroll while I was overseas, however, the Red Cross paid me every week so I had a little extra spending money. There was nothing much to purchase as I was already getting everything free.

During my "volunteer work" I met a very nice Red Cross worker by the name of Faye Anderson. She was from Minnesota and was very dedicated to the war effort. Some of the Red Cross girls were out to enjoy the company of GIs but Faye was not like that at all. She enjoyed her work and would not leave her duties as some of the other girls did. (We will meet Faye Anderson later in this story.) When I wasn't working for the Red Cross, I was on the beach playing volleyball. My health was returning and my game was improving too.

A rumor was spreading around that some GIs had high-jacked a truck carrying meat. The MP's came around and wanted to know if any of the stolen meat had showed up in the Red Cross section. The Red Cross had a large refrigerator, which would be the logical place to conceal the meat if you had taken it. That's exactly where the meat was! I was told to keep quiet. Later I enjoyed the steaks with several of the MPs. The eggs that I confiscated between my daily rounds were a rare treat for breakfast. Enough said.

Throughout my time in the hospital, we had many visits from the USO (United Service Organization). These were traveling Hollywood shows put on for the service personnel. I remember seeing Kay Kyser and his nutty group. Jack Benny and Jerry Colona were very popular with the troops. The only girl I can remember was Betty Hutton. One show in particular that stands out in my mind as the best was Joe E. Brown. He had lost a son fighting in the Pacific (so I was told) and never gave a show in any other war theater. He entertained the Americal Division while on Fiji and later on Cebu. The Americal Division made him an honorary member and later the United States Government awarded him the Bronze Star.

One advantage of working with the Red Cross enabled me to get some front row seats near the stage. I should have had a camera with me because I did see many famous entertainers.

There were other hospital units in our area, some of them showed better movies than we had at the 1st Convalescence Hospital. I visited one of these and saw the movie entitled, "The Story of Dorian Grey". The screen was set up in a graveyard and the seating was on grave markers. It was an eerie place to view that type of movie. It started to rain, so I never saw the finish.

It was on 6 August 1945 that a B-29 bomber named Enola Gay, loaded with the Atomic Bomb took off from Tinian Island. Five and one half-hours later at 8:15 a.m. it dropped its Atomic Bomb on Hiroshima.

We received this unbelievable news on Leyte. Who ever heard of an Atomic Bomb? Could you really wipe out a whole city with just one bomb? Should we celebrate now or wait until later? We all anticipated that the war would soon be over.

On 7 August 1945 I celebrated my nineteenth birthday quietly and somewhat alone on Leyte. The day started the same as any other day.

Rumor stated that the Japanese Government was going to surrender. Suddenly everything broke loose on Leyte. They were celebrating my birthday...not really! Guns went off in the harbor aboard the Navy ships. Searchlights were turned on and the whole sky was illuminated with beams going back and forth. On land, it was everyone for himself. Warehouses were broken into and hand grenades were thrown into the ocean. Jeeps were driven off piers into the Pacific. Bullets were flying all over the place and it was just like a war zone. I stayed close to the Hospital because I did not want to get hit on the last day of the war. No one can imagine the joy that I felt in my heart at this time. Was this really the end of the war?

I wanted to get back to my outfit. The hospital was undecided what to do with the sick that were in the wards. Those that were critically wounded were shipped out and back to the states. Soldiers with jungle rot were being sent back to the states. Would I be on my way home soon?

On the 22nd of August I was transferred to the 4th Casualty Camp. This is not where I wanted to be. At any Casualty Camp, they could transfer me to my old unit or reassign me. If a ship were going to where my Division was, maybe they would put me on that sailing list. In the meantime, we cleaned up after the mess of our celebration a few days before. Some guys were assigned to clean out the latrine or another disgusting job. Most were sent to KP duty. I didn't want to do manual work while waiting for a transfer back to Cebu. When these details were being assigned; I quietly slipped away into the underbrush until evening. I then returned to camp and kept watching for a way to get out of this Casualty Camp.

Saturday the 25th of August I recognized a lieutenant from the Americal Division and heard he was returning to Cebu by way of an LST that evening. Dare I ask him to find room for me on board that ship? "Come along, we'll give it a try," he responded, "You want to get back to the 182nd and so do I."

With these words of encouragement, I accompanied the lieutenant to the beach area and sure enough there were some LSTs at dockside. This officer reported aboard and asked the Skipper if he had room for another GI. This was going to be the LSTs last voyage and the captain had no objection to another person on board. There were no cabins to sleep in, but the deck was going to be my bed. In order to get off the Island of Leyte and return to my buddies in the Americal, I would have taken a canoe.

I left Leyte without telling anyone. Maybe I am still AWOL (absent without official leave) but so far no one has come after me. I remember leaving the Island of Leyte once before and heading for Cebu, but that was 149 days earlier. What a difference this trip was. No convoy, no blackout and not knowing where I was going! I didn't sleep all night but gazed out into the open sea. The waves were very calm and the fluorescent fish could be seen below the surface of the deep blue waters.

What could I expect when I landed on Cebu? I had no orders transferring me back to the Americal. Once I had landed I would have to make my way back to Cebu City and find my unit. Would Company "G" still be on duty? Maybe taking this craft was not the best way to go. Maybe I should have stayed on Leyte. There were many doubts going on in my mind but I was determined to locate my buddies. I was convinced this was the right thing to do.

The two medical documents as shown on pages 167 and 168 as well as others printed throughout this book are parts of my medical records while in the hospitals on Leyte.

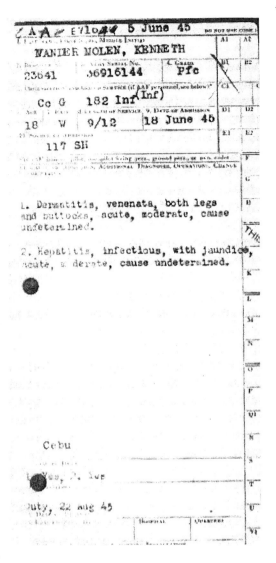

I do have more in a file that I have kept separate from this book. I do not have copies of my service record because all were destroyed in a fire at a St. Louis storage facility. The only records now available to me are the medical records that were stored in another building.

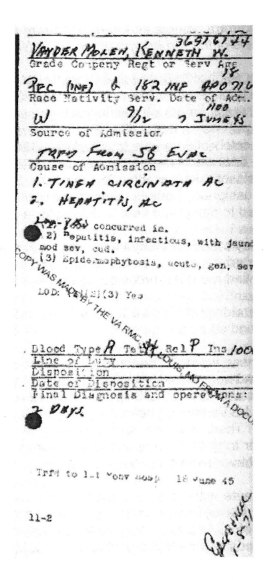

VANDER MOLEN, KENNETH W.   36976174
Grade Company Regt or Serv Age
                                    94
PFC (INF) 6 182 INF APO 716
Race Nativity Serv. Date of Adm.
                          /100
W   9/12   7 JUNE 45
Source of Admission
TRFD FROM SB EVAC
Cause of Admission
1. TINEA CIRCINATA AC
2. HEPATITIS, AC

1.-(AC) concurred in.
2) Hepatitis, infectious, with jaun
mod sev, cud.
(3) Epidermophytosis, acute, gen, ser

LOD: Yes (3) Yes

Blood Type A Te Rel P Ins /00
Line of Duty
Disposition
Date of Disposition
Final Diagnosis and operations:
2 DAYS

Trfd to 1st Conv Hosp 18 June 45

11-2

I have to admit at picking up souvenirs. The Philippine Peso was
what the Red Cross paid me while in their "service". The Japanese
money was taken from an enemy who didn't need it anymore. I
tried to sell these souvenirs but there really isn't much market value
for these bills.

Detroiters Win Honors With American Division

THE "AMERICAL" (33rd Infantry) Division in the Philippinos boasts some fighting Detroit and Michigan soldiers to rival those in the famous "Red Arrow (32nd Infantry) Division, whose exploits are being chronicled daily by John M. Carlisle, The News war correspondent.

The two outfits fought side by side on Luzon to sweep the island clean of Japs. Enemy resistance was declared ended officially by Gen. MacArthur recently, although mopping up continues.

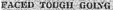
Van Wynsberghe

One Detroit hero was Pfc. Albert C. Van Wynsberghe, mentioned in one of a series of overseas dispatches received Tuesday.

FACED TOUGH GOING

It was tough going for Van Wynsberghe's outfit, attacking a Jap-held ridge under withering fire. When the assault faltered and threatened to turn into retreat, the Detroiter sprang to his feet and led a charge.

"Come on, let's give these so-and-so's some of their own 'Banzai'!" Van Wynsberghe yelled. His courage was contagious. Other Yanks followed.

As the Detroiter ran at the enemy, more and more Yanks rallied to help him. Soon the one-man charge was a full-scale attack. The Jap position was over-run, the last Jap on the ridge killed, and a strategic point won.

Van Wynsberghe lives at 5364 Hereford avenue.

Another Detroiter, Sergt William A. Nokes, 133 Hilldale avenue east, fought a one-man covering action which enabled his pinned-down platoon to withdraw with few casualties. Had it not been for his bravery, the platoon would have fallen victim to a Jap ambush.

COVERED RETREAT

The action took place against a Jap line on broken Yamashita Line in the northeast corner of Luzon. Nokes tied a piece of rope to a light machine-gun, forming a sling, and stood up in the face of heavy enemy fire, shooting to cover the temporary American retreat. His gun silenced two pillboxes.

Then, spotting a Jap patrol of 30 men trying to flank his outfit, he wheeled and sprayed them. Six died on their feet, several other Japs were killed or wounded as the patrol beat a hasty retreat. Through it all, Nokes suffered only an eyebrow scratch.

He kept up his covering fire until the last Yank had withdrawn, then rejoined his outfit.

Disregard for his own safety in laying a vital communications wire through heavy Jap fire won the Bronze Star Medal for Corp. Max Reynolds of Pinckney, Livingston County.

Another outstate soldier, Sergt. Erwin Burdick of Sidney, Montcalm County, took his patrol within 35 yards of a Jap strongpoint, then jumped to his feet and led an attack. Six Japs were killed.

FOUGHT WITH DISTINCTION

Other Detroiters who "fought with distinction" in the "Americal" Division included: Tech. Sergt. Fred Stroup, 21802 Moross road, who landed with the first assault waves to hit the island and later participated in a nine day reconnaissance patrol deep behind enemy lines.

Staff Sergt. Max Staniszewski, 3885 Evaline avenue, Hamtramck; Sergt. Hugo M. Cleva, 3326 Edsel avenue South; Corp. Elmer A. Nycholas, 8025 Manila avenue; Tech 5th Gr. Earl C. Enochs, 8115 Radford avenue; Pfc. Kenneth V. VanderMolen, 2662 Manistique avenue; Pfc. Duane A. Ryan, 4874 Dickerson avenue, and Pfc. Gerd G. Schaefer, 15774 Riopelle street, all of whom were in on the final "round-up" of Japs.

Other outstate soldiers mentioned in the dispatches were: Pvt. Paul F. Frust, Caledonia; Pfc. Charles W. Furniss, Leroy; Staff Sergt. Robert F. Oberlin, Bannister, an Sergt. Henry L. Wellman, Lake George.

My parents saved this clipping from the Detroit News. I don't know when it appeared. It is very interesting to note how they list the Americal Division as the 33rd Infantry. The Division never had a number just the word, Americal Division.

The 33rd Infantry Division did fight in the South Pacific but they were stationed in the Hawaiians Islands.

This is the only time that I had my name in newsprint, so look very carefully, and maybe you will find it.

I am surprised at the listing of PFC Duane A. Ryan and PFC Gerd G. Schaefer as they were in the same squad with me on Cebu.

I noticed that they printed my name as PFC Kenneth V. VanderMolen. While in Chicago during my induction, I first noticed the "V" middle initial. It should have been "W".

Cebu Battle Costs Japs 5,000 Dead

Island Group Ours, Says M'Arthur

MANILA, April 21.—(P)—With the death of 5,000 Japanese on Cebu Island, Gen. MacArthur announced today the "virtual conclusion" of the Central Philippines campaign.

Liberated in this 33,000 square mile Visayan islands area are more than 6,400,000 Filipinos.

This leaves the "only remaining enemy armies completely ir

OUR LOSSES LIGHT

Our losses in this campaign were extraordinarily light, due largely to the enemy's continued inability to diagnose our point of attack and to understand our local tactics of combat," MacArthur declared.

Twenty-fourth Division troops which landed on Mindanao Tuesday widened their beachheads at Malabang and Parang and by Thursday had thrust 16 miles inland along the Cotabato-Davao road to the town of Manuangan, north of the immense Libungan marsh.

15-MILE ADVANCE

From Malabang, U. S. troops pushed 15 miles northeast to the shores of Lake Lanao, a former Moro stronghold, 700 feet above sea level.

From Cebu came reports of a dramatic end to the sharp cleanup battle Thursday, with Japanese forces dispersing under the impact of heavy blows on flank and rear by Americal division troops.

Five thousand dead were left on the battlefield and considerable equipment was captured.

171

These clippings in the local newspapers were there to "inform" the American people how the war was going. General MacArthur was a great one for announcing great victories before they happened. He wanted nothing but good news printed in the papers.

The first line in this communicate on page 171, is dated 21 April . He announces the death of 5,000 Japanese on Cebu Island and the "virtual conclusion" of the Central Philippine campaign. It's no wonder that the folks back home thought that we would be home as the war was ending.

Where was I on 21 April? I believe we were still on the eastern shores of Cebu, trying to push the enemy back into the hills. I never saw General MacArthur on the Island of Cebu, although I understood that he did fly over Cebu to get a look at how the war was going.

On Sunday morning, 26 August 1945 I returned to the Island of Cebu.

My stay on Leyte was mostly in the TACLOBAN DROME area. If you can locate the City of Tacloban, you will note an arrow pointing out the Hospital and farther south you can locate the Replacement Depot. Going farther south, find Highway 2 and the city of PALO. Base K was located here. That's where all the action was planned.

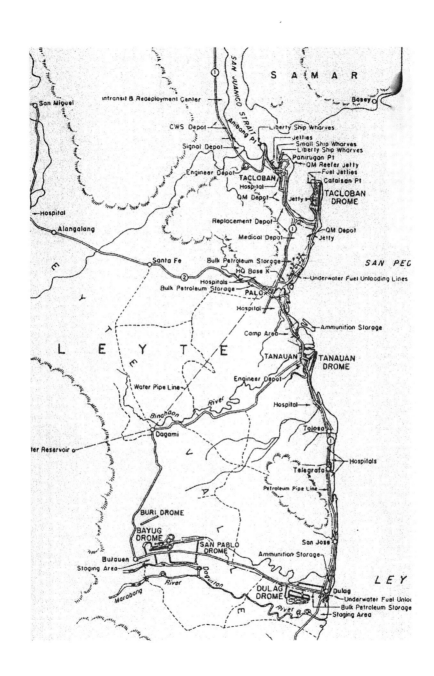

Chapter XIII
CEBU AGAIN
August 1945

The LST landed right up on the beach and opened the forward doors, dropping its ramp. I walked out onto the dry ground of Cebu. My lieutenant was nowhere to be found, I was on my own. I noticed some soldiers and asked them where the 182nd Infantry might be. They informed me that our Division had gone through some intense training for the invasion of Japan. The Americal Division was designated to be the first wave to hit the beach on the invasion. I was glad that the war was at an end. I had many questions to ask these soldiers but that had to wait, as I wanted to find my unit.

All seemed so different since I left Cebu in June. It was like I was in a different world. There wasn't any enemy action. I could walk down the highway without any fear. I understand that on 1 July, my division had been transferred from Lieutenant General Robert L. Eichelberger's Eighth Army to the command of Lieutenant General Walter Krueger's Sixth Army. The reason for the change was the upcoming invasion of Japan was to take place in early November.

All the time I was in the hospital from June to August, I was unaware of what was going on. I understand from reading and asking questions that Company "G" were in classrooms, attending lectures on how to understand the Japanese. Strict censorship was imposed but most GIs understood what was coming next, the invasion of Japan.

I became aware much later on my return from Leyte that I would have been assigned to the Americal Division. I was glad of that. I was hoping that I could find my buddies, if they were still around.

The first plan called *Operation Olympic* was to be the invasion of Kyushu Islands. I would have been attached to XI Corps with the 43rd Infantry Division, 1st Cavalry Division and the Americal Division on that trip.

175

After landing on the Japanese soil and seeing the amount of material that Japan had stockpiled for such an invasion, I know now that would have been a one-way trip.

Major General William H. Arnold, Commanding General of the Americal Division was instructed to locate the Japanese Army and inform them that Japan had surrendered. This was going to be a real problem, because the Japanese Army did not know that the Emperor of Japan had surrendered. General Arnold ordered several thousand leaflets prepared, and on 17 August, dropped over areas where troops were known to be hiding. The Japanese did not at first believe his message and called it propaganda. On 18 August, more than three thousand leaflets were printed and dropped along the northwest coast of Cebu.

16 August 1945

TO: All Japanese on Cebu.

This is to inform you that Japanese forces throughout the world have surrendered by order of his August Majesty the Emperor of Japan. On 14 August 1945, it was officially proclaimed that Japanese wherever they might be, would lay down their arms having realized that peace was the only solution to a hopeless cause. Now that your Emperor has come to an honorable agreement we feel that you on CEBU should come to us as we have always wanted you to.

In the past some of you have taken advantage of our guarantees of fair and kind treatment. Now that all hostilities have ceased, lay down your arms and come to us. You will be treated fairly according to the rules of Hague and Geneva Conventions.

There is one point where you can assemble and be collected: BAGSAC

Come to the above point unarmed during daylight hours waving this leaflet.

COMMANDING GENERAL AMERICAN FORCES ON CEBU.

The above leaflet was dropped by order of General Arnold,
Commanding General,
Americal Division

I have obtained some copy prints of the leaflets, which were dropped. These actions happened while I was making my way back to Cebu.

It is very interesting that in the surrender notice, General Arnold uses the phrase; You *will be treated fairly according to the rules of Hague and Geneva Conventions.*

The Japanese never signed the rules of Hague and Geneva Conventions. The name SACSAC was a village on the main costal highway but very near to the northern shores of Cebu. There was one highway that encircled the Island of Cebu. I passed through Sacsac on my way to headquarters, which was located in Liloan at this time. Liloan was at the 18.8 km highway marker.

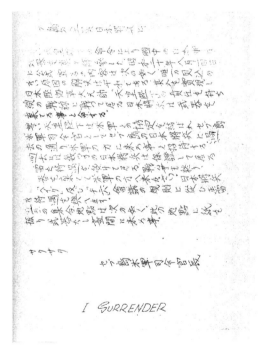

The original Japanese pamphlet shown above. The only English word "I SURRENDER" was meant for American personnel.

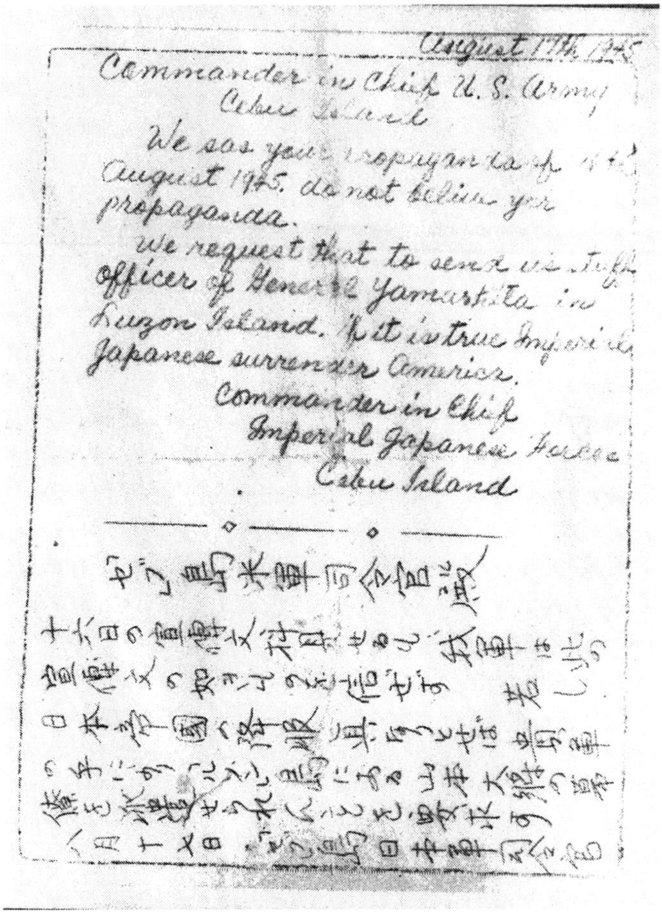

August 17th 1945

Commander in Chief U. S. Army
Cebu Island

We saw your propaganda of
August 1945. do not believe your
propaganda.

We request that to send us Staff
Officer of General Yamashita in
Luzon Island. If it is true Imperial
Japanese surrender America.

Commander in Chief
Imperial Japanese Forces
Cebu Island

Translation:
August 17th 1945

Commander In Chief U.S. Army Cebu Island.
We saw your propaganda of 16[th]August 1945; do not believe your propaganda. We request that you send to us a Staff Officer of General Yamashita in Luzon if it is true that Imperial Japanese surrender to the America.

Commander in Chief Imperial Japanese Forces   Cebu Island

178

21 August 45

TO: Commander of American Forces on Cebu

I received your kind message from 1st Lt HOSAKA, who was sent to your headquarters, at 1200 on 20 August.

I have faith in your veracity and am positively convinced that Japan has surrendered. At the same time, I wish to express my sincere thanks for the kind treatment accorded the lieutenant.

I am sending the following persons to your headquarters. They will be at the 84 kilometer road marker at 1000 on 22 August. It is requested that auto transportation be sent to that location.

Chief of Staff: Col OKABAYASHI
Staff Officer: Maj DOI
Staff Officer: Capt UEDA
Staff Officer: 1st Lt HOSAKA
NCO's: 2
Privates: 2

/s/ KATAOKA
Lt Gen
CG, Northern Cebu Forces

...so on with my journey.

Monday, 27 August I located some of my buddies from the 182nd Infantry. It was great to see guys from my outfit. They were on a mission to locate Japanese soldiers who wished to surrender. Headquarters was informed that a large group of soldiers could be found near road marker 81.3 km. The Division sent out about forty enlisted men with a Colonel in charge. Toward evening this group had made contact with a Japanese soldier who spoke English. He informed them that about 2,000 troops were ready to surrender and were located just a few miles away. This message was relayed quickly by radio to the headquarters located in Liloan. Liloan was

179

at the 18.8 km. highway marker. I remained in the area, aware of the overwhelming enemy forces just over the next hill.

The next morning there were numerous Americal troops nearby. They were all dressed up in neat suntan uniforms. They had the Americal shoulder patch insignia on their sleeves and helmets. These were not the same rag-tag outfit that I had last seen on Cebu. I observed what was taking place from where I was standing. I noticed that the Japanese soldiers were all in

military formation. Officers were in front with their swords in hand. On command, the enemy soldiers broke ranks and stacked their rifles. Machine guns and heavy weapons were then stacked in neat piles along with boxes of ammunition. The Japanese solders were now disarmed.

The date is 28 August 1945. The Japanese have put down their weapons and as we know from history the surrender was signed on 2 September 1945 in Tokyo Bay, Japan.

Leading the officers was Major General William H. Arnold. I was on the other side of the road but had a good view of what was happening. This was a part of history, which I will never forget.

The Japanese on Cebu wanted to surrender and so General Arnold asked General MacArthur what he was to do with over 2,667 enemy prisoners of war. MacArthur reply was to do nothing but send all the weapons on to Manila. General Arnold's reply was that he had given all the weapons to his soldiers. I don't want to use the word "souvenirs", but I guess that is what it was.

The Japanese prisoners seemed to be in good shape. Some of the troops were located on the Island of Samar and came over to Cebu at eventide. Many of the soldiers were carrying white boxes with them, which we found out later were the remains of comrades who had died while fighting on this island. These remains were being returned to their homeland. I counted at least six nurses in this group of prisoners.

The soldiers were loaded onto trucks and returned to Cebu City. General Arnold had set up this camp just for these internees. Our camp looked about the same with tents all in neat straight rows. When I finally got to camp, I was assigned to one of the tents as viewed above. Within just a few days, these troops were on their way home to Japan. They left before we did.

The Japanese Lieutenant General Kataoka unbuckled his Samurai sword and gave it to the Americal General William Arnold.

Japanese rifles and Samurai swords become "available" as souvenirs.

The trip back to Cebu City wasn't a very pleasant trip for most of these prisoners of war. As the trucks went through the cities along the highway, rocks and garbage were thrown at them. We had placed one guard in every truck and they were hit with some of that debris as well.

After leaving the surrender area, I started walking along the highway to where I was told I might find Company "G". An empty truck drove by and stopped for me. I accepted a ride to Liloan,

Approaching the town, I jumped off the truck and started to walk down the road to locate my buddies. I was hopeful that I would find my brother Gordon.

Many years later, after some communications with Gordon, he related that he saw me walking along the road and then called to me. What we did the next couple of days I am not sure. I did know that we were not going to stay too long on Cebu.

On Thursday 30 August the 77th Infantry Division landed on Cebu to take over the operation of the Americal Division. Our Division was now relieved of all responsibilities on the Island of Cebu. It was later reported that over 9,800 Japanese soldiers had surrendered during this the last week of August.

Many years after the war, while living at Breton Woods in Grand Rapids, Michigan, I had the privilege of meeting the late General Arnold's wife. I also was introduced to one of his sons. I had quite a long talk with them.

Lieutenant-General William Howard Arnold (1901-1976) was the Commanding General of the Americal Division. After the war he was Commanding General of US Forces in Austria and later was Commanding General 5th Army. His son related to me the trouble that his father had with General MacArthur about the surrender on Cebu. I was given a copy of a top-secret note between MacArthur and Arnold. MacArthur did not want the surrender on the field. The Cebu surrender was not to be scheduled before the formal surrender, which was planned for on or after 2 September. It was to be called a Non-Formal Surrender. The secret message which is

185

just part of a whole communication between Generals MacArthur and Arnold is as follows:

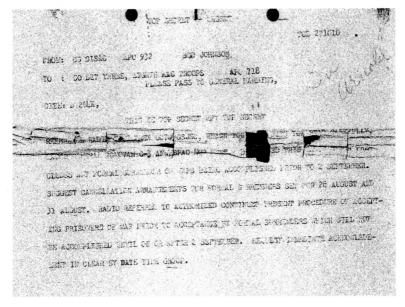

TOP SECRET URGENT

FROM: CG SISAC   APO 932   SGD JOHNSON
TO: CO DET THREE, EIGHTH AAC TROOPS   APO 718
              PLEASE PASS TO GENERAL HARDING,
CITE: D 264X,
              THIS IS TOP SECRET RPT TOP SECRET

(some words here are unreadable due to fold in paper)

PRECLUDES ANY FORMAL SURRENDER OF JAPS BEING ACCOMPLISHED PRIOR TO 2 SEPTEMBER. SUGGEST CANCELLATION ARRANGEMENTS FOR FORMAL SURRENDERS SET FOR 28 AUGUST AND 31 AUGUST. RADIO REFERRED TO AUTHORIZED CONTINUED PRESENT PROCEDURE OF ACCEPTING PRISONERS OF WAR PRIOR TO ACCEPTANCE BY FORMAL SURRENDERS WHICH WILL NOT BE ACCOMPLISHED UNTIL ON OR AFTER 2 SEPTEMBER.   REQUEST IMMEDIATE ACKNOWLEDGMENT IN CLEAR BY DATE TIME GROUP.

Now you can understand why so many Japanese swords have shown up in the United States, it seems that General Arnold let everyone take one home.

Early on Friday, 31 August I headed to the beach to board a ship; its destination would be Japan. I was issued another rifle and other necessary equipment. On the beach, I noticed a group of Red Cross Volunteers who were giving out coffee and doughnuts to soldiers waiting to board. To my amazement, one was Faye Anderson, who I had helped while I was in the hospital on Leyte. We were all standing around with time on our hands; I told this group that I was going over and give a kiss to one of those lovely beauties. "No way," was the reply from a few, but some dared me to do it. I was ready for that challenge.

I walked up to Faye Anderson; she was surprised and happy to see me. I told her of the bet that I had made with the other guys. I asked if I could give her a kiss to impress my fellow comrades. (My soldier friends did not know that I was acquainted with Faye). She replied by throwing her arms around me and giving me a real passionate kiss. The other guys just yelled, hooted and wished they were in my place. My face was really red because I didn't believe that she would favor me with such an affectionate hug. I always thought that Faye was sweet and now she proved it. Then it happened. These fellows decided that I would be the first one to kiss a Japanese young lady. Some were even betting money. I had a lot to live up to.

At 0925 we started to board the APA-134, USS Bland. By 1200 this vessel recorded seventy-eight officers and 1,240 EM on board. We were headed out to sea and bound for Japan. Our convoy carried the American Division using nineteen transports, two liberty ships with a total of 1,112 officers and 17,733 EM. This was the first time that our Division was at full strength.

My memory is a complete blank on the details leaving the Island of Cebu for Japan. My brother Gordon recounts that as we boarded the ship, each of us were required to call out our name and serial number to check if we were on the sailing list.

As I approached the gang-plank I called out, "Private First Class Kenneth Vander Molen, 36916144."

The officer could not find my name of the list. He doubled checked his list and said, "There must be a mistake, I have the name Gordon Vander Molen but no Kenneth. Two people can't have the same name." Claiming there must have been a mistake in the orders, I was told to move on board.

Just before departing Cebu I was issued summer khaki, or in Army language, suntans. These were a light yellow color that looked better than the olive drab color of our fatigues. I also received new combat boots. One of the strangest pieces of new issue was sunglasses.

Chapter XIV
JAPAN
September – October 1945

We took our last look of Cebu as our ship steamed out of the harbor bound for the Island of Japan. The distant hills slowly faded away. My thoughts lingered on the events of the past five months. Some of my buddies sacrificed their lives for this victory. This was a bittersweet reflective moment.

Life aboard ship was more lighthearted than when we first came across on the USS GENERAL BUTNER, which seemed like a thousand years ago. Our food was better and we were given freedom to roam aboard ship. We were able to be on deck at night and could see other ships in the distance. However, this was no pleasure cruise, as we had to keep all of our equipment in good order. We cleaned our rifles and received instructions in our duties as occupation troops.

One curious thing I noticed was that most of the old timers were not with us. All the guys who fought on Guadalcanal had remained in Cebu and their ranks were being filled with replacements. Most of these newcomers were still wet behind the ears, now we were the real veterans. Later we heard that the fellows who remained on Cebu were shipped back home while we sailed for occupation duty in Japan.

I had never received one day of pay while overseas. I had a large sum of American money coming to me. The company clerk interviewed each of us regarding the pay we had accumulated. The Army pays us on the 30th of the month provided we signed the payroll on the 15th. If you do not sign the payroll, you do not get paid. I did have some Japanese money on me because I seized currency from dead soldiers. We were informed that our "Japanese money" would be of no good because the United States Government was going to issue occupation money to the troops. Many GIs threw the bogus money over the side, but many more used the worthless money in card games. The smart ones kept the bills when we landed on Japanese soil, as we were paid in Japanese currency. Never trust what the Army tells you as the truth.

There are quite a few interesting facts about our campaign on Cebu that can be found in the book, *UNDER THE SOUTHERN CROSS by Captain Francis D. Cronin*. This book recalls all of the action of the Americal Division. Please excuse me for boasting about the activities of my Division but it is important for people to know what we did.

The intelligence-gathering unit is called Division G-2. They were able to report that the operation against the enemy had been successful. Reports showed that 9,958 Japanese had been killed or found dead by the Americal Division units. In addition, 380 prisoners of war were taken, representing the largest number taken in any of the Americal's campaigns. Up to 30 June, our entire Division had suffered the staggering total of 10,566 casualties. Of these, 2,427 were actual battle casualties; the remaining 8,139 included officers and men who fell before the onslaught or recurrent malaria, yellow jaundice, dysentery, skin rashes and other tropical diseases. Because all required treatment, often evacuation and replacement, these men too were casualties of the campaign. The fighting on Cebu itself brought death to 9,321 Japanese during the 96-day campaign. To attain this result, men of the Americal killed an average of 97 enemies per day.

On the morning of 2 September the USS Battleship MISSOURI, anchored peacefully in the harbor of Tokyo Bay. At the direction of General MacArthur, Baron Mamora Shigemitsu, acting on behalf of the Emperor of Japan and the Japanese Government moved forward to a table on which was placed the documents of surrender. Bending over, he slowly affixed his signature to the documents. Following this, on behalf of the Japanese Imperial General Headquarters, General Yoshijiro Umezu stepped forward and signed quickly. The time was 9:04 a.m. Japan has now surrendered!

General MacArthur moved forward, sat down and signed the instrument of surrender. It was now 9:08 a.m. and it was official. This was now VJ-Day!

On the 9th of September our convoy entered the waters of Japan. It was a beautiful day as we approached land and entered the waterways to Tokyo. I was standing on the deck looking out toward the shoreline and could see the many gun emplacements. All of these large guns were pointed toward our ship and I was glad that the war had ended. If we had to invade Japan, these very guns would now be firing upon this ship and we would have been blown out of the water. I am very glad that President Truman gave the go ahead order to drop the atomic bomb. We would have suffered many casualties approaching the soil of Japan.

While I was looking over the countryside my sunglasses slipped off from my nose. I moved my hand up quickly to replace them on my nose but hit the glasses instead and they fell into the harbor of Japan. Maybe someday I will go back to Tokyo and see if my sunglasses are still in the deep waters of Tokyo Bay.

Shortly, a pilot boat arrived along side our ship; a rope ladder was dropped so the Japanese pilot could come aboard. His duties were to direct our ship through the minefield and safely into the dock. One of the new replacements standing next to me was surprised to see this Japanese and wanted to get a better look at him. I really wasn't interested in seeing what he looked like, but was praying that we could trust him. All he had to do was to direct our ship into a mine and blow us all up. I still did not trust the Japanese people even up to this point. Our ship was guided safely along the wharf; we tied up, and I (invaded) set foot on the soil of Japan without getting my feet wet.

The 182nd Infantry stayed that first night along the dock area maintaining a night patrol. Martial law was in force allowing us to shoot anything or any person who moved after 6:00 p.m. Our rifles were loaded and we were ready to use force, if needed. The Eighth Army Headquarters was set up near the dock area. Some of these fellows who had never been in combat wanted to see what the Japanese people looked like but more likely to pick up Japanese women. We were not allowed to contact any women but it seems like the GIs from Headquarters never heard that order. After a few drinks of Saki, these "heroes" would wander into the streets disobeying the order of curfew. We had orders to shoot and we did. We usually aimed high and they really took off, back to their quarters.

The next morning, we boarded trucks and left the city area and headed inland toward Fuchinobe Station. From our perspective we could view the landscape and the people. I saw many working in small garden plots, as we drove by they looked up at us in wonderment. No doubt we were the first Americans they had ever seen. I was not aware of any young people only older couples and many small children. It seemed like a whole generation of young people was missing. The truck drivers were getting more nervous the farther we got away from the large population of the city. They had heard rumors that our convoy was going to be attacked and did not care to go any farther. Since we were just short of our destination, we unloaded from the trucks and proceeded toward some buildings in the distance. The trucks turned around and retreated to the safety of the city.

Division Headquarters moved its command post to Fuchinobe Station, northwest of the dock area and set up in the Sagami Ordnance School land Arsenal. The Americal now became the first full Infantry Division to reach Japan by ship after VJ-Day. Moving to our assigned area of occupation the Americal Division was to cover more than 1,650 square miles of land, approximately six hundred square miles greater than the land area of Rhode Island.

Our Company took over one of the buildings in the Engineering College Complex. We entered the building only to find rodents had taken over the place. There was a large drill area in front of the building so we set up our tents for the first night. We did not sleep in large type tents but in our two man pup tents. For some of the new guys it was a rough night, but I slept well. I guess I was hardened to sleeping on the ground. This did bring back memories of my days in the ROTC at Southeastern High School. We had field day trials and one of the requirements was setting up our two man pup tents. This was the last time while in service that I slept on the ground.

The next morning we scrutinized our new home. This was a two-story building resembling a dormitory. There were rooms along one side of the building while the other side was left open. In this large area was the usual tub for bathing. According to Japanese custom the officers bathed themselves first in the tub, and then after they had left, the enlisted men were allowed to take a bath. Of course they used the same water the men used before them. I surely didn't like that system, as I preferred a shower. We immediately set our goal on getting showers set up. Large empty containers were set on a frame and from this was attached a showerhead. We filled the container with hot water and stood underneath, pulled the rope and down came refreshing hot water over our bodies. This was better than the Japanese tubs. We smashed the tubs inside the buildings to make more room for tables and chairs. The building was scrubbed clean and we even washed the windows. This was going to be our new home away from home.

The rooms along the side were about 14 feet by 14 feet in size. They all had windows facing the drill field and flagpole. Four GIs were assigned to each room, now we had a place to put our rifles and duffel bags. We were getting to look more like an Army of occupation. Each morning at reveille we stood at attention while the American flag was run up the flagpole and the band played the National Anthem. We did the same at night as the flag was lowered this was called retreat. Things were becoming more "chicken" as we were required to salute all officers.

While getting acquainted to this new life style, whom did I see, but Jack Morton heading in my direction. I hadn't seen Jack since I left Cebu in early June. I walked up to Jack and yelled, "Hi Jack, you son-of-a-gun", or maybe words along that line.

He looked at me and said that his name was Lieutenant Jack Morton and that as an officer I was to salute him.

The hardest task at this time for me was saluting Lieutenant Morton. He taught me all about combat and how to survive; now I was required to address him as Lieutenant Morton instead of Jack. It was at that very moment that he recognized me and threw his arms around me and I got a big bear hug. This was the first and only time that I was hugged by an officer.

Every morning Japanese farmers would pull up in a wagon and empty our latrines using a long handled bamboo shovel to empty them. They wanted our human waste for fertilizing their garden crops. That was the reason why we were not allowed to eat any fresh produce from local farmers. Most of the produce from these farmers looked good but this was not the time to acquire diarrhea. When we heard the sound of the wagon wheels on the dry ground some one would always yell out, "Here comes the honey wagon."

The water supply was from an artesian well that ran all the time. It was cold, fresh and clean. With this water supply we were required to shave. Some shaved using the cold water but most of us heated the water. There was a small propane tank in each room to heat our water.

The mess hall was close to our barracks and we were getting into a routine. I was wondering when I was going home but we still had a job to do as occupation troops. Each morning groups of soldiers were loaded unto trucks and sent out into the countryside to locate the military and industrial installations. We were always on the lookout for weapons. Whenever I was out on such a mission we never found anything unusual, but there was one incident that stands out in my memory.

Our group had a lieutenant in charge; we loaded on to trucks and headed for a town to explore the possibilities of locating weapons. We disembarked just outside the town and proceed to check building by building. Usually two or three GIs were together. We made no move to smash down doors but were very careful in how we conducted ourselves. If we came in view of the Japanese civilians they would bow their heads and looked at the ground. We could not talk with them as we were ordered to have no communication with civilians, besides, we did not know their language. It would have been interesting to speak with these people because they did seem very nice. Civilians were different than the soldiers we had encountered on Cebu. These civilians were the innocents; they just wanted to get on with the business of living.

When we were about to leave this area, the lieutenant noticed a building that had not been checked. The lieutenant and I walked over to investigate what was inside. It was a school with a classroom of children around the age of five to nine years. The teacher was sitting at his desk and the children were reading their books like any typical classroom. As we entered the teacher stood up respectfully and with good English welcomed us to his classroom. While the lieutenant questioned him, I walked around the room looking at the work the children were doing at their desks. I viewed the drawings that were displayed on the walls surrounding the classroom. They were not the pictures of houses, farms, families or nature studies but war pictures. They showed Japanese aircraft shooting down American planes. The teacher was embarrassed and wanted to take the pictures down immediately. We had a great officer in charge and he told the frightened teacher that the pictures could remain where they were. His reason for doing so was that these children didn't understand war or the true meaning of the pictures they had drawn. I am sure that the teacher was really relieved to hear that. The lieutenant then asked if the children knew how to play volleyball. With a very positive answer to that question we spent the rest of that day playing volleyball with the class. It was great to see children smiling. The teacher was most surprised at our friendship with the children. Just two months before we were killing their fathers.

On 15 September 1945 the Military Vicar of Catholic Chaplains of the Armed Forces said Mass for the Catholic servicemen stationed at Fuchinobe. It was the Most Rev. Francis J. Spellman, who later became a Cardinal. I did not attend that service but if I had known that later he would become a Cardinal, I would have gone, maybe!

We had a small Japanese radio in our room and could tune in broadcasts from the Armed Service Radio Network. I remember hearing the Army/Navy football game. I am sure that the Army team won that year. While sitting on the window ledge overlooking the drill field, I began to notice that the walls seemed to be moving back and forth. A glass fell from the table smashing against the floor. I saw the flagpole sway slightly even when there was no movement of wind. It was very quiet as these strange things were happening. Then I realize that we had just witnessed an earthquake. It was a moving experience!

On 24 September, the 97th Infantry Division arrived in Japan and became the first Infantry Division to reach the Pacific from the European Theater of Operation. They were to replace the 43rd Infantry Division as that division was scheduled for movement as a unit to the United States for deactivation.

The point system went into effect. This was the method used to determine which veteran would be shipped home. Servicemen received one point per month for service in the states and two points for each month overseas. We received five points for each wound, five points for each battle star and five points for any medals that were received for combat bravery. Men with high points from the Americal Division were transferred to the 43rd Infantry Division and the low point men from the 43rd were sent to the Americal Division for continued service in Japan.

When I added up my service time, I had twenty-one points and I needed 85 points to go home. I was going to be in Japan for another five years!

Something happened that would change my Army experience completely. I was called into the orderly room and told to report to the first sergeant. He had studied my service record and noticed that I could type. He informed me that Regimental Headquarters needed clerk/typists. Why did they wait so long to find out that I could type? I was transferred to Service Company. No more drilling, no more looking for weapons, no more marching, no more standing retreat and no more eating with all of my former comrades. I moved all of my meager belongings into the building housing the Service Company.

I was assigned my own glass covered office desk and typewriter. The sergeant in charge introduced me to the GIs around the office and gave instructions on how to do things the right way, the wrong way and the Army way. There were about twenty-five GIs

196

assigned to this office. Every one seemed to have a pin-up girl under the glass on their desks. I needed a pin-up girl that I could call my own so I found a picture in a magazine of a pretty young girl by the name of Linda Van Loon. Since I was Dutch, Linda Van Loon was going to be my pin-up girl.

We did not have computers in those days so anytime a soldier was being transferred to another Division, his orders had to be typed out completely. We used stencils and printed out orders on sheets of paper that were 8½ by 14 inches. These were run through the stencil copy machine usually in triplicates. Each morning after mess we were given the names of service men being transferred to other outfits. No one moved to any location until his orders were cut and delivered.

With many guys wanting to go home and the Army wanting to send everyone home as fast as possible, we were kept very busy. I mentioned to my sergeant that Gordon was also a typist and we sure could use another man. He didn't hesitate transferring him to our section. Gordon started to work in the same office but in the finance section.

Page 197 shows the Morning Report that on 5 October 1945, Gordon and I were transferred to Service Company. If you look close you can see that Gordon has ASR 28, while my ASR is 23. These are the points that we received at this time for movement on going home. Gordon received the extra five points because of his being awarded the Purple Heart.

My new circumstances allowed me to write home more often. Our mail was not being censored. I resumed my correspondence with Mary Margaret Liddane. I really cared for her and looked forward to seeing her whenever I returned from Japan. I had her graduation picture in my duffel bag for safekeeping. I was falling in love. She promised that she would write to me while I was overseas. I was really flying on cloud nine and I was in love with this really nice girl. She had red hair.

There were advantages for me to be a clerk in Regimental Headquarters. We heard the latest gossip because we were in the building where all the action took place. We saw generals come and go. Reports and promotions were cleared through this office.

During the Cebu campaign a newly appointed Second Lieutenant named Verl F. Scott was assigned as platoon leader of "C" Company. During the Japanese occupation a newly appointed First Lieutenant named Verl F. Scott was assigned as the Regimental Personnel Officer.

Upon entering any new country the black market seemed to come alive. Soldiers are given cigarettes and beer. If you didn't smoke or drink, we could sell these items to the local population for any amount the traffic would bear. To stop the money from the black market getting back to the United States; enlisted men were allowed only $50.00 each month to send home. This was done by means of U.S. Postage Savings or money orders. If a person had more than the allotted amount of cash to send home we needed the authorization of the personnel officer. Lieutenant Scott usually kept a few pre-signed slips in his desk and if he wasn't around we were authorized to dispense them. Some GIs had more money to send home than the allowed $50.00 because of a good hand at poker. It was quite easy for some fellows in the Regimental Office to authorize a larger amount and sign Verl F. Scott's name to the request. A person could make a little extra himself by doing this. Now, I didn't say that I would do anything like that, did I?

One of my tasks was to fill out the necessary forms, which would allow a service man to be sent home earlier. I worked with the Red Cross in regard to servicemen who had to go home on emergency leave. This was usually because of a parent who died or child being seriously sick. Farmers needed help in bringing in the fall crop; so many farm hands were given an early discharge. The Red Cross would request that these servicemen be released from service duty. My instructions were to find out what he was doing and how important his job was and if his task could be taken over by another GI. We had many letters that had to be sent from one unit to another to expedite this request. In order to save space on the request we would type on the bottom of the letter the following: "Request acknowledged receipt by endorsement thereon." This was one line that the Army used on all its communications between units. Sometimes there were as many as ten endorsements on one request for leave.

On 14 October, the Americal Division was listed as a Category IV unit and this meant redeployment to the United States for prompt de-activation. The Americal Division was going home! Despite the official word much more work remained to be done before the division could be relieved. More enemy materials had to be destroyed. The vast stores of ammunitions that the Americal Division had collected had to be turned over to the U.S. Navy for disposal. Much of this was placed on board ships and dumped at sea in waters at least three hundred feet deep.

We were all given another Typhoid immunization shot on 18 October 1945.

199

According to the latest rumor received from XI Corps Headquarters, the 1st Cavalry Division was set to begin the progressive relief of the Americal Division in Kanagawa Prefecture on 25 October. The relief of the last of the division troops was to be completed by the evening of 5 November. This rumor was just too good to believe!

Being in the Regimental Headquarters we were able to read most of the communications regarding the deployment of Infantry Divisions. More troops wanted out than we had ships to return them home. I surely did not believe that the Americal Division would go home by the 5 November date.

Toward the end of October I attended a meeting in a large indoor theater where officers were trying to sell the idea of enlisting into the Regular Army for just one more year. They promised us that we would be home for Christmas. Their message was to have us sign up now and take a ninety-day furlough. Most of the fellows had the points to get home without signing up for more duty time. There were many of us who figured that we would be in Japan for at least another year as the occupation force. I wanted to see what they were selling so I secured a copy of the order.

The requirements called for us to have been overseas for at least nine months and assigned to a combat unit to qualify. I took the copy back to my office and read it over very carefully. We had only two days in which to sign up for this GOOD deal. I read the small print and it said that I would have to serve the one year enlistment plus furlough time. I could take thirty days if I wanted. The enlisting officer did not say that to all the troops. He wanted every enlisted man to sign up for ninety days. I talked it over with Gordon and we both decided to enlist for one year with a thirty-day furlough. We went back to see the enlistment officer and signed up for one year in the Regular Army, plus the thirty days. Was it a good decision? Only time will tell. At least now we knew when we would be out of the service.

This is the only photo taken of me while overseas in Japan,
September 1945.

Chapter XV
GOING HOME
November 1945 – January 1946

On 25 September 1944, I was *drafted* and assigned into the (AUS) Army of the United States. If I had *volunteered* I would have been assigned into the (RA) Regular Army. On Wednesday 31 October 1945, as per REG ARMY AR 615, CONVIENIENCE OF THE GOVT CIR 76 HQ USAFRAC 9/2/45, I volunteered to serve in the Regular Army.

Why did I enlist or volunteer to be part of the Regular Army now? When I was drafted in September of '44 the term of service was for the duration of the war plus six months. History told me that the First World War didn't end officially until around 1930. I have only twenty three points and I needed eighty five points to be discharged. By enlisting now my discharge date will be 1 December 1946. During this special re-enlisting period most GIs signed up for the ninety day leave, but my brother Gordon and I signed up for only thirty days. Did we make the right choice? It will be shown later that we had.

There are some advantages of being in the Regular Army. The Army pays the Regular Army first and then the draftees. They pay first by rank, then name. A draftee named Private First Class Kenneth Vander Molen would be one of the last to get paid. As a member of the Regular Army I could be buried in Arlington Cemetery. I would still be getting my extra $10.00 a month for the Combat Infantryman's Badge and twenty-five cents each month would be taken out of my pay for Old Soldiers' Home Benefit.

I was kept very busy in the Regimental Office of the 182nd Infantry. I did have an occasion to visit the nearby towns. My responsibilities did not give me time to visit Tokyo or any other large city. I knew that several of the fellows in our outfit were able to visit the atom bomb blast site of Hiroshima and Nagasaki.

There were two divisions from the European Theater of Operation heading our way that really created a problem. These fellows had more discharge points then we did, so most remained on the ship and were transported back to the states. My time, as I mentioned, before was spent filling out forms.

Soldiers going home had to have their duffel bags checked by the officer in charge of embarking. This was to prevent soldiers from taking home items that they may have stolen or looted from Japanese civilians. Also, there were many Japanese pistols, which had been taken from enemy corpses and the possible danger of alcoholic "Sake" being smuggled into the States. It was permitted to take one battle sword and flag. A few GIs were able to smuggle Japanese pistols into the States.

On 4 November, the USS SEA WITCH moved out into Tokyo Bay and the first of the Americal Division troops were on their way home. In the next two weeks I typed up the orders for the rest of the Division. I could say that I was the last one to turn off the lights at Regimental Headquarters.

On Sunday, 18 November 1945, I boarded the USS GENERAL ERNST and departed the shores of Japan. We were finally heading in the right direction. I remember looking to the western skyline and seeing Mt. Fuji in all its glory. Japan slowly drifted away but for the longest time Mt. Fuji could be seen on the horizon. This was a glorious ending to our occupation.

The seas were blue and calm but I was excited. I was going home. I recall very little of this home bound trip except that they put out a ship's newspaper. It was very informative as they reported the distance we had traveled. On one day we were very close to the Aleutians Islands. It was cold out on deck at night but few complained; most of the fellows just wanted to be free to walk around. It was quite different than when we came over. Now there were lights on the ship and the guns were covered up. We were not required to do any details aboard ship.

On the evening of 29 November we entered Puget Sound. In the distance we could see a constant streak of car headlights beaming across the waterways. As I watched, it seemed so incredible that these lights were on cars driving on American soil! That was the first and most remembered view we had of the United States. We could see the sky getting brighter and brighter as we were approaching the city of Seattle. Our ship made a turn and this great city with all the bright lights seemed to be saying to us, "Welcome Home." Along the dock we saw a large sign that read, "PORT OF SEATTLE." I made it home!

The ship tied up at Pier 42 that evening, but no one slept that long night. We had to wait until morning before debarkation. I just stood on the deck and looked at the lights all night. The dawn did not come too soon for me. Early the next morning people began to appear near the gangplank and we rushed to the rail to yell messages to them. Some asked if they would call their parents, sweethearts or wives. Much money was thrown down to the dock so those messages could be sent informing loved ones of their safe arrivals. An announcement on the PA system instructed us to remain below decks until our units were called for debarking but we wanted to see the action and refused to go below. The captain stopped the debarking until the main deck was clear. Some GIs refused to move from the railing and it took a stream of water from the fire hoses to encourage them to get below deck. In a matter of a few hours our unit was called topside and I made my way down the gangplank and on to solid American soil.

I walked along the dockside and boarded the waiting trucks. It was a real effort to climb into these trucks. Before leaving Japan we were issued our OD's (olive drab) winter type clothing. These were of wool material and much heavier than the suntans that we wore during the Japanese occupation. We now had on the wool overcoat and that made it hard to climb into the truck. It was chilly outside and the warmth of this heavy clothing was necessary. We sat along either side of the truck and everyone seemed very quiet but I'm sure that all of us were impatient to get home. We drove from the dock area and headed for Ft. Lawton near Seattle.

As we entered the front gate, the sentry on duty asked if there were any Regular Army soldiers on this truck. Most of the fellows said that anyone who signed up to serve in the Regular Army was crazy and there were no crazy soldiers on this truck. Without saying a word, I slipped off the truck and reported to the sentry.

There were about five other fellows who also jumped off when I did; we were given a lot of cat calls. They thought we were crazy to love the Army so much that we would want to serve more time. The truck drove on with its occupants laughing and yelling. The sentry informed us that we were to eat in a different mess hall and would be getting our orders very shortly to start our furloughs. We headed for the barracks and then the mess hall. We were given a special color pass to get into this special mess hall. Once inside, we could order anything we wanted. We sat at tables with white tablecloths and were given any kind of food just for the asking. This would only last for one day, but I was there for most of that first day. The first item I ordered was a bottle of milk. Next was meat with plenty of fried potatoes. I had ice cream with a whole can of nuts, then more milk and ham and eggs. More and more milk. I don't believe that I drank water all the time I was in that mess hall. We slept in real beds all the next day. We had free phone calls the following day and I called my parents to inform them of my safe arrival.

I also had time to write a letter to Mary Margaret Liddane. I wrote and told her that I was now in the States and shortly would be in Detroit. I explained that I wanted some time to think things over before we met. I believe I was getting cold feet about some of the things that I had written her while overseas. It must have sounded like a "Dear John" letter. Later when I did return to Detroit and called her, she informed me that she had gotten married and was living in Ann Arbor. I was glad that happened; now I was free.

We all were given passes and I headed for the bright lights of Seattle. It was raining of course. I went to a barbershop and got a good American hair cut. I found a tailor shop and had my PFC stripes sewed on my uniform. I had an Americal Division shoulder patch and that was sewn onto my left sleeve. This was the first time I wore that emblem. I was ready to see the sights. I did not see Mt. Rainier because of the weather.

I noticed that all service men were being treated extremely well. We never paid a fare when we rode on the bus. If we were standing in line to get into a restaurant, the owner would make sure that we were put at the head of the line. There were USO facilities where everything was free to us when we entered. I suppose there were many famous people serving as USO entertainers but I can't recall meeting any of them.

On 1 December I received an enlistment allowance of $381.00 The next day the last units of the 182nd Infantry Regiment reached Seattle. I spent about five days at Ft. Lawton, Washington. We didn't have much to do as we were waiting for our paperwork to be completed. We ate well and were given liberty to leave the post. On Wednesday the 5th of December, I boarded a train bound for Michigan with a stop first at Ft. Sheridan, Illinois. We were to receive our furlough papers at Ft. Sheridan and then permitted to proceed home for our leave.

This was not a troop train but rather a civilian train going east. I was in a group of about thirty GIs; assigned to a special Pullman car. This was a combination of coach and sleeper cars. In the daytime hours they served as coach and in the evening they were transformed into sleeping compartments. It was a comfortable way to travel but somehow the train didn't seem to be going fast enough for most of us. It stopped at every small town along the way. I remembered stopping in Billings, Montana and one of the guys ran into the depot and got a map of the train schedule. We had an idea of which towns we were in and at what time we would get there. The schedule was mostly wrong. We ate in the dining car and the food was excellent. We were issued some meal tickets for food on the train and the service was great. Whenever we walked through the rest of the train, people would stop and ask us where we fought. The most stupid question was, did we know their son? I suppose everybody missed someone in the war.

It was cold going through the mountain areas but the scenery was beautiful. Most people don't appreciate their own country until they have been away from it for a period of time. That was true of my feelings as we left the mountains and the train gathered more speed. We headed toward the state of Illinois and finally stopped in Highwood, Illinois. We gathered our duffel bags and entered Ft. Sheridan. Can you imagine my surprise when I was assigned to the same barracks that I occupied when entering military service? I located the bed that I had first slept in ages ago. It seemed like a miracle that I am in the very same place where I started my "journey".

We arrived at Ft. Sheridan on Saturday 8 December. The next morning was spent getting our records up to date. This was quite a process because the clerks should have been better informed about our enlistment. I was given a copy of my enlistment and noticed that the clerk had written on my records that I was given a ninety-day furlough. I made sure that my personnel records had stated my furlough would be for thirty days and not ninety days. The clerk also went through a checklist of equipment, which were issued to me upon entering the service. I was short one fork and had to pay thirty-five cents for a replacement. They never asked about the rifle that I had left in Japan. I wonder who had to pay for that piece of equipment. I should have charged the government for all of my personnel belongings, which was in my duffel bag left behind on Leyte.

On Monday morning, 10 December I boarded a train for Detroit and home. Later that day (since my parents did not have a car) Gordon and I took a taxi and headed for 2662 Manistique. I walked up the front steps with Gordon just ahead of me. Mother and Dad were at the door to welcome us home. Tears of joy abounded. There was so much to talk over with our parents. They were obviously concerned about the wound Gordon had received and rightly so. Perhaps I was somewhat envious of the fuss they made over him. They couldn't have understood that I was also a causality of war. I had spent sixty-three days and nights in continuous combat and over eighty days in the field hospitals on Leyte. My parents were unaware of this. I made up my mind that I wouldn't say anything about what I had seen or gone through. I have kept all of these feelings within myself for many years and writing this book has helped me unburden my soul.

There were not too many of my friends around town so just what do I do with thirty days on my hands? There was no reason to go back to Southeastern High School as I was still in service. I was Regular Army and did not have to purchase any civilian clothes. They were in short supply anyway.

I attended First Christian Reformed Church on Sunday and since a lot of the servicemen were not home yet, there were young ladies waiting for a date. Gordon was going with a neighbor girl so his time was spent with her. I was somewhat free to go wherever I wanted to. One afternoon, six girls from church invited me to go with them to a bowling lane and so I escorted them. We took the streetcar as no one had a car. The fare was six cents and of course being in uniform, I did not have to pay. This was a very cheap date, six girls for six cents each. I did pay for their bowling games. The cost was fifteen cents a game. The pinsetter usually got ten cents for setting the pins, pushing the cost to twenty-five cents a game. I took each of the girls' home, gave them each a kiss goodnight. Except the last girl, Terry DeGroot, I stayed with her for a little longer. I went to her home and we did a little necking. (That is a slang word for kissing). When I got home, my Army shirt was full of lipstick. Terry had placed her head on my shoulder and strands of her hair were entangled in my service ribbons. I had a hard time telling my mother just what was going on. After going out with all of those girls from church I decided I was not ready to get involved with any girl at the present time. I was thinking seriously of staying in the military service.

I did make a trip downtown to the Hudson Department Store to look up Mary Margaret Liddane. I entered the store and had no idea which department she worked. I just walked around from floor to floor glancing over all the merchandise and trying to locate Mary Margaret. Why I never asked anybody, I will never know. While on the elevator, I happened to look in the glove department and there was Mary selling some gloves to a customer. She looked wonderful but I did not stop to talk with her. After mailing the "Dear John" letter to her, I figured she wouldn't really want to talk with me.

While attending church, we had the flag with all the service stars on it and I noticed that there was one gold star on the flag. It was for Herman Batts who was in my eighth grade class. He enlisted in the U.S. Marines and was killed on the island of Tawara. His brother Philip was also in our eighth grade class. He served in the U.S. Navy but did not see any action. There were two fellows from

209

church who were prisoners of war and quite a few who were wounded.

Remember the war scrapbook we started when I was still in high school? I located it and as I turned the pages my thoughts reflected on the events that happened after I last worked on the book. Little did I know at that time what Gordon and I would be experiencing. Dad had kept the book current. It was difficult for me to read the details of various battles. It was time to put my war experiences behind me. I closed the book with intentions of reading it sometime in the future.

For many years I thought that the books were water damaged. On one occasion many years later, I asked Gordon what had happened to the War Books, which we started and had been taken care of while we were in service. Gordon stated that the books were still at his home in Eastpointe, Michigan. I have made a few attempts to locate then.

As was my habit, I attended the Old Year Night service and then the next morning attended the New Years Day service at church. My thirty-day furlough was fast coming to an end. On the 11th of January 1946, I was to report to the Commanding General at Ft. Sheridan, Illinois. Gordon and I boarded the train and departed for Illinois. We were retracing the same route we had taken in September 1944. This photo was taken while I was home on furlough. Shortly after this I returned to active duty to be stationed at Ft. Sheridan, Illinois.

Chapter XVI
FT. SHERIDAN
January – March 1946

Gordon and I reported to Ft. Sheridan for re-assignment on 11 January 1946. This Fort is a Reception Center for newly selected draftees entering into military service. This is where they would take a battery of tests to determine what job they are best qualified to perform in the military. They entered as civilians and left as "soldiers." I entered Ft. Sheridan as Regular Army and reported for duty. The Army personnel were very confused with our arrival. We had orders to report but Ft. Sheridan didn't know how to handle our arrival. Let me explain the problem.

While in Japan, I signed up for a one-year enlistment plus furlough time. The date was 31 October 1945. Part of this enlistment was served while I was on duty overseas. I did not leave Japan until late November and started my furlough beginning on 11 December 1945. After my furlough time was up, I reported to Ft. Sheridan as ordered for re-assignment. According to Army regulations, any enlisted man with ten months left on his enlistment could not be sent overseas. They wanted men that would be overseas for at least a year. That is the reason why the enlisting officers were eager to have us sign up for a ninety-day leave. Maybe signing up for the Regular Army wasn't such a bad deal after all? It was now the Army's move.

After looking at my records, someone noticed that I was classified as a clerk/typist, which in the Army is listed as MOS-405. I was questioned a little more as to what kind of work I did while overseas in Japan. They were looking for personnel that could do typing and clerical work. They finally asked if I would be willing to be assigned to Ft. Sheridan for the duration of my enlistment.

"Yes sir," was my answer, loud and clear!

While waiting for my orders I was temporary assigned to the MPs unit at Ft. Sheridan. MP's were the Military Police on the post who carried out the orders of the Commanding General. I had experience with weapons so I was sent over to the MP's barracks. I was assigned a cot and a place to store my clothes and personal effects. Part of my uniform included a black armband that I wore on my right sleeve; it showed an MP in white letters. I was now a policeman.

My first job was to direct traffic at the Headquarters Building. I had to stand out in front and wave the jeep traffic around the building. I did not issue any tickets but just kept the traffic moving. It was fun for a while but then my arm got tired from waving it back and forth. The silly part was the civilians who wanted to have a picture taken of them standing beside me.

One evening there was a fire on the base and I had to go out and direct traffic around the fire. This put me close to where all the action was. There really is a lot of authority in that little black band with the letters MP on them.

Each afternoon two of us had to take the jeep and go to the railroad station. Our job was to guard the mail as it came off the train and transferred to our jeep for delivery to the camp. I would watch the US Postal Clerks throw the mailbags into the waiting jeep. We had to keep our eyes open for any person or persons who might want to steal the U. S. Mail. One thing wrong with this whole procedure, we never had any bullets in our guns.

I was not a regular MP therefore, I was never allowed to do anything that demanded armed force. I could not enter a bar and handcuff a drunken soldier. That was left to the official MP's.

Even though I wasn't an official Military Police, I made the most of it and played the part right to the end of my tour of duty. One night I was stationed at the main gate with orders to stop every vehicle and check out the driver and any passengers. I was instructed to ask for their Army serial number and if he did not know it, he was not allowed to leave the post. My instructions were to stop *all vehicles* and that is what I was going to do. Approaching my post at the main gate was a General's car. You can always tell a General's car by the red flags attached to each front fender. These pennants have two gold stars on a red field indicating that there was a Major General in that car. Military courtesy demands that you salute the flags even if you can't see the General in the rear. Normally you would salute the car and let the General pass through the gate. My orders were to stop *all* cars leaving the post. This General's car was leaving the post and I was going to stop him. I did. The driver stuck his head out of the front window and wanted to know by whose authority was I stopping the General's car?

I said that my orders were to stop all cars leaving the post and I didn't care if he was a General, I had my orders. I looked into the back seat and saw the Major General and he looked at me with a smile. He saw my service ribbons and knew that I was no rookie. He commended me for following my orders. I replied "Thank you, sir" saluted him and told the driver to carry on. I was in my glory that night. The other MPs on duty just laughed and could hardly wait until morning to tell the other guys that I had stopped a General's car.

On 18 January, the papers came through from Washington DC stating that Gordon and I were assigned to Ft. Sheridan. I was attached/unassigned to the Fifth Army, which was headquartered at Chicago. My direct assignment was to the Army Ground Forces Liaison Office (AGF) and I wore the shoulder patch of that organization on my left sleeve. That patch was round with three horizontally stripes of blue, white and red. I wore the Americal Division Patch on my right sleeve. This was a blue shield with four white stars forming the Constellation of the Southern Cross.

I reported to the Colonel in charge of the AGF attached at Ft. Sheridan, Illinois. My assignment would be in the records department. Future instructions would come from his second in command. This was a first lieutenant and he introduced me to the other soldiers on our group. There were twelve GIs that made up this AGF Office. I was shown to the barracks where I was to be housed. It was really a great place because I did not have to clean up the barracks; German POWs were assigned to do that task.

Our group was attached/unassigned to Ft. Sheridan. This meant that the camp supplied us with all the necessary items to live on site but all of our orders came directly from Washington DC. We were not under the control of Ft. Sheridan or of any of its officers. We were issued a Class A pass, signifying that we could leave camp at anytime and return at anytime. All other soldiers had a curfew hour to be back on base.

Our office was just a short walk from the barracks that I now called home. In about ten more months I would be out of the service. I began to like this Army life and was very seriously thinking of staying in service. I talked with Gordon about it; maybe he would also stay in for another hitch. He didn't seem too much interested in that idea. He had a girlfriend at this time and was thinking that he had enough of Army life. I wanted to stay in service and this was the first time that I had considered separating from my brother. I really didn't know how my folks would go for the idea but I would trust God to lead me in the right direction.

My assignment orders came directly from the Army Ground Forces Headquartered in Washington DC. These were transmitted by telegraph (TWX) to the AGF unit at Ft. Sheridan. These orders indicated a number of recruits that would be assigned to the United States Ground Forces. There are three branches of service that an inductee could be assigned to: the US Ground Forces, US Service Force or the US Army Air Force. The Ground Forces are the fighting units, which include the Infantry, Paratroopers, Tank Corps, Engineers and Field Artillery.

My direct orders were to assign a certain number of draftees into the Infantry. At this time there was still a need for the Infantrymen. Armed with this authority, I was directed to get the best of the incoming recruits. The other fellows in our office would then assign the remaining draftees to other units of the AGF.

When entering Ft. Sheridan, these raw recruits were issued uniforms and usually sat around until they were assigned. Before they could get into their new uniforms, the medical officer had to make one final check of these men. He was looking for any skin diseases that could be carried on to the new clothes and cause a rash. He would check if they had flat feet and the condition of their teeth. They just had a physical before they arrived but the Army

214

always did things twice. They would have another thorough check-up. Early every morning a group of about fifty men would be marched over to the warehouse where they would be getting their new Army clothes. This group would all be in this large room with benches on both sides. They carried a small duffel bag into which they would put their civilian clothes for shipment home. While these men were going into the warehouse, someone would call the doctor to come over and give his final OK. This is where I came into the picture.

I would address these fellows before the doctor came in. I would inform these recruits that a medical doctor would be coming into the warehouse for one final examination. They were to remove all of their clothes and place them into their small duffel bag that they had carried with them. Always someone would ask, "Do I have to take off ALL of my clothes?"

My further instructions to them were to stand on the benches when the doctor came into the warehouse. All recruits had a clipboard in hand with their service records to date. It indicated where they were born, their age, religion, blood type and if they had any contagious diseases. I had to explain to these troops that the doctor was an officer in the United States Army and should be treated with great respect.

At this point the fun for me would begin. I would say, "Now when the medical officer comes into this building SHE will give you your final examination." When I would say the word SHE, all kinds of words came at me. These were like, "I ain't standing naked in front of any woman," or "How come we don't have a real doctor look at us." Most of the guys were in a state of shock to think that SHE was going to look at all of these naked bodies. I would say, "Gentlemen, you are in the Army now and this Doctor is an officer and SHE is neither a male or female but an officer in the United States Army." This usually didn't set too well with some of these tough guys. I would then look out of the window and report that the Doctor coming this morning was a HE and that SHE was going to meet the group coming in the afternoon. So goes the jokes that were played on new recruits. Just before the arrival of the doctor I would shout the order, "Attention" and these raw recruits would "sort of" come to attention. They were relieved that the doctor was a HE.

I would follow the Doctor as he gave each fellow a quick check over and I mean a quick one. He would grade these fellows according to a set pattern. They were classified, as "A" if all looked good. Maybe if you were wearing glasses the doctor would mark you as a "B" and so on down the list. I was only interested in the fellows who he marked "A". If my orders for that morning called for twenty one men for the Infantry, I would look for twenty one men in the "A" grouping. I would place the letter "I" on the right hand corner of their clipboard indicating Infantry. Most of the recruits were in the "A" classification so I didn't have much of a problem getting my quota.

I liked to talk to these new guys and see just how they liked being in the Army. If a fellow would give me a "difficult" time, I would put the letter "I" on his papers, he was in the Infantry. If a group of new soldiers came in from Detroit, I would see to it that most of them did not get into the infantry. One time a group came in from Grand Rapids, and most of these guys had Dutch names. I would talk with these fellows, being Dutch myself; they were not assigned to the Infantry. I remember one wise guy by the name of Gritter; I asked him if he was Dutch, and he replied, "What's it to you?" Of course you know he went into the infantry.

After I made my selection, the rest were assigned to other branches of service. Most of these were assigned without being seen by the person assigning them. Only the Infantry was hand picked at this time. After I picked these men, our unit would cut the orders sending these men to their new assigned post. It was the same routine as September 1944 when I came into Ft. Sheridan; someone assigned me to Camp Robertson in Arkansas, now I was doing the same thing to these new draftees.

While I was working in the warehouse, I had the opportunity to get some shoulder patches of all the units that served in the Army. I should say, I borrowed the patches of units that served in the Army. Later, I put them in a box and shipped them to my home in Detroit.

216

They remained there for over forty five years. I was able to attach these patches on a large wallboard made especially for them.

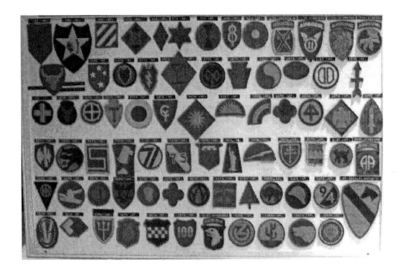

While working in this building, I became acquainted with the medical officers stationed at Ft. Sheridan. I still had trouble wearing combat boots due to jungle rot. I had one of these officers write a medical excuse for me so that I wouldn't have to wear heavy combat boots. The Army doesn't just give you an excuse without getting a reward in return. This medical officer needed a pair of low cut shoes and I knew a guy in the section of the warehouse dealing with shoes. He was a veteran from the Pacific. When I asked him for a pair of shoes for the medical officer he gave them to me with no questions asked. One good deed deserves another. The officer got his shoes and I got my medical excuse.

Life was good at Ft. Sheridan. I would play baseball on weekends. I did write letters to my parents but I admit I could have written more often. It was easier to make a phone call. I also wrote letters to my Aunt Lou De Vries in Grand Rapids, Michigan. She was my favorite Aunt. Aunt Lou lived at 833 Oakhill SE and her door was always opened, that is, if you knew where she kept the keys to the door.

I posed for a photo next to the World War I artillery piece located near the main administration building. Ft. Sheridan was responsible for our daily needs such as clothes, meals and transportation. I was issued a Class "A" pass. This pass was only issued to our "attached-unassigned" unit while stationed there. This meant that I could leave the post at any time. Near the Fort was the small town of Highwood, Illinois. There was a USO located in town and many of the local townspeople would invite some of the lucky fellows to their homes for a home-cooked meal.

They had a roller rink inside the USO building. It was very small but I tried skating there a few times. There were always girls around who would skate with soldiers. They had a small bar; beer was only ten cents for a very cold mug. For one dollar we could sit at the bar and drink most of the night. The Military Police made this  one of their first visits while going through the town. If any one looks the least drunk, they would haul you out and back to camp. Ft. Sheridan wanted to always keep on good terms with the city of Highwood.

Ft. Sheridan was a Separation Center; many fellows who had just been discharged would head first for Highwood to celebrate with a glass of beer before boarding the local train to Chicago and home. Most would walk into the USO and say, "The drinks are on me."

Everyone in the place would get a glass. I paid for very few drinks. I hope you don't get the idea that I sat around all night in Highwood because that wouldn't be true. They always had good cookies and homemade cake available to serviceman. It was nice to talk with the girls that came to show hospitality.

My cousin, Elaine Zylstra, wanted me to come to Grand Rapids. She wanted to introduce me to her friend. Elaine was now working at the Bergsma Brothers Furniture Company. She wrote a couple of letters to me and encouraged me to make the trip to Grand Rapids. I was told that Aunt Lou would be pleased to put me up at her house so I would have a place to stay. This sounded like a good idea, I needed to get away from the Army routine.

On 1 March, I was promoted to corporal and would be making $100.00 per month. I informed Elaine that maybe by the end of March, I could get time off to come to Grand Rapids. I checked out the train schedule and could easily make a trip to Grand Rapids for a weekend.

Friday morning 22 March, after I had completed my assignment for the day, I left Ft. Sheridan heading for Highwood. I purchased a ticket on the Chicago Northwestern Railroad, which took me to Chicago. The cost of the ticket was $1.00. Arriving in Chicago I walked over to the Union Station and bought a ticket bound for Grand Rapids, however I do not remember the cost of that ticket. The train pulled out of the station heading south around the southern shores of Lake Michigan. The train made a stop at Gary, Indiana. We continued on through Benton Harbor, Holland and finally arrived at the Union Station in Grand Rapids, Michigan. The station was a large covered yard and departing the train I had to cross over the train rails to get into the station itself, which was located on Ionia Avenue. I located a city bus that took me near 833 Oakhill SE. I knocked on the door and was welcomed by my Aunt Lou.

Supper was on the table. The home cooked food was delicious and the conversation was spontaneous. It was neat just sitting in a large living room with loving people around to share experiences. No one was wearing a uniform. I seemed out of place in uniform.

(It was mandatory to keep my uniform on because I was still on active duty).

That evening I slept like a baby in a large bed upstairs. The next morning Aunt Lou had my breakfast prepared. This day would be the best of my life. That afternoon I was to have a blind date with a young lady by the name of Jeanne Tuinstra. Elaine had planned the whole date. Right after lunch, we were to going bowling at Ryan's Bowling Alley on South Division and then in the evening we were to take in a movie. What a wonderful day this was going to be, I hoped!

Chapter XVII
JEANNE
March – December 1946

"The Lord moves in mysterious ways His wonders to perform".

Aunt Lou suggested that whenever I came to Grand Rapids her house would be open to me. Upon arrival my instructions were to reach my hand through the milk receiver and turn the key in the back door and enter the house. I then had the run of the house. Aunt Lou's first husband had died and she married a gentleman from Portland, Michigan by the name of Lue De Vries. Now I had an Uncle Lue and Aunt Lou.

Cousin Elaine was the youngest of the family but only one-year-older than I. When my parents came to Grand Rapids before the war, we usually stayed with Aunt Lou. I would spend time with Elaine. We sometimes took the bus downtown and went into the different stores. We went to the Ramona Amusement Park located very near to Reed's Lake. On occasion we would swim in Reed's Lake. There was also a steamer that went around the lake. After a day of fun, we relaxed with an ice cream cone from Rose's Ice Cream Shop.

Elaine and I went downtown one day to show me something that was really great. We got off the bus on lower Monroe Street and proceeded to Wurzburg's Department Store. She entered with me at her heels, heading straight for the escalator. This moving stairway only went from the main floor to the mezzanine. Elaine went on the escalator and turned around and came right back down. "Isn't this great?" she asked. I just stood there and thought how crazy these people are from Grand Rapids. In Detroit, at Hudson's Department Store, the escalator went from the first floor to the fourteenth floor. It was a thrill for Elaine, but for me it was silly.

I wanted to know more about this young lady that I was taking out on a blind date. Elaine said that Jeanne was working with her at Bergsma Brothers Furniture Company on Hall Street. We were to meet her at Ryan's Bowling Lanes. I hadn't done much bowling so

I really wasn't very interested in going, but I had to be nice to my host.

We drove to Ryan's bowling establishment and walked in. I was introduced to Jeanne Tuinstra. She had red hair and really didn't say too much. We started to bowl and I noticed that she bowled left-handed. This seemed very strange because when she was writing her score down, she used her right hand. I asked her why she did this and was informed that her brother Robert, was left handed. He had taught her to bowl left-handed. Jeanne was a good bowler. Since I was keeping score, I made sure that I won at least two of the three games. I can't remember Elaine's score. The cost of bowling was twenty-five cents per game and we paid ten cents for shoe rental. Nothing was automatic as they had "pin setters" who worked fast behind the scenes setting up the pins as quickly as we knocked them down. A good pinsetter could work two lanes at the same time. He usually got a tip after the games. We would throw a quarter down the lane after we had finished our games.

After three games I was about to call it quits. My date with Jeanne was only for bowling and that was it. As far as I was concerned, she was a sweet girl, nice to be with but, I really didn't know much about her. After the games, I helped Jeanne with her shoes and at that time Elaine said in a soft voice, that could be heard by everyone within fifteen feet, "Well, aren't you going to ask her?" What could I do now? So I asked her what her plans were for the evening, maybe we could take in a movie. Jeanne replied that she was very busy that night as she had made plans with a couple of girlfriends and besides; tomorrow being Sunday, she didn't want to stay out too late.

Now Elaine got into the act again, seeing as Ken was in town only for this weekend, it would be nice for Jeanne to go out with cousin, Ken. Elaine went so far as to say that she would be glad to go along on the date with us. She was going out that evening with her boyfriend so we could double date. Finally, Jeanne said that she would go out only after she canceled her date with her friends. She made it clear to me that she had to be home early as she had to study her Sunday School lesson. There was no need to ask her what church she belonged to, I figured if she was a friend of Elaine; she had to be Christian Reformed.

That evening, at Aunt Lou's house, Elaine told me that her boyfriend was sick and her date was cancelled. I was glad because this would also end my evening date with Jeanne. Elaine said not to worry as she had a plan. Elaine was really determined to get Jeanne and me together. She mentioned that her brother, Dutch, and his girlfriend, were going out for the evening. They would love to double date with us. They could be our chaperones. I agreed only if Elaine would call Jeanne and explain this new arrangement. Jeanne said "yes".

Later on that evening, Dutch, his girlfriend, and I arrived at 1700 Boston Street. It was a brick house with lots of trees around it. I didn't enter the house as Jeanne was standing outside waiting for us. She got in the backseat and I put my arm around her. Jeanne didn't seem to object. She had on a black coat with a scarf around her head. Jeanne knew Dutch and they got to talking about some of the action around town. Dutch's girlfriend was very friendly and this made for good conversation. We drove downtown and went to a movie. I don't remember the picture but after the show we headed straight home.

As we were traveling along Lake Drive, the lights on Dutch's car went out. We really couldn't make our way home in the dark. We drove to the first gas station we came to that was GI Johnny's. It was on the corner of Lake Drive and Diamond Street. They figured out that the trouble was an electrical short in the car's lighting system and decided to put the car up on the hoist. Jeanne and I stayed in the backseat as the car went up in the air. We figured that the trouble would soon be found but it lasted at least two hours. What to do with all that time on our hands?

We talked. I was beginning to realize this was really a neat person. She was very interesting to be with and she was funny, but had some real strong feelings about life. I got to know a little about her brothers and sisters. Her older sister Doris had served during the war with the WAVES and was stationed in Philadelphia. The other sister was Marie married to Jack Post. Jack had served in the Army but never left the states, serving in California. Her older brother Gerald, was a sergeant in the Army with the 42nd Infantry Division and served in Europe. The youngest brother was Robert. He had been a second lieutenant in the Air Force and was now discharged as we had enough pilots by the end of the war.

Repairs were finally made on the car and we were lowered to the ground floor. It was really late; in fact it was now Sunday morning around 1:00 a.m. and we had yet to arrive at 1700 Boston. Dutch drove the car to the top of Boston hill and into the driveway. Outlined against the glass front door was the figure of a large woman. It was Jeanne's mother. Knowing that I was going to be in trouble with Mrs. Tuinstra, I took the cowardly way out. I opened the car door, walked Jeanne part way to the front door, said my good night and hopped in the car. We drove off to 833 Oakhill S.E. I had been in combat with the enemy and had no fear and yet now I was a coward.

I could not sleep that night because I was miserable. This was really a nice Christian girl and I behaved badly. It really bothered me, so before 7:00 a.m. that Sunday morning, I walked about two miles from Oakhill Street to Boston Street. I knocked at the side door. Mrs. Tuinstra opened the door. I was somewhat frightened at this time, so I apologized for keeping her daughter out so late on a date. "We had car trouble and there really wasn't anything we could do about it," I explained apologetically.

Mrs. Tuinstra quickly responded, "Jeanne already told me about your misfortune with the car. Next time call to let us know that you would be late."

I asked, "What church will you be attending this morning?"

"Burton Heights Christian Reformed Church." Mrs. Tuinstra replied,

That was kind of an unfair question to ask, as I already knew they were Christian Reformed. I had to redeem myself. I then suggested that I would like to attend church with them. At this time Mrs. Tuinstra inquired as to where my home was and what church I attended. Short and to the point, "I was born in Detroit and am a member of the First Christian Reformed Church of that city." With that statement I had won a great victory!

She seemed pleased and invited me into the kitchen area. We had coffee together before the other family members awakened. We had a pleasant talk and I told her about my time in service. I explained I was scheduled to be out of service by the end of December. We talked about her sons and daughter who were in the service. We conversed about our belief and faith; it was just great talking with her. I believe that I told her more about my experiences in service than I did my own mother. I had a real feeling that this is where I belonged. Jeanne finally appeared and seemed surprised to see me there.

After breakfast we all went to Burton Heights Church. It was a very large church about the same size as my Detroit church and the people were very friendly. I remember that the minister of the church was Rev. Henry Evenhouse. After the morning service we went back to the Boston home as I was invited to have dinner with the Tuinstra family.

At the table was Mrs. Tuinstra's mother Mary. She was quite elderly and talked with a heavy Dutch accent. She had a friendly smile and was very interested in the things going on around her. After a very delicious meal, Mr. Jacob Tuinstra read *The Meditation* from "The Banner" that took a very long time to read. The family then seemed to go into other rooms while Jeanne and I sat in the living room and talked.

Later in the evening we again returned to Burton Heights Church. I had to return to the train station by 10:00 p.m. as that was the last train leaving for Chicago. I packed my small bag and Dutch, his girlfriend, and Jeanne took me to the train station. I remember holding Jeanne's hand until we got to the train station on Ionia Street. I got out of the car and headed for the train. Jeanne called me back and leaned out of the back window of the car and gave me a kiss. Actually our first kiss! The love bug bit me.

I boarded the train and found an empty seat next to the window. I was hoping that I might get another view of Jeanne as the train pulled away. It was dark and the engine smoke obstructed my view. I don't remember getting back into camp as it was just like a dream. I was in love! The first chance that I had I wanted to write Jeanne a letter. This was not as simple as it may seem. You see I didn't know how to spell her last name and I had also forgotten her home address. Love is so blind.

After contacting Elaine I was able to address a letter. After a few days of anxious waiting I received a letter from Grand Rapids. It was from Jeanne and this started a romance that continues to this day.

A few days later an envelope was thrown onto my bunk. My eyes were drawn to some strange markings on the back of that envelope. There was a funny, yet familiar message on the back. S.W.A.K. was plainly visible with little red hearts drawn around it. It didn't seem characteristic of Jeanne to write this on our first letter. Later, I was to find out that this writing was not by Jeanne but by Kenneth Bergsma, her boss. After Jeanne had written this letter to me she asked Ken to mail her letter at the Post Office. He replied that he would and seeing the address of a serviceman, Ken decided to play a joke on her. He was the one who had scribbled those initials on the back of the envelope.

While stationed at Ft. Sheridan, I began writing to Jeanne every opportunity that came along. All these letters which I wrote to her and which she wrote to me were saved and have been placed into memory books. Our letters were inserted into plastic sheets to protect them. There are eight volumes altogether. They are kept on our bookshelves and can be reviewed at any time. From this point in my journal I will be referring to these letters and to specific dates that are taken from them. As I read these letters over, I recalled other events that had happened. One of these reminded me about the time I took a bus from Detroit to Chicago. I do not recall that bus trip; just because I can't remember doesn't mean that it never happened. I think that the letters are more correct than my memory.

On 11 April 1946 I answered that first letter, the one with the S.W.A.K. on the back. For those of you who do not know, those letters stand for *Sealed With A Kiss*. I inquired about the meaning of the lettering on the back of her first letter. Jeanne denied writing anything on the back of the envelope and it remained a mystery for a couple of months. I also inquired about her phone number, which was CHerry 3-2759.

21 April was Easter Sunday. I wired a dozen red roses to Jeanne from Ft. Sheridan. I sent another picture of myself to her but I had not received any photos from her up to this time.

I took the General Educational and Development Test on 27 April and passed. This GED test took over six hours; I was able to acquire my High School Diploma. It was made up of mostly questions that could be answered by multiple choices. Southeastern High School was told that I passed the test and would

be able to graduate with the class of 1946. I checked with my commanding officer to see if it was possible for me to have a short furlough so that I might graduate. With all the Army red tape, I didn't think that I would be able to do it. You never know until you try.

I finally got a picture of Jeanne. It came in a leather picture frame that I was able to keep on my desk at Ft. Sheridan. It was autographed, "Especially for you, Jeanne."

I was eager to see Jeanne again. I asked Elaine if it was possible for them to come to Chicago. I figured if Elaine came along as a chaperone, Mrs. Tuinstra would let Jeanne come.

I suggested 30 May to Elaine as this was a Memorial Day holiday and I could get a few days off. We got paid on the last day of the month so I would have some extra cash in my pocket. I told Elaine that there were many servicemen at camp and I was sure that I could get a blind date for her. After all, she had set me up with Jeanne; I wanted to return the favor. Did my plans work out as I had anticipated?

I received notice that I would be allowed time off to graduate from Southeastern High School on 19 June. All of my former classmates had graduated with the class of 1945 while I was in service. My parents would be celebrating their 30th Wedding Anniversary on 22 June. In one of my letters to Jeanne I suggested that this might be

 an opportunity for her to meet my parents. I didn't get an answer to that question right away. I was eager for my parents to meet Jeanne because I knew that they would like her as much as I did. I was still working on the idea that Elaine and Jeanne could come and visit with me in Chicago.

Every day was the same, get up, go to the office, check in at the warehouse, eat, write letters and then to bed again. I played baseball for Detachment B as that was

the unit I was assigned to. I played left field and sometimes second base.

Mother's Day was 12 May and I called my mother from camp to wish her a happy Mother's Day.

I started to count the days left in the Army and it now was 202 days. It seemed like a lifetime! When writing my letters I would always include the number of days left to serve on my enlistment. When I talked to Jeanne on the phone she told me that she had a very bad cold. After that phone call, I ordered a dozen roses to be sent to cheer her up. There is nothing like flowers to leave a good impression with a girl. I received another picture of her.

Jeanne went before the consistory of Burton Heights Church on Monday, 20 May to make Profession of her faith. She answered all the questions that were asked of her and a date was set for appearing before the whole church. I was thrilled to hear that news. When I found out the date, I was disappointed because I could not get the time off to come to Grand Rapids. Some of the other fellows from our unit were already on leave. I had to do some of their work.

I did most of my letter writing at the USO in Highwood, Illinois. They had a real nice area set aside for writing. It was not too smart to spend time in camp because if anyone would see you sitting around they would find a job for you to do. There were still new recruits coming into Ft. Sheridan every day. My class "A" pass allowed me to leave the post whenever I wanted to.

The US Government had an allowance for each man in camp. This was called "A Company Fund" or as we called it " Our Company Fun." The new recruits had no idea there was money set aside for them to enjoy a Company Party. Somehow we never told them. We had all this money on hand so why not throw a party? We usually did this once a month. Only the permanent personnel were invited; we all accepted readily. We would have all kinds of cold cuts and party snacks. We could not have any beer at these parties, but we did eat well.

I was able to get into Chicago almost every weekend using my pass. Chicago was a great town to visit as they did everything for servicemen. Great Lakes Naval Training Center was located just north of Chicago; there were many sailors in town as well as Army personnel. Everything was free. Buses, ballparks, the zoo, streetcars, museums and most restaurants offered free coffee to servicemen. This was a great town to visit while in uniform. There were very few MPs (Military Police) or SPs (Shore Patrol) around.

I would leave the Fort around 4:00 p.m. and catch the train leaving Highwood Station heading for Chicago. The train came every hour and took one hour to get into the loop. I would proceed first to the Serviceman's Center across from the Congress Hotel to secure a room for the night. There was no charge at the Serviceman's Center. Our beds were bunks in a very large room holding about 150 other GIs. If we had any valuables we could place them in the safe in the lobby. Some GIs were in the habit of carrying large sums of money for gambling purposes. If they wanted to gamble, Chicago was the place to be.

In the morning we could have coffee and doughnuts or Coke and cookies. They even had a table with hot dogs and cold cuts so that we could make a sandwich. There were always small groups of musicians who played chamber music while we ate our breakfast. We could check with the front desk and see if they had free tickets to the movies. If the circus was in town, we could get tickets. It was a little different with the ballparks. We had to wait until the fourth inning before we were allowed in, then we could sit in any of the empty seats. Chicago had two ballparks so there was always a game going on. Since we didn't have to pay a bus fare we would ride about three or so blocks and jump off. I even went to the Science and Industry Building plus a few other museums in my spare time.

On some weekends, midget auto racing was the thing to see. We would go over to Soldier Field to watch them race. I remember seeing Tony Bettenhauser as he raced his car around the dirt track. He had a shiny blue racer with the number 24 painted on the side, a real favorite of the crowd. His son, Tony Jr., won the "Indianapolis 500" years later. These races ran until quite late in the evening and we would have to hurry to catch the last train leaving for camp. The last train for camp left the Chicago Station at midnight. I remember seeing many times, soldiers and sailors running to catch the last train home.

Once on board most fell fast asleep. When the train got near Highwood, the conductor would wake all the soldiers up. He would do the same as they came to Great Lakes Naval Station.

T/5 (Technical Corporal) Marion Hulst was a member of our unit and came from Sheldon, Iowa. He was a schoolteacher and a very nice fellow. We went together to Chicago and checked in at the Servicemen Center. We arrived a little late as most of the tickets were taken. They had a couple of tickets for the Chicago Athletic Club on Michigan Avenue. We took the tickets and headed down Michigan Avenue. Neither of us had ever been to an athletic club before, so we didn't really know what we were getting into. We found the place and at the front desk we inquired if they had anything going on. He mentioned that we could use their swimming pool so we went swimming. We took the elevator to the twentieth floor. We were given swimming trunks and towels. After changing, we located a very large pool. The two of us were the only ones there, so into the pool we jumped. Hulst was not convinced that we were on the twentieth floor. Every so often he would leave the pool just to look up and down the street below. He just couldn't figure out how all that water could get up so high and not spill over the sides of the building.

If we wanted a pass, we went to the Orderly Room and asked for a pass. If we needed articles of clothing we went to the Orderly Room and filled out the necessary papers for whatever we needed. If we had mail, we got it from the Orderly Room. If anybody sent a telegram, we picked it up at the Orderly Room. From that Orderly Room the sergeant in charge could contact anybody in the barracks by use of a speaker system. While sitting on my bunk, I heard my name coming over the intercom wanting to know if I was present. I yelled that I was present and he stated that there was a telegram for me. I started for the Orderly Room only to my surprise; he started to read that telegram over the intercom. The message came over **loud and clear,**

KENNETH RESERVE ROOM FOR TWO IN CHICAGO FOR MAY 29TH 30TH 31ST FONDEST LOVE, JEANNE.

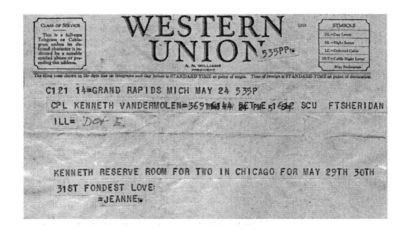

WESTERN UNION

C121 14=GRAND RAPIDS MICH MAY 24 535P
CPL KENNETH VANDERMOLEN=369 BETHE SCU FTSHERIDAN
ILL= Def E,

KENNETH RESERVE ROOM FOR TWO IN CHICAGO FOR MAY 29TH 30TH
31ST FONDEST LOVE:
=JEANNE.

This meant that Elaine and Jeanne had accepted my invitation to come to Chicago. Everyone in the barracks heard that message.

The two girls wanted me to get a room for them at a hotel in Chicago. I smiled and said out loud, GREAT! Not everyone in that barracks understood what the telegram meant because all my buddies were hooting and hollering. I explained that the room for two was for my cousin and her girlfriend and of course everyone said, "Yea, yea, your cousin, we believe you, yea, yea!"

Later they started yelling, "Have a great weekend in Chicago with your cousin." How could I make these guys believe that I was making a reservation for my cousin and her girlfriend? I didn't even try to explain, it was impossible.

That weekend I made the usual trip to Chicago to make a room reservation for Elaine Zylstra and Jeanne Tuinstra at the Congress Hotel. This hotel was next to the Serviceman Center and would be convenient for all of us. I tried to get one of my buddies to come and double date with Elaine. I asked Marion Hulst if he would like to double date my best cousin, a great person. Hulst was still laughing over the telegram and didn't believe that there was going to be another girl in Chicago for him. He kept saying that he didn't want to spoil my weekend in Chicago. Maybe Gordon would help me out, so I asked him to accompany Elaine. He said that he would come along after I promised to pay for everything.

Gordon and I went to Chicago and checked into the Serviceman Center. We then went to the Congress Hotel where Jeanne and Elaine were waiting for us. So off we all went. We did crazy things for the next three days. We went to Riverview Amusement Park and did all the exciting things that everyone would do at a fun park. They had a large parachute jump located in the center of the park. Jeanne and I decided to take the plunge. We got into a swing and were strapped in tight, the chute gradually moved to the top. Suddenly, after a pause, they let us freefall. We were floating in air. I was beginning to "fall" for Jeanne in a big way. We bought cotton candy and ate hot dogs. We returned the girls to their hotel around 10:30 p.m. I checked into the Serviceman Center for that night. Gordon went back to camp that evening. I was left with taking care of two young ladies.

The next morning, I walked across the street to the Congress Hotel. I went to the lobby desk to call the girls room and wake then up.

We ate breakfast in the hotel and then off for another day. We went strolling down Michigan Avenue and did a lot of window-shopping. Carson Pirie Scott was the store that was most interesting to them. We went to a couple of museums and walked along the waterfront. Elaine had a camera and took several of pictures of us. It was still quite chilly at this time of the year and servicemen wore suntans. I wanted to be alone with Jeanne. Elaine finally caught on that we should have a little time by ourselves. Jeanne and I walked in the park just across from the Hotel. We went back to the hotel room and Elaine went into the bathroom and

said that she was going to take a shower. I believe that this was the longest bath anyone ever took. Elaine must have been swimming in the tub. The three-day visit soon ended.

As the girls got their bags together, I escorted them to a waiting taxi and directed the driver to bring them to the Union Station. I returned the room keys to the main desk. The clerk then asked if I was checking out. I replied that the girls had the room and I was just returning the room key. He then mentioned that the girls had not paid their bill and presented me with the full amount. What was I to do? So I paid the bill. After three days on the town, even though servicemen didn't have to pay for most items, I still was short of money. After paying for their room nothing was left in my pockets and I had to report back to camp. The girls were on their way to the Union Station with joy in their hearts and tears in their eyes while I was left with nothing in my pockets!

I got to the Chicago and Northwestern train terminal and looked around for anybody that I might know, who could loan me some money to get back to camp. All I needed was one dollar and I

wasn't about to beg strangers in the station. I saw the sign, *Travelers Aid*, and if anybody needed aid, it was I. Approaching the desk I told my story to the young girl behind the desk. All I needed was one dollar. After my story she told me that she would personally give me the money to enable me to return to camp. I did not want any charity so I told her that I would give her one Japanese Yen as security. When I returned later, I paid her the dollar and she returned my Japanese Yen. People were very trusting in those days.

There was a change in Army Command for the Chicago area. I was no longer in the Army Ground Force Liaison Office but was assigned to the Fifth Army Area Command. The other guys in our unit were assigned to different jobs but I kept assigning recruits and new draftees. I continued to type orders. I still went to the warehouse and processed the men through their entrance into the Army. I had to change the shoulder patch from Army Ground Force to the Fifth Army shoulder patch. I wore the Americal Division patch on the right shoulder while the 5th Army patch went on the left sleeve.

I made a habit of calling Jeanne every Sunday. On one such Sunday, Jeanne had not quite gotten home from church but her Grandmother Mary had answered the phone. She was really Dutch and her English was broken. I found her to be very interesting and had quite a long conversation with her. I asked her to tell Jeanne that I had called. On the next Sunday I talked with Jeanne and she informed me she would be making her Profession of Faith the following week. I was really getting serious about this Christian young lady and I was falling deeper and deeper in love.

According to our love letters, I wrote Jeanne on the 4th of June. I told her many things I did during the war in the Philippine Islands. I also bought her a necklace, as the one she had was broken. One of my letters mentioned that I put the broken necklace on my dog tags. I don't remember but that's what the letter said so it must be true.

I called my Mother on the 6th of June to inform her that I would be arriving in Detroit around the 13th of June. I called Jeanne and invited her to come with me to Detroit. This would be her first meeting with my parents.

On 7 June Grandmother Mary Sietsema died. I sent flowers on this sad occasion. Jeanne's Profession of Faith was scheduled for that week but because of the death it was rescheduled for the following week. I wished I could have been there.

I graduated from Southeastern High School on 18 June. I was wearing my uniform because I was still on active duty. After they had called the names of all the class members, they called my name. I went across the stage and received my diploma. I don't recall if my parents were in the auditorium or not. It was a long time ago.

Jeanne came to Detroit to meet my parents and frankly it wasn't the best of meetings. My folks were very much into their 30th Anniversary celebration on 22 June. She met many of my parent's friends and everyone was in a party mood. My parents seemed disappointed in my selection of Jeanne as my girlfriend. They couldn't figure out what I saw in this girl from Grand Rapids and why couldn't I find a nice girl in Detroit? I guess they wanted me to stay at home since I recently returned from overseas. I brought Jeanne back to Grand Rapids on the train and I returned to Detroit.

Many words were exchanged after I returned from bringing her home. I did promise my folks that I would not leave Detroit or make any future plans until I was twenty-one. When I reached that age I could vote and also would be able to leave home on my own. My Detroit stay at home would only be a little over a year, this would keep my parents happy.

On 30 June, Jeanne and a couple of her girlfriends were going to Grand Haven to spend a week at the beach. Elaine was included in the bunch. My understanding was that all they did was to lie around the beach, get a sun tan and watch the boys go by. I remember getting a post card from Jeanne with my address written in sand. She must have written that address in glue and then poured sand over the card. Today that card is still readable.

I recall going on a picnic with Jeanne's brother Bob and his girlfriend, Lois De Witt. We enjoyed a picnic lunch at a park near Ionia. That evening, Aunt Lou had company and all of her beds were full. It seemed the inn was full for the night. Jeanne made arrangements with her folks for me to stay overnight at their house.

239

 They really didn't have any extra room so I shared sleeping accommodations with her brother. I slept in the same bed with an Army Air Force lieutenant. He was all spit and polish and I bet that if he had entered combat; he would have done his duty to the fullest.

July was a very hot month. On 13 July, I was transferred to Detachment "E" while Gordon stayed in Detachment "B". Gordon and I had been together most all the time we were in service. This is the first time that we were going to be attached to different units. I checked with the Company Commander about the transfer and was told that the Army was realigning the way they handled new recruits. Our group was being cut down from thirteen Enlisted Men to only four. I have no idea what Gordon was doing as he was not with me from this time until our discharge from service. I was to continue to perform the tasks that I had done. I reported each morning to the warehouse; worked with the doctors while inspecting the new troops. I continued to assign men to the Infantry and to the Armored Forces as well. Most of the Armored Forces were sent to Ft. Knox located in Kentucky. The Infantry was being sent to (IRTC) Infantry Replacement Training Centers located throughout the south. I was classified as attached/unassigned and able to keep my Class A pass. We also were informed that the pay for certain grades would be increased and I received an increase of $30.00 per month. This means I was making a total of $130.00 per month. The reason for the raise was to encourage men to re-enlist.

The Army warehouse was quite an operation. I got to know the GIs working there and most of the fellows knew just what my assignment was. If they had a friend coming through the camp and didn't want them attached to the infantry; they would give me their name and I would assign them to the Service Forces. One good turn deserves another.

We never had to clean our room as the Army supplied a civilian to clean it. He was quite a large fellow and was eager to work at any job the government assigned him. He was not allowed to take any money from us for his services. Since we all worked at the warehouse, we would see to it that he got some underclothes and socks. The socks were mostly olive drab color. Once we gave him a carton of soap from the PX (Post Exchange), which was almost impossible for civilians to obtain.

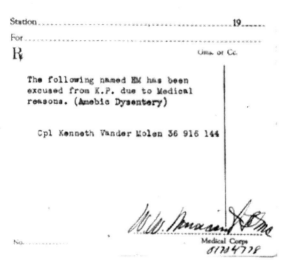

In the Army, it isn't what you do, it's who you know. One day a medical officer approached me and wanted to know if I could get him a pair of black shoes. Officers had to pay for their own and there were not many shoe stores around. I asked his size and said I would see what I could do. He got his shoes. Now he asked what he could do for me. Since he was a medical officer, I suggested that maybe I could get a medical excuse from KP. I told him that I got jungle rot and jaundice while serving overseas. He told me to come to his office and wrote me out an excuse. He also added that I shouldn't wear OD shirts because I had a skin rash. I got my excuse!

On 7 August 1946 I was twenty years old. Would anyone remember my birthday? I heard a summons over the intercom to report to the Orderly Room at once. The corporal also mentioned that it looked like a birthday cake. I rushed over and sure enough, there was a full size cake shipped by the Post Office. It had gone through the mail and had remained in an upright position. Jeanne had ordered this cake shipped with a cellophane cover over the top and it arrived in excellent condition! Naturally, the other fellows heard the announcement on the intercom about a cake in the Orderly Room. Someone brought ice cream plus a few bottles of Coke and we had a real party. All the fellows thought that this girl of mine was crazy sending a cake by way of the Postal Service. They all wished that their girls had sent them a cake when it was their birthday. I also received a tiepin in another box that came later from Jeanne. Clarence and Grace sent me a tie. I put that tie on and affixed the tiepin. I was a civilian for just a few minutes and it felt great. The next day I treated the three fellows that were assigned to my unit to a steak dinner and a few beers in Highwood. The bill came to $11.03. One of the fellows was Marion Hulst, the same fellow who turned down a blind date with my cousin Elaine.

I wanted to hitchhike to Grand Rapids. There were quite a number of GIs who would use that form of transportation. I talked with a couple and figured if they could do it, I could too. All you had to do was to use your right hand finger. Sounded easy.

On 22 August I stood outside of Ft. Sheridan, stuck out my thumb and immediately got a ride into Chicago. I thanked the driver and waited for another ride. Three cars passed me but the fourth one stopped and picked me up. I rode all the way to Grand Rapids and it didn't cost me a cent. What a way to travel! Hitching a ride was remarkable. In Chicago there was a location where all you did was wait and people would drive up and say, "How far are you going soldier?" I was able to get to Grand Rapids faster using this method than by train or bus. Airplanes were really unheard of in those days. We had no fear that somebody might want to rob or kill us. We wore a uniform, we were heroes; we had it made.

It was interesting hitchhiking and meeting diverse drivers. Most all the folks were just common everyday people. They appreciated what we had done during the war. They usually asked what theater of operation I was in, when I would say the Pacific, they would ask about certain units. It seems everyone had somebody in service and wanted to know just a little bit about what it was like out there. These were great times to be a serviceman.

While hitching outside of Highwood an elderly couple drove up and asked if I knew how to get to St. Johns, Michigan. They mentioned that they needed to drive through Chicago and would prefer not to. I told them I would be glad to get them through Chicago, I got behind the wheel. These were really nice people; they had a son who was killed in the war so they would only pick up soldiers, not sailors. We had a lovely time traveling around the lake area toward Grand Rapids. We stopped for something to eat in Benton Harbor and I paid for their meal. When we got on Clyde Park Avenue and Grandville Avenue, I told them I would leave them because I could get a cross-town bus to Aunt Lou's house. I directed them in the direction of St. Johns. They were really sorry to see me leave them, as they were so friendly. I often wonder what happened to the people I met in my hitchhiking experiences.

I decided that I could use the "free route" to Detroit over a Labor Day weekend, so I left the camp and got a ride starting in Highwood, then to Chicago and another hitch to Michigan City, Indiana. I was standing by the curb when a fellow drove up in an older Oldsmobile and asked me where I was going, I replied "Detroit." He was going as far a Kalamazoo, so off we went. I was never so scared in all my life, as this guy pushed that Olds up to 98 mph. He kept saying he had eighty-eight horses under the hood and had the reins in his hand. He was in control as we went speeding down the road. I believe this was the first time I wished a policeman would stop us and give this fellow a ticket. One thing was certain; I made it to Kalamazoo in record speed.

I picked up another ride to Plymouth, Michigan where I went into a restaurant to phone home to tell my folks that I was in town. While phoning, a fellow said that he was heading into Detroit and I could ride with him. The front seat was loaded with boxes so I got in the back seat; he turned his car away from the curb and just then had a flat tire. I could have stayed to help him fix the tire but I wanted to get home. I got out of the back seat, stuck my finger out and the first car that came by picked me up. I was off to Detroit. That was the shortest ride I ever had while hitchhiking. I wonder if that fellow is still trying to fix his flat?

Even though the war had ended, we were still running men through the induction center at Ft. Sheridan. My letter relates that on 5 September, 519 men went through the center. On the 13th of September, we ran a record of 714 enlisted men. I did not work on Saturday because only the colored personnel came through at that time. We had a segregated Army at that time and all the colored troops went through on Saturdays. They were not destined for the infantry as most all went into transportation groups. They made excellent truck drivers but sad to say, they were not allowed into the ranks of Army Ground Forces.

Hitching a ride back from Grand Rapids was just as interesting as leaving from Chicago. I would usually arrive in Grand Rapids late Friday night and go out on a date with Jeanne. We always went to church together at Burton Heights Christian Reformed Church. I usually had Sunday dinner at the Tuinstra's. This was a scrumptious meal as Mrs. Tuinstra was a great cook. After the meal, Mr. Tuinstra would read *The Meditation* from The Banner then close with prayer. I would sometimes help with the dishes while Mr. Tuinstra took his Sunday nap. In the evening after church we enjoyed a light supper. I would then hitchhike back to camp. I understood that the Tuinstra's did not like me traveling on Sunday even if I had to be back in camp early Monday morning. Bob Tuinstra, along with Jeanne would usually drive me to Chicago Drive in the Grandville area and I would hitchhike back to camp. We generally waited until midnight before I left for my return to camp.

On one occasion a trucker stopped and asked, "Where are you going?"

"Ft. Sheridan," I answered.

"Good," he said, "I'm going to Milwaukee."

It was great being up in the front seat of that huge truck, the miles just kept speeding away. We struck up a good conversation, mostly about how rough it was being a civilian during the war. He said that his wife was having quite a time getting the clothes clean because of the soap shortage. I asked him for his name and address. I promised him that I would get a case of laundry soap and mail it to that address. He offered me $5.00 for my trouble but I refused. After all he took me back to camp at no charge, why would I charge him for his services?

On another occasion, after Jeanne left me off in Grandville, there were a couple of sailors standing on the corner waiting for a pick-up. Usually I wanted to hitch by myself because most people would not stop for two people even if they were in uniform. It was getting late; finally a car drove up.

"Where are you going?" the driver asked the sailors.

"To the Great Lakes Training Center." they answered. Great Lakes was located just fifteen miles north of Ft. Sheridan.

"I'm heading for Ft. Sheridan, is there still room?" I immediately replied.

Then an answer to prayer, the driver called to me, "I have plenty of room and am heading in the direction of Chicago." I got in the back seat with one sailor while the other sailor took the front seat. I settled into my corner and soon fell asleep. After some time, the car came to a stop and the sailors jumped out and I with them. Where was I? Which direction is north? What town was this? I looked at my watch and it was 4:00 a.m.

I was hungry and saw a gas station open and went there to use the restroom. A car pulled up and the two sailors disappeared. The gas attendant informed me that I was in South Chicago and there should be traffic heading north. All I had to do was wait. I waited, and waited and waited. Only two or three cars passed me, most of the traffic was heading in the opposite direction. Finally, as the light of dawn was appearing I realized I was thumbing in the wrong direction. I should have been on the other side of that highway where all the traffic was headed into Chicago. I learned a hard lesson; never fall asleep in a car while hitchhiking. I did make it back to camp on time.

September was spent working in camp and making trips to Grand Rapids. I lived for the weekends when I would see my Jeanne. There was one time when I didn't make it back to camp on time and I was restricted to the camp for one week. At least I didn't have to pull KP or some other duty. I still ran 301 men through the system the last week of September.

The railroad workers decided to go out on strike. We were all confined to camp. President Truman said that the Army would take over the railroads if the train personnel went on strike. President Truman was our commander in chief and he wanted to know who could take over the rail system. We were then instructed to look over the personnel records (Form 20) of everyone in camp. We had to find out who had any experience or were qualified to operate trains. With no computers, we had to read each person's record. Everyone was restricted to camp except the four fellows working for the Army Ground Forces.

Using my Class A pass I headed for Chicago. It was strange being in Chicago at this time. It looked like I was the only soldier in town. There were MP's and SP's standing on the corner. They approach me and asked the reason for being there and why wasn't I confined to camp? I showed my pass and they respond, "Keep moving soldier." The Serviceman Center was closed. Nothing was going on in Chicago so I returned to camp. The next day the striking railroad men went back to work. The camp was let loose and everyone escaped to town except me, I had already been there.

Some of the recruits being processed through Ft. Sheridan were assigned to Ft. Knox, Kentucky for their basic training. Orders were usually given for a group of fifty with a non-com in charge, instructing them to report to the Commanding Officer at Ft. Knox. I asked my Commanding Officer if I could be assigned as a group leader. This would give me an opportunity to visit with my brother Clarence, and his wife, living in Cincinnati, Ohio.

Since things were slow in the warehouse I was given the opportunity to transport a group of enlisted men to their next training base. In these orders, I received a voucher to purchase room, meals and a return train ticket. All of these vouchers had a cash value, if I did not use the train ticket, I could turn it in for cash. After the troops were delivered to the Commanding Officer of their training base, I was to return by the fastest route possible back to Ft. Sheridan.

Orders were cut and I was given the task of delivering forty-seven men to Ft. Knox, Kentucky. I carried forty-eight tickets to cover the men and myself, as we were using the Union Pacific Railroad to transport these troops. Early Thursday morning on 25 October, I assembled my "troops" and found only forty-six men instead of forty-seven. Somehow they had counted wrong, I now had one extra meal ticket. We all boarded the Chicago Northwestern Railway leaving Ft. Sheridan at Highwood. We arrived in Chicago, "marched" after a fashion, to the Union Station and located the train for Kentucky.

One railroad coach was allotted to my group. I set up my office in the private room at the end of the coach. Each soldier had a seat of his own because there were only forty-six in our group. Most of these guys had never been away from home and some were even homesick. I made arrangements with the cook on the train to serve us all at once. At mealtime we marched to the dining car. I gave the porter forty-six meal tickets but kept one for myself. I intended to return that unused ticket for a cash refund when returning to camp. We did the same procedure for supper that night. This allowed me another meal ticket to turn in later.

We were due to arrive at Ft. Knox around 4:00 p.m. on Friday, which we did precisely on time. My orders were to turn these recruits over to the Commanding Officer, then return to Ft. Sheridan by the fastest means possible. While in Ft. Knox, I asked a mess sergeant if I could eat supper at his mess and I was granted that privilege. I located an empty barracks and retired for the evening. This saved me using my housing voucher, another item that could be turned in for a cash rebate.

I had breakfast the next morning at Ft. Knox and hitchhiked to Cincinnati, Ohio. I picked up a quick ride and arrived in Cincinnati by early afternoon. I took a bus to 3293 Victory Parkway, the address of brother Clarence. I spent the rest of the day with them. On Saturday night, their church was having a Youth Meeting and Clarence asked if I was interested in going, I accepted. There were many young people in attendance. They had a film that was going to be shown to the group. It was a fun evening. Most of the kids were just a year younger than I was, but it seemed like my uniform made me appear much older. I talked with them about what it was like in the Philippines and Japan. It was good to get to bed that night as I had a long day ahead of me. I slept on their living room couch and it wasn't very comfortable.

Sunday morning I attended church with Clarence and Grace. They had a guest speaker who was an Army Chaplain. I recognized his shoulder patch from the 41st Infantry Division. This unit had fought in the Philippine Islands mostly on the Island of Mindanao. He was also stationed in Japan. I was able to talk with him after the morning service. Once again the young people asked both Chaplain Graham and myself about our experiences.

After dinner, Clarence drove me to the Central Railroad Station in Cincinnati. This was a very large railroad terminal; in fact, it was the largest railroad terminal I had ever seen. It had paintings on the walls and ceiling, the place echoed with the sound of many people saying their hellos and good-byes. I was going to take the train back to Ft. Sheridan as I didn't think that I could make it back in time for Monday morning reveille. Just as I was about to board the train, an MP stopped me. He wanted to see my traveling orders and where I was heading.

I had to talk fast in this case. I didn't have any traveling papers except the orders allowing me to enter Ft. Knox with recruits. I told the MPs that I had just returned from overseas and was given the opportunity to deliver troops to Kentucky. If time allowed, I thought I might take the side trip to Cincinnati and see my brother whom I hadn't seem for quite some time. I stuck with that story but he kept questioning me about traveling without papers. My Class A pass wouldn't have been the best thing to show him as it allowed me to travel only 200 miles beyond Ft. Sheridan. He was about to call Ft. Sheridan and find out why I was in Ohio instead of on my way to Illinois, when another MP came in and interrupted him. There was a disturbance inside the terminal and they needed all the help he could muster. The MP that was questioning me directed me to the next train heading for Ft. Sheridan. He told me to get going and away I went.

I arrived in camp before reveille and headed for the Orderly Room. I turned in my unused meal and lodging vouchers and received cash for them.

The first of December was fast approaching and my enlistment would soon be ended. I was told that I could expect a Terminal Leave from 11 November, but would have to return to Ft. Sheridan by 1 December 1946. I informed them that my enlistment would end on that day. Did they expect me to return to get discharged from Ft. Sheridan?

They had a real problem with this terminal leave question. They had never discharged a soldier who was in the Regular Army. According to regulations, I had to return to my place of enlistment to receive my discharge papers. That is why they wanted me to return to Ft. Sheridan, Illinois. I told them to look closely at my enlistment papers because I had enlisted in Yokohama, Japan. This would mean that I could demand a trip to Japan and they would have to pay my fare plus mileage from Japan to Detroit. After some discussion and, no doubt, some messages to Washington DC; it was decided that I would go on my Terminal Leave and didn't have to report back to Ft. Sheridan. I would do all the paperwork before leaving Ft. Sheridan, and then they would send my discharge papers to my home in Detroit. I wrote my last letter to Jeanne on 5 November and told her that my Army life was soon to end. I was given my Honorable Discharge on 1 December 1946. I had served my country two years, two months and eight days.

All of these events happened many years ago. I can remember a lot of good times and a lot of tough times. I remember the times spent in foxholes, attacking enemy strongholds and eating anything to stay alive. I remember the hospital experiences, the trip to Japan and the arrival in Seattle. As I look back I know that I was not alone as God was with me always. I had no fear that I was going to die. I knew in my heart that I would make it back to the States. I put my trust in God. My faith was unwavering. I look back and see God's direction every step of the way. He guided me to re-enlist so I would meet Jeanne. What more could I want? His way was the best way.

I recall a sign that I saw on the highway and it said,

IF YOU WANT TO HEAR GOD LAUGH,
TELL HIM YOUR PLANS.

Honorable Discharge

This is to certify that

KENNETH W. VANDER MOLEN, 36916144, PRIVATE FIRST CLASS

Army of the United States

is hereby Honorably Discharged from the military service of the United States of America.

This certificate is awarded as a testimonial of Honest and Faithful Service to this country.

Given at   APO 716

Date   31 OCTOBER 1945

FLOYD E. DUNN
COLONEL, 182ND INFANTRY
COMMANDING

251

ENLISTED RECORD AND REPORT OF SEPARATION
HONORABLE DISCHARGE

1. LAST NAME - FIRST NAME - MIDDLE INITIAL		2. ARMY SERIAL NO.	3. GRADE	4. ARM OR SERVICE	5. COMPONENT
Vander Molen Kenneth W		36916144	Pfc	Inf	AUS

6. ORGANIZATION	7. DATE OF SEPARATION	8. PLACE OF SEPARATION
Ser Co 182 Inf	31 Oct 45	APO 716

9. PERMANENT ADDRESS FOR MAILING PURPOSES	10. DATE OF BIRTH	11. PLACE OF BIRTH
2662 Manistique Ave, Detroit 15, Mich	7 Aug 26	Detroit, Mich

12. ADDRESS FROM WHICH EMPLOYMENT WILL BE SOUGHT	13. COLOR EYES	14. COLOR HAIR	15. HEIGHT	16. WEIGHT	17. NO. DEPEND.
	Blue	Blonde	5' 9"	173 lbs.	None

18. RACE			19. MARITAL STATUS		20. U.S. CITIZEN		21. CIVILIAN OCCUPATION AND NO.
WHITE X	NEGRO	OTHER (specify)	SINGLE X	MARRIED OTHER (specify)	YES X	NO	Fir cleaner

MILITARY HISTORY

22. DATE OF INDUCTION	23. DATE OF ENLISTMENT	24. DATE OF ENTRY INTO ACTIVE SERVICE	25. PLACE OF ENTRY INTO SERVICE
	25 Sept 44	25 Sept 44	Chicago, Ill

SELECTIVE SERVICE DATA	26. REGISTERED YES X NO	27. LOCAL S.S. BOARD NO. 17	28. COUNTY AND STATE Wayne, Ill	29. HOME ADDRESS AT TIME OF ENTRY INTO SERVICE 2662 Manistique Ave, Detroit Mich

30. MILITARY OCCUPATIONAL SPECIALTY AND NO.	31. MILITARY QUALIFICATION AND DATE (i.e., infantry, aviation and marksmanship badges, etc.)
Clerk typist 405	None

32. BATTLES AND CAMPAIGNS
Battle of the Southern Philippines

33. DECORATIONS AND CITATIONS
Asiatic Pacific Theatre Ribbon w/ 1 star   Good Conduct Medal
Philippine Liberation Ribbon w/ 1 star   Combat Infantry Badge

34. WOUNDS RECEIVED IN ACTION
None

35.	LATEST IMMUNIZATION DATES				36.	SERVICE OUTSIDE CONTINENTAL U.S. AND RETURN		
SMALLPOX	TYPHOID	TETANUS	OTHER (specify)		DATE OF DEPARTURE	DESTINATION		DATE OF ARRIVAL
14Oct44	18Oct45	25Nov44	Typhus21Feb45 Chhlera21Feb45		17 Feb 45	Pacific Theatre		17 Mar 45

37.	TOTAL LENGTH OF SERVICE					38. HIGHEST GRADE HELD
CONTINENTAL SERVICE			FOREIGN SERVICE			
YEARS	MONTHS	DAYS	YEARS	MONTHS	DAYS	Pfc
no	4	23	no	8	14	

39. PRIOR SERVICE
None

Enlistment Allowance $.....Paid
Accts. of F. D. KELLER, 1st Lt., F. D.

40. REASON AND AUTHORITY FOR SEPARATION
Reenlistment in Regular Army AR 615-365 convenience of the Govt Cir 76 Hq USAFPAC 22 Sept 45

41. SERVICE SCHOOLS ATTENDED	42. EDUCATION (Years)		
	Grammar	High School	College
None	8	3	no

PAY DATA

45. LONGEVITY FOR PAY PURPOSES			44. MUSTERING OUT PAY		45. SOLDIER DEPOSIT	46. TRAVEL PAY	47. TOTAL AMOUNT, NAME OF DISBURSING OFFICER
YEARS 1	MONTHS	DAYS 7	TOTAL $	THIS PAYMENT $	None $	$	$

INSURANCE NOTICE

IMPORTANT IF PREMIUM IS NOT PAID WHEN DUE OR WITHIN THIRTY-ONE DAYS THEREAFTER, INSURANCE WILL LAPSE. MAKE CHECKS OR MONEY ORDERS PAYABLE TO THE TREASURER OF THE U.S. AND FORWARD TO COLLECTIONS SUBDIVISION, VETERANS ADMINISTRATION, WASHINGTON 25, D. C.

48. KIND OF INSURANCE			49. HOW PAID		50. Effective Date of Allotment Discontinuance	51. Date of Next Premium Due (One month after 50)	52. PREMIUM DUE EACH MONTH	53. INTENTION OF VETERAN TO		
Nat. Serv. X	U.S. Govt.	None	Allotment	Direct to V.A.			$ 6.40	Continue	Continue Only	Discontinue

54. REMARKS (This space for completion of above items or entry of other items specified in W. D. Directives)
Certified for Michigan Veterans Military Pay

56. SIGNATURE OF PERSON BEING SEPARATED	57. PERSONNEL OFFICER (Type name, grade and organization — signature)
Kenneth Vander Molen	JOHN A. ABBE, 1st Lt, 182nd Inf

WD AGO FORM 53-55
1 November 1944

This form supersedes all previous editions of WD AGO Forms 53 and 55 for enlisted persons entitled to an Honorable Discharge, which...

Army of the United States

Honorable Discharge

This is to certify that

KENNETH   W   VANDER MOLEN

36 916 144   CPL   DET E 5012 A^SU

Army of the United States

is hereby Honorably Discharged from the military service of the United States of America.

This certificate is awarded as a testimonial of Honest and Faithful Service to this country. Asiatic - Pacific Theatre Ribbon

Given at   SEPARATION CENTER
FORT SHERIDAN ILL

Date   1   DECEMBER 1946

J A CARROLL
MAJ   CAV

253

ENLISTED RECORD AND REPORT OF SEPARATION
HONORABLE DISCHARGE

1. LAST NAME - FIRST NAME - MIDDLE INITIAL	2. ARMY SERIAL NO.	1MARR46	4. ARM OR SERVICE	5. COMPONENT
VANDER MOLEN KENNETH W	36 916 144	CPL	BI	RA 13MOS

6. ORGANIZATION	7. DATE OF SEPARATION	8. PLACE OF SEPARATION
DET E 5012 ASU	1 DEC 46	SEPARATION CENTER FORT SHERIDAN ILLINOIS

9. PERMANENT ADDRESS FOR MAILING PURPOSES	10. DATE OF BIRTH	11. PLACE OF BIRTH
2662 MANISTIQUE AVE DETROIT MICHIGAN	7 AUG 26	DETROIT MICHIGAN

12. ADDRESS FROM WHICH EMPLOYMENT WILL BE SOUGHT	16. COLOR EYES	16. COLOR HAIR	17. HEIGHT	18. WEIGHT	17. NO. DEPEN.
SEE 9	BLUE	BLOND	5-11	175	0

18. RACE	19. MARITAL STATUS	20. U.S. CITIZEN	21. CIVILIAN OCCUPATION AND NO.
X	X	X	FUR CLEANER 5-57.610

MILITARY HISTORY

22. DATE OF INDUCTION	23. DATE OF ENLISTMENT	24. DATE OF ENTRY INTO ACTIVE SERVICE	25. PLACE OF ENTRY INTO SERVICE
	31 OCT 45	31 OCT 45	JAPAN

SELECTIVE SERVICE DATA	26. REGISTERED X	27. LOCAL S.S. BOARD NO. 17	28. COUNTY AND STATE WAYNE CO MICH	29. HOME ADDRESS AT TIME OF ENTRY INTO SERVICE SEE 9

30. MILITARY OCCUPATIONAL SPECIALTY AND NO.	31. MILITARY QUALIFICATION AND DATE (i.e., infantry, aviation and marksmanship badges, etc.)
CLASSIFICATION SPECIALIST 275	COMB INF BADGE MM/W M 1 RIFLE

32. BATTLES AND CAMPAIGNS

SOUTHERN PHILIPPINES LIBERATION LUZON

33. DECORATIONS AND CITATIONS ASIATIC PACIFIC THEATER RIBBON W/2 BRONZE BATTLE STARS
PHILIPPINE LIBERATION RIBBON W/2 BRONZE BATTLE STARS VICTORY MEDAL

34. WOUNDS RECEIVED IN ACTION

NONE

35. LATEST IMMUNIZATION DATES				36. SERVICE OUTSIDE CONTINENTAL U.S. AND RETURN		
SMALLPOX	TYPHOID	TETANUS	OTHER (specify)	DATE OF DEPARTURE	DESTINATION	DATE OF ARRIVAL
OCT 44	OCT 45	NOV 44		ENLISTED	PTO	31 OCT 45

37. TOTAL LENGTH OF SERVICE				38. HIGHEST GRADE HELD			
CONTINENTAL SERVICE			FOREIGN SERVICE				
YEARS	MONTHS	DAYS	YEARS	MONTHS	DAYS		
1	0	2	0	0	29	CPL	18 NOV 45	USA	29 NOV 45

39. PRIOR SERVICE

AUS 25 SEP 44 TO 31 OCT 45

40. REASON AND AUTHORITY FOR SEPARATION

CONVN OF GOVT AR 615-365 15 DEC 44 TWX WCL 46706 24 SEP 46

41. SERVICE SCHOOLS ATTENDED	42. EDUCATION (Years)		
NONE	8	3	0

PAY DATA VO 1252

43. LONGEVITY FOR PAY PURPOSES		44. MUSTERING OUT PAY	45. TRAVEL PAY	46. TOTAL AMOUNT, NAME OF DISBURSING OFFICER
YEARS	MONTHS			
2	2	TOTAL PREV PD	THIS PAYMENT NONE	$15.50	213 66 J J MURRAY MAJ FD

INSURANCE NOTICE

IMPORTANT IF PREMIUM IS NOT PAID WHEN DUE OR WITHIN THIRTY-ONE DAYS THEREAFTER, INSURANCE WILL LAPSE. MAKE CHECKS OR MONEY ORDERS PAYABLE TO THE TREASURER OF THE U.S. AND FORWARD TO COLLECTIONS SUBDIVISION, VETERANS ADMINISTRATION, WASHINGTON 25, D.C.

48. KIND OF INSURANCE				49. HOW PAID		50. Effective Date of Allotment Discontinuance	51. Date of Next Premium Due (One month after 50)	53. PREMIUM DUE EACH MONTH	54. INTENTION OF VETERAN TO
Nat. Serv.	U.S. Govt.		Allotment	Direct	V.A.				
X				DEC 46		JAN 47	6 40	X	

55. REMARKS (This space for completion of above items or entry of other items specified in W. D. Directives)

LAPEL BUTTON ISSUED
ASR SCORE 2 SEP 45 10
ON TERMINAL LEAVE FROM 11 NOV 46 TO 1 DEC 46
Certified for Michygn Veteran Military pay

56. SIGNATURE OF PERSON BEING SEPARATED	57. PERSONNEL OFFICER (Type name, grade and organization - signature)
Kenneth Vander Molen	R L STEWART WO JG USA

This form supersedes all previous editions of WD AGO Forms 53 and 55 for enlisted persons entitled to an Honorable Discharge, which will not be used after receipt of this revision.

THE UNITED STATES OF AMERICA

TO ALL WHO SHALL SEE THESE PRESENTS, GREETING: THIS IS TO CERTIFY THAT THE PRESIDENT
OF THE UNITED STATES OF AMERICA AUTHORIZED BY EXECUTIVE ORDER, 24 AUGUST 1962 HAS AWARDED

THE BRONZE STAR MEDAL

TO   CORPORAL KENNETH W. VANDER-MOLEN, UNITED STATES ARMY

FOR   meritorious achievement in ground combat against the armed enemy
during World War II in the Asiatic Pacific Theater of Operations.

GIVEN UNDER MY HAND IN THE CITY OF WASHINGTON
THIS   20th   DAY OF   February 19 90

THE ADJUTANT GENERAL   SECRETARY OF THE ARMY

Postscript: 1946 and Onward

On 7 August 1947, I left Detroit to make Grand Rapids my home. I did marry Jeanne Tuinstra on 17 June 1949 and we were blessed with six children who are now married. They are Kenneth J (Trudy Hessels), David J (Ruth Roskam), Andrew J (Gayla Lankheet), Doris K (Evan Heerema), Karla K (Bill Zeilstra), and Susan K (Nico Damsteegt). We were also blessed with eighteen grandchildren, and eight great-grandchildren.

I worked eighteen years for Fruit Basket Flowerland with Jeanne. In 1967, I left their employment and worked for W.R. Grace & Co. until I retired in 1989. Jeanne retired shortly thereafter. We have really enjoyed our retirement years together traveling to many foreign countries. Our travels have taken us to England a number of times and also most of central Europe. We were fortunate to be able to travel to China, Mexico, Alaska and the Holy Lands. Our travels have also included cruises in the Caribbean area, Hawaiian Islands and crossing the Atlantic aboard the QE2.

We have owned all of our homes. Our honeymoon home was on West Avenue. With the help of Ted Hoekstra, I built our next home on Rosewood S.E. This was the home that held our best memories of a growing family. Later, as our family began to down size we moved to a home on Argus Drive S.E. Next a condominium suited our leisure life style on Edington Court S.E. Jeanne and I moved again in 2002 to an independent living facility under the leadership of the Holland Home.

Since I last wrote this book in 2001, I have revised it, added a few more memories, and also pictures. As of this printing in 2012, much has happened in my life. In June 2009, there was great joy, we celebrated our 60th wedding anniversary. In July 2009, there was a great loss, as Jeanne passed away.

My brother, Gordon passed away in 2011. After my brother Gordon's death, his son Scott shared a letter with me.

Dear Uncle,
My father and I were very close but like you said you knew him better than anyone. My dad and I spent many times together on trips or beside my hospital bed and we shared a lot.
Many times I heard the story of how you met after he was wounded. He told me what poor condition you were in and how he feared he could loose you. Dad told me, you should have gotten a "purple heart" for the suffering you went through.
When I was thinking of a "keep sake" to send

you, I recalled his
story: It was not a
story of one brother
being wounded and another
one being ill. It was
a story of one brother's
love for another. I
hope you will understand
why my brother and I
wanted you to have our
father's "dress purple heart"
as a keep sake. I'm sure
he would be pleased.

Scott

Please know Uncle you are
always welcome to come
and visit. I have plenty
room and would enjoy
showing you some of the
southwest ..)

WORLD WAR II
Organization of the Army

12 Infantrymen equal Squad

3 Squads equal 1 Platoon

3 Platoons equal 1 Company

3 Companies equal 1 Battalion

3 Battalions equal 1 Regiment

3 Regiments equal 1 Division
(9,354 Infantrymen equal 6,160 Staff Support)

3 Divisions or more equals 1 Corps
(Entire HQ=196)

3 Corps or more equals 1 Army
(Entire HQ=778)

3 Armies or more equals 1 Army Group

3 Army Groups or more equals The Army Ground Forces

Abbreviations often found in Morning Reports.

APO	Army Post Office	opns	operations
aptd	appointed	PAR	paragraph
ar	arrest	Pers	peronnel
asgd	assigned	Plat/Plt	platoon
asgmt	assignment	qrs	quarters
atchd	attached	reld	relieved
BC	Battle Casualty	Repl	replacement
Bn	battalion	reptd	reported
DP	disbursement point	rd	reduced
det	detached	RTD	Returned to Duty
disch	discharged	SIA	Seriously Injured in Action
D/D	dishonorable discharge	Sk	sick
DOI	Died of Injuries	SWA	Seriously Wounded inAction
DOW	Died of Wounds	trfd	transferred
DS	detached service	unasgd	unassigned
d	temporary duty	vic	vicinity
dy	duty	W	wound
EM	enlisted men	WIA	Wounded in Action
FOD	Finding of Death		
Fr	from		
hosp	hospital		
IIA	Injured in action		
jd	joined		
LD	Line of Duty		
LIA	Lightly Injured in Action		
LV	leave		
LWA	Lightly wounded in Action		
MOS	Military Occupational Specialty		
MIA	Missing in Action		
NBC	Non-battle Casualty		
Nco	Non-commissioned officer		
NLD	not in line of duty		
No	number		

"Wounds" usually meant that they were caused by enemy action.

"Injuries" usually meant that they were caused by accidents, premature explosions of our own mortar shell, etc.